SALES & CELEBRATIONS

SALES &

Sarah Elvins

CELEBRATIONS

Retailing and
Regional Identity in
Western New York State,

1920–1940

Ohio University Press • Athens

Ohio University Press, Athens, Ohio 45701
© 2004 by Ohio University Press
Printed in the United States of America

Ohio University Press books are printed on acid-free paper ⊚ ™

12 11 10 09 08 07 06 05 04   5 4 3 2 1

A version of chapter 5 appeared as "Shopping for Recovery: Local Spending Initiatives and the Great Depression in Buffalo and Rochester, New York" in the *Journal
of Urban History* 29, no. 6 (September 2003): 670–93.

Library of Congress Cataloging-in-Publication Data

Elvins, Sarah.
 Sales and celebrations : retailing and regional identity in Western New York State, 1920-
 1940 / Sarah Elvins.
   p. cm.
 ISBN 0-8214-1549-2 (cloth : alk. paper)
 1. Retail trade—New York (State)—History—20th century. 2. New York (State), Western—Economic conditions. I. Title.

HF5429.4.N56E48 2004
381'.1'09747909042—dc22

                                                                    2003028115

For my parents and Chris

Contents

Illustrations

Acknowledgments

In the course of researching and writing this book, I have incurred many debts. I would like to thank my dissertation supervisor, Marlene Shore, who first encouraged me to pursue my doctorate. Marlene and the other members of my committee—Christopher Armstrong, Molly Ladd-Taylor, and Marc Stein—provided valuable feedback at every stage of this project and stood as fine examples of teachers and historians. I was fortunate to be part of a lively community of scholars in Toronto, many of whom commented on early versions of this work. Thanks go to Alexandra Mosquin, Lisa Levenstein, and members of the Toronto Consumer History Reading Group, particularly Daniel Robinson, Steve Penfold, Jeet Heer, and Joseph Tohill, for their insights. Alison Isenberg of Rutgers University closely read and thoughtfully critiqued every chapter. David Nye of the University of Southern Denmark gave sound advice about framing this project. I have also greatly benefited from conversations about history with students and faculty during years spent at the University of Winnipeg and the University of Notre Dame. Special thanks to Tamara Myers, Serena Keshavjee, and James Hanley. New colleagues at the University of Manitoba, in particular Tina Chen, David Churchill, and Adele Perry, have been enthusiastic and supportive.

A number of archivists and librarians were crucial to the success of this project. Karl Kabelac and Nancy Martin at the University of Rochester's Rush Rhees Library, the staff at the Buffalo and Erie County Historical Society, Carol Sandler at the Strong Museum, Rick Meier of the Rochester Gas and Electric Corporation, the archivists at the State University of New York (SUNY) at Buffalo, and Al Bartovics at Harvard University's Baker Library all brought to my attention resources I would never have discovered on my own. Lynda McCurdy Hotra shared materials relating to the history of her family's department store in Rochester. Two Ontario Graduate Scholarships, funding from the Faculty of Graduate Studies at York, and an Alfred D. Chandler Jr. Traveling Fellowship at Harvard University made research trips possible. A portion of chapter 5 appeared previously in the *Journal of Urban History*, and I would like to thank editor David Goldfield as well as the anonymous readers who offered comments. I must also express my heartfelt gratitude to the Great Lakes American Studies Association and Ohio University Press for their support of this manuscript.

Friends and family also played an essential role in bringing this work to completion. Lili Kim and Dennis Meletiche opened their homes in Rochester and Buffalo to me. Gum Fa Ng provided essential technical expertise. Julie and Nathan Elliott were a great help during a year in South Bend, Indiana. Finally, this book is dedicated to three people who have provided unstinting encouragement and support over many years. My parents, Wayne and Naomi Elvins, instilled a love of history and learning in me from an early age. They also took me on shopping trips to some of the department stores in Buffalo and Rochester that figure prominently in this book. My husband, Chris Frank, was happy to talk about this project when I wanted to but was also adept at taking my mind off it when necessary. He has helped me in more ways than he knows.

Introduction

This book is a study of retailers in western New York State in the years from 1920 to 1940. Their story illuminates urban life in the interwar period, the development of the American mass market, and most important, the persistence of local identities in the face of sweeping economic and cultural changes. My research had its start in a deceptively simple question: How national was the national market of the 1920s and 1930s? The early twentieth century is seen as a heyday of consumer capitalism. Americans were exposed to an abundance of mass-produced goods, and new institutions—including mass-market magazines, mail-order catalogs, department stores, and professional advertising agencies—worked to spread the creed of consumerism across the nation. Although the consumption of goods was certainly not a new phenomenon in American life in the early twentieth century, it seemed to take on a new significance and attain an unprecedented scale in the interwar period. Older inhibitions to spending, though not completely erased, were downplayed in a culture that increasingly equated success with the acquisition of goods. Problems in distribution, which had hampered national marketing efforts in the nineteenth century, were largely conquered. Production technology had been honed to the point that standardized, packaged goods were cheaper and more plentiful than ever before in the nation's history and were incorporated into the daily lives of rich and poor, rural and urban, native-born and newcomer.

Tracking the changes in production, marketing, and retailing in this time period provides only part of the story, however. More challenging is the task of determining just how Americans understood their participation in this national market. Did a new sensibility accompany the extension of these trade networks? What did it mean for people across the country to adopt similar products in their daily lives? How did the meaning of the selling of goods in America change over the course of the nineteenth and early twentieth centuries? The conventional view assumes that these developments had a homogenizing effect. Influential early works by David Potter and Daniel Boorstin emphasized the unifying potential of consumption—in other words, goods brought

Americans together and allowed them to share experiences in a way they never had before. This shared experience muted class or regional differences that had divided them in the past—consumption helped to forge a new national culture during the late nineteenth and early twentieth centuries.[1]

The retailer—in particular the department store—has been identified as one of the main catalysts of this change. In cities in both North America and Europe, the store became a meeting place, a pilgrimage site, a location to visit and revisit. And while enabling the acquisition of goods was at the heart of the store's purpose, the mundane act of ringing up sales was at times subsumed by a larger significance. Stores presented a new cultural vision in the United States, one that fully embraced the possibilities of commercial capitalism. William Leach argues that department stores symbolized "the very essence of the consumer revolution."[2] Not only did they supply material goods to customers, they also offered a spectacle of light, mirrors, and display that thrilled and sometimes even overwhelmed visitors.[3] Yet in focusing on the store as an instrument of national transformation, historians have paid little attention to regional variations in the buying and selling of goods. In one sense, it is not surprising that much of the scholarship on retailing in this period has focused on developments in the nation's largest cities. Institutions such as Macy's, Wanamaker's, or Marshall Field's became synonymous with innovation and success in retailing. The concentration of publishers and advertising executives in New York, Chicago, and other major cities similarly contributed to the sense that, in addition to the advertising campaigns themselves, more general attitudes and business practices originating in these centers eventually radiated out to encompass the rest of the nation. When merchants in regions beyond New York, Chicago, Philadelphia, or Boston are mentioned at all, their stories are often assumed to simply follow those of the "leaders" in the big city.

The transformation of America into a "land of desire" did not, however, entail a simple, one-way expansion of goods and retailing practices from the metropolis to the rest of the nation. The reality was much more complicated. In the early decades of the twentieth century, consumers in different parts of the country had very different levels of interaction with new retailing phenomena. For most Americans, a trip to Fifth Avenue or Michigan Avenue was an occasional experience at best. Their day-to-day participation in a "national market" was through local stores. Well into the 1920s and 1930s, regional variations persisted in terms of the availability of goods and, more important, the retailers who supplied these products. The hinterland did take from the metropolis, to be sure, but many residents and merchants in smaller towns and cities took pride in their local institutions and their ability to put a local spin on national trends and innovations.

Buffalo and Rochester were home to a number of independent merchants who acted as both civic leaders and cultural brokers. Merchants were participants in public life on a level unattainable by any other type of business. Physically, stores occupied prime space in the center of the city, becoming landmarks for tourists and locals alike. The owners and managers of department stores, usually men with long-established roots in the community, were among the most prominent figures in civic life in smaller cities. They dominated local trade councils, headed "Main Street" improvement drives, and were a huge presence in daily newspapers. Yet smaller retailers—grocers, druggists, even managers of the branches of chain organizations—also participated in public life in ways that went beyond the simple sale of goods. Culturally, the store became a site of fantasy, entertainment, and leisure. In some ways, the role of the retail business in these cities was, I would argue, even more prominent than that played by the department store in larger centers. Because Macy's and Filene's were located in such huge metropolises, they had to compete with nightclubs, movie houses, museums, theaters, and even crowds of people in the streets for the attention of urbanites. In smaller cities, this competition was not quite so fierce, and the store's role in bringing the latest trends to the community was heightened. Although Buffalo and Rochester were home to a range of entertainments, stores dominated the cultural landscape in ways that their New York and Chicago counterparts did not. They were, in many ways, the main game in town. Movie stars and sports celebrities might never have visited Rochester if Sibley's department store had not brought them in for autograph sessions; no other businesses had the budget to sponsor city parades like the retailers of Buffalo did; no other destination was as alluring for women with leisure time, children at Christmas, or even businessmen seeking a luncheon place.

A regional study of retailing and marketing also helps to counterbalance the tendency toward a national perspective that has characterized much of the writing about the history of consumption. Scholars of advertising have been understandably drawn to the profusion of national ad campaigns that dominated the pages of mass-market magazines. Roland Marchand's masterful dissection of the scenes of modern life depicted in ad campaigns, for example, suggests that advertisers created a new national language, complete with its own parables and guides for behavior. Similarly, historians of marketing have looked first to those companies that managed to succeed on a countrywide scale.[4] But by turning the lens around to observe not the spread of these goods outward across the nation but a community's reception of a newly advertised item or a chain store branch, we can explore a range of different issues. Did consumers make distinctions between locally made goods and those that came from other areas? Did local retailers view branded goods as allies or foes in their fight to remain competitive? Did national brands acknowledge any regional variations in the marketing of their goods?

Scholars focusing on the mass media have examined not only the advertisements but also the stories and articles in periodicals such as the *Ladies' Home Journal* and *Saturday Evening Post*, for these also encouraged the consumption of goods as the key mode of individual expression in modern society.[5] Here, too, a local perspective brings new questions to light. Richard Ohmann has suggested that while these magazines may have been sold across the United States, geographic representation in their pages was not so democratic. Stories concentrated on a few major cities (primarily New York, Boston, Philadelphia, and, to a lesser extent, Chicago and Los Angeles) and did not include other cities or smaller towns as part of the "social space" of modernity. In their stories, photographs, and articles, magazines reported the fashionable parties of New York society, the vacation homes of the rich in Sag Harbor, the activities of celebrities on Broadway or in Hollywood. The vast regions of the United States west of the Mississippi, south of the Mason-Dixon Line, or, for that matter, in areas of New York State north of Yonkers simply were not visible in the pages of the medium.[6] A closer look at this unseen America can test the universality of the mass magazine's cultural dominance. How did those who lived outside the designated circuit of places inhabited by the wealthy and fashionable understand their own position? Did they aim to imitate the urban lifestyle depicted in the mass media, or were there ways for them to carve out their own spaces and their own styles within their own communities? Retailers in smaller communities often used national magazines to validate the fashionability of their wares. Buffalo might not have been featured in stories or ads in national periodicals, but Buffalo retailers and consumers often used the magazine not to emphasize their exclusion but to assert their own participation in the mass market.

Not everyone has accepted the notion that a new national culture effectively effaced differences between Americans during the early twentieth century. A growing number of scholars have suggested that the buying and selling of goods could enhance distinct group identities in America. The purchase of particular items might enhance an individual's sense of belonging to an ethnic community. Workers could gain a sense of class consciousness not only from experiences shared in the workplace but also in items purchased during leisure time.[7] This book explores a different dimension of identity and the market, using a local perspective to highlight the friction and the variation inherent in the spread of American consumerism. Well into the 1920s and 1930s, regional identity remained central to the way in which merchants in western New York State both ran their operations and presented themselves to customers. Residents of Buffalo and Rochester would have bristled at the suggestion that they lived in the shadow of Manhattan; retailers would have rejected the notion that they simply imitated Fifth Avenue.

Historians who have paid attention to region as a dimension of consumer history have focused primarily on the South and the rural West (or Midwest) as distinct worlds where the buying and selling of goods was part of a complex negotiation of modernity.[8] This approach is not surprising: if American consumerism is thought of primarily as an urban phenomenon centered on the middle class, then farmers in Wisconsin who joined a Grange purchasing cooperative or southern sharecroppers who tried to resist the monopoly of the local merchant seem by definition to be exceptional cases. We might expect rural consumers to be different; we might predict that merchants serving poorer populations in the South faced different issues than urban retailers with more affluent customers. In contrast, western New York might not seem a likely place to look for variations in American consumerism. Surely, if anyone participated in a national culture of consumption, this view holds, it would be residents of communities on the main rail line to Manhattan. Was it difficult to resist the sheer economic and cultural power of the nation's largest city? Did not the consuming and retailing practices of New York City quickly become the practices of New York State and eventually the entire nation? Cultural historians not specifically interested in consumerism have also posited this model of cultural dominance. Some unapologetically present New York as the symbol not only of America but also of Western culture in the twentieth century. In explaining why she has chosen to study New York in the 1920s, for example, Ann Douglas argues that this decade saw America seize "economic and cultural leadership of the West" and New York become recognized as "the world's most powerful city."[9]

Yet what is striking is the extent to which Buffalo and Rochester retailers and consumers maintained a distinct identity throughout the 1920s and the 1930s. Local patterns of buying and selling persisted. In their advertising, in their management techniques, and even in terms of the types of goods they stocked, merchants had their own particular perspective. The appeal of region as a selling tool suggests another dimension of the appeal of consumer culture in the early twentieth century. Gary Cross contends that commercialism triumphed in America because it was able to substitute a community of goods for any meaningful political community.[10] Indeed, local identity served as a powerful selling tool for many retailers. At a time when chain stores were an increasing presence in the area and when national advertising and mail-order catalogs let people all over the nation know about new products, merchants in Buffalo and Rochester asserted that they alone could really understand local needs—they did not defer to New York (or Paris or London, for that matter). Using a language of localism, they encouraged patrons to spend their money in institutions with ties to their hometowns. Retailers also encouraged area residents to view patronizing "home" stores as a form of civic expression. This effort was more than a cynical marketing technique, however. For both retailers and consumers in Buffalo and Rochester, consumption could serve as a means to express a sincere pride in the area or even as a rallying point in a program of civic activism. The notion that place continued to matter even as national networks of distribution were blanketing the country is not one many scholars have explored. Critics of modern culture often point to a sense of "placelessness" as one negative outgrowth of the spread of commercialism.[11] This study shows that locality remained fundamental to the way in which American consumers negotiated the mass market well into the 1920s and 1930s.

Western New York State is, in many respects, an ideal laboratory within which to view this interplay. Buffalo and Rochester at the turn of the twentieth century were booming cities whose potential seemed almost unlimited. They were home to world-class architecture, society families, streets of stately homes, and rapidly expanding industries that drew new residents each year. Indeed, local boosters often made claims that Buffalo would become the next Chicago and that Rochester might someday rival New York (or at least St. Louis). Buffalo, New York State's second largest city, was home to over half a million people. In the 1920s, it ranked eleventh among American cities by population (in contrast, it would rank fiftieth by 1990). Moreover, it boasted more millionaires per capita than New York City. In 1920, Rochester had a population of almost three hundred thousand in its metropolitan area and a diversified economy, which included cutting-edge technical and manufacturing companies such as Kodak and Bausch and Lomb. The populations of both cities climbed steadily over the course of the 1920s, attracting new settlers and workers. Established residents were optimistic about the possibilities for success in the region. Both cities had active civic and business organizations that trumpeted their local advantages.

Buffalo and Rochester can tell us a good deal about the experiences of average Americans in these decades of both unprecedented prosperity and unmitigated economic distress. The census data indicating America's shift from a rural to an urban population serve as a standard point of departure for any undergraduate lecture about the emergence of "modern" America. In 1920, 51 percent of the U.S. population lived in cities, a majority for the first time. The definition of an urban population, however, set a relatively low bar for admission. Any community with a population of 2,500 or more was eligible for "city" status. Only three cities at the time had populations of 1,000,000 inhabitants or more, with nine (including Buffalo) in the category from 500,000 to 1,000,000 and thirteen (including Rochester) ranging from 250,000 to 500,000.

In other words, although most Americans were urban dwellers, not all lived in cities the size of Chicago or New York. A sizable group resided in smaller or midsized cities. In fact, while 10,245,532 lived in cities of 1 million or more, 10,764,607 lived in cities of 250,000 to 1 million.[12] Living in one of these midsized cities was perhaps even more of an "average" urban experience than was living in New York, Chicago, or Philadelphia. Observers at the time took this for granted: for example, in 1920, when the U.S. Bureau of the Census faced the task of finding a "representative American city" in which to study the economic and social conditions of the nation's homemakers, it selected Rochester as the case study.[13] For historians, urban life has often meant life in the nation's largest cities. Yet to fully understand the nuances of urban life in the early twentieth century, studies of other communities are essential. New York was not and is not America. Works that purport to be national in scope yet focus on only a few metropolitan centers obscure the heterogeneity of the nation's experience. Scholars have paid a disproportionate amount of attention to the experiences of retailers and consumers in big cities; a closer look at midsized cities adds a new dimension to this history.

An exploration of buying and selling in Buffalo and Rochester illuminates how Americans in midsized cities participated in the emerging mass market. The spread of new trade relationships did not simply eliminate local traditions and identities. Merchants in Rochester and Buffalo played on local sentiment in an effort to adapt to a changing climate of selling. As chain stores entered the region, area retailers used a language of localism to encourage patrons to spend their money in institutions with ties to their hometowns. Mass marketers, as well, acknowledged the power of the local, tailoring ads to refer to local people and combat their perceived status as interlopers. By taking a closer look at western New York, one can gain a greater understanding of how local variations and loyalties could often coexist with and occasionally challenge the hegemony of national culture.

The chapters that follow will explore the particularities of retailing in western New York. Chapter 1 traces the broad history of the region and looks at the roots of its enduring retail institutions. From the vantage point of the twenty-first century, Buffalo and Rochester do not immediately spring to mind as exemplars of American progress. Although the region is still home to many proud local residents, it has suffered a decline as a result of deindustrialization. Current conditions have made it harder to imagine these two Rust Belt communities as real contenders for national and even international prestige. These preconceptions must be set aside. The story of the rapid development and growth of western New York demonstrates that retailers and residents had good reason to feel optimistic about their futures. As chapter 2 reveals, area merchants took on a range of roles in the community—hosting a variety of entertainments for the local population, spearheading downtown development projects, and participating in charity drives. Perhaps even more than their New York City counterparts, department stores loomed large on the local cultural scene. Chapter 3 examines how the increased ease of transportation and the spread of national media made Rochester and Buffalo stores more aware of their competition in New York City. Retailers drew on their history and ties to the area in their advertising to encourage western New Yorkers to shop at home. They reassured patrons that they offered goods comparable to those found in stores in Manhattan, and they asserted their ability to serve the local market in a unique way. They also used the mass-market media to promote their capacity to stay up-to-date on trends in fashion.

Chapter 4 looks at the way Rochester and Buffalo stores grappled with the "chain store problem" in the 1920s and 1930s. Just as local retailers took pains to differentiate themselves from New York City stores, they drew on a language of localism to put chain store branches in a bad light. Chain branches were criticized as interlopers with no interest in community affairs. At the same time, however, many retailers watched chain business practices with interest, adopting those that looked promising while strenuously asserting their own "independent" status. Chapter 5 explores how the emphasis on local spending that stores had cultivated during the 1920s became the foundation for the region's approach to the crisis of the Great Depression. In Rochester and Buffalo during the early 1930s, the debate over the Depression was, for the most part, limited to the role played by the private individual—in particular, the private consumer—in turning the so-called slump around. With an almost messianic zeal, local business leaders embarked on campaigns to put more local dollars into circulation through pledge drives, citywide sales, and private employment initiatives. It was only after initiatives to harness the power of local consumers came and went that western New Yorkers turned to more far-reaching solutions involving federal intervention. Chapter 6 examines the persistence of downtown merchants as cultural brokers even during the hard times of the late 1930s. Many reinvested considerable amounts in expanding or updating their facilities, underscoring their continued faith that conditions in the region would soon turn around. The chapter also touches on how even national manufacturers tailored their advertising to sell to western New Yorkers. By using testimonials from Buffalonians and Rochesterians, a number of national advertisers put a more familiar face forward in newspaper and magazine campaigns. This chapter continues to explore how the very definition of what was "local" and what was "national" was being renegotiated in the 1920s and 1930s.

Although each chapter in this volume is organized around one central theme, they are linked by a common thread: the assertion by retailers that their interests were inseparable from the community's interests. In prosperous times, merchants drew attention to the services they provided to local citizens; in times of crisis, area residents were instructed that by spending their dollars at home, they could help to restore prosperity. The use of retailing conditions as a measure of local economic health was not limited to the merchants alone; local boosters, newspaper editorial writers, and area politicians saw local spending as a goal to be encouraged. And consumers, as well, made choices about where to spend because of their feelings of attachment to local businesses. The persistence of these local loyalties complicates our understanding of the evolution of the American mass market, challenging the notion that the cultural patterns and business practices of larger cities such as New York and Chicago were simply replicated across the rest of the nation. The merchants and consumers of Buffalo and Rochester did experience some profound changes in the ways they sold and bought goods in the 1920s and 1930s, yet some of these changes had a particularly local emphasis.

A REGION DEVELOPS

IN ORDER TO TAKE A CLOSE LOOK at the business and cultural life of western New York in the 1920s and 1930s, it is essential to have a sense of the area's history. The settlement and development of Buffalo and Rochester in the nineteenth century laid the foundation for the region's participation in America's consumer economy during the twentieth. This chapter traces the broad contours of the area's history, paying special attention to the growth of retail institutions. Many of the large department stores that came to dominate the physical and cultural landscape of Buffalo and Rochester had modest beginnings and developed in tandem with the communities in which they were located. The tremendous influx of immigrants into western New York made it a destination of choice for many retail entrepreneurs, who hoped to tap into an ever-expanding market. Over the course of the first two decades of the twentieth century, both cities would develop concentrated downtown retail districts where department stores and other merchants attracted customers from throughout the region. The overall pattern throughout this period was one of tremendous growth. Both Rochester and Buffalo came a long way in a relatively short span of time. By the 1920s, local boosters who crowed about the advantages of the two cities had convincing evidence to back up their claims. The tremendous faith in the local economy and the sense of western New York as an important and distinct market that characterized retailers in Buffalo and Rochester in the interwar period was based on an understanding of the history of the region as a site of expansion and innovation.

The frontier town of Buffalo was originally surveyed by Joseph Ellicott of the Holland Land Company in the 1790s, and there were twenty houses in the settlement by 1804. Skirmishes with the British (the settlement was burned to the ground by British soldiers in December 1813) combined with Buffalo's geographic isolation to limit the village's growth. Located at the junction of the Niagara River and Lake Erie, Buffalo needed a more direct connection with eastern trade routes to encourage future growth. Local settlers watched with interest as New York's legislature debated the creation of a waterway to connect Lake Erie to Albany on the Hudson River, thus providing a water route from the Great Lakes to the Atlantic Ocean. A group of Buffalo entrepreneurs, led by Samuel Wilkeson and some prominent dock merchants, took the initiative to have Buffalo designated the western terminus of the canal by dredging Buffalo Creek and creating their own harbor and pier.[1] In 1823, Albany lawmakers officially chose Buffalo as the terminus of the waterway, and the opening of the Erie Canal two years later brought a flurry of economic activity and population growth.[2] The route reduced the cost of transportation between Buffalo and the Hudson River from $100 to $10 per ton, encouraging an increase in shipments of wheat, corn, oats, and meat from the West and manufactured goods from the East.[3]

Ships brought people as well as goods to Buffalo. Some migrants stopped only temporarily in the city before heading farther west, but many stayed. Irish immigrants, in particular, flocked to Buffalo's old First Ward to work initially on the building of the canal and later on the docks, loading and unloading shipments of grain. By 1832, the year that the charter of the city of Buffalo was approved, the local population (also affected by an influx of German immigrants) had grown to ten thousand. New residences and public buildings sprang up at a rapid pace, many constructed by local businessman Benjamin Rathbun. The technological achievement of Clinton's Ditch (as the canal was sarcastically called, with reference to New York governor De Witt Clinton) became a basis of local pride, and the tremendous flow of trade was a continual source of amazement. Thirty-six thousand tons of manufactured goods were shipped west from Buffalo in 1836.[4] The editor of the *City Directory* that year felt confident enough in Buffalo's position as the link between the East and

West that he christened the city the "GREAT NATIONAL EXCHANGE."[5] Even as the rest of the nation suffered financial setbacks during the panic of 1837, the stream of traffic on the lake and canal continued to rise. The city was emerging as a hub of international renown. In 1842, Buffalo became the site of the world's first steam-powered grain elevator.

The new waterway ushered in a similar period of expansion in Rochester. Located at the junction of the Erie Canal and the Genesee River and surrounded by rich farmland, the city was in a good position to profit from the increased commercialization of agriculture. The area was surveyed by Col. Nathaniel Rochester in 1810, but the success of the settlement was ensured by the canal's opening. From the start, Rochester was designed as a mill town, to capitalize on the Genesee River falls. By 1820, Rochester had acquired the nickname "Flour City," as it became a magnet for grain milling in the rich farmlands of the upstate region. As the community's exports of flour grew, a constant influx of newcomers was attracted to the city. In 1835, Rochester's economy entered a new phase, one that prompted a change in moniker. As the "Flower City," it became home to a sizable plant and nursery industry. Both milling and nurseries remained important aspects of Rochester's economic identity, but the clothing manufacturing sector emerged as the largest industrial employer by the middle of the century. Shoe manufacturing also became increasingly important, for a number of leading firms set up factories in the central district of the city. Woodworking, brewing, leatherworking, and tanning were other significant local industries.

In these early years, Rochester was notable not only for its economic growth but also for its social upheavals. It was the leading city in western New York's "Burned-Over District," so christened due to its intense religious activities. The city was convulsed with the Second Great Awakening in the 1820s and 1830s.[6] The religious revivals climaxed with the arrival of Charles Grandison Finney, who appeared in Rochester in 1830 and began a six-month campaign of daily prayer meetings and individual conversions, which united and invigorated the city's Protestants. The city became the site of another type of religious mania in the late 1840s when sisters Margaretta and Kate Fox first claimed to communicate with the dead, leading to the development of the Spiritualist religion. Although the religious impulse eventually waned, it would exert influence on many subsequent reform movements in the region. In later years, Rochester would become the home of numerous prominent abolitionists and women's rights activists, including Frederick Douglass and Susan B. Anthony. Rochester women were actually the first in the country to vote in a national election, as

the city was the site of a test case in 1872 in which fifty women (led by Anthony) voted and were eventually arrested in an attempt to determine the scope
of the Fourteenth and Fifteenth Amendments to the Constitution.[7]

Just as the building of the canal had spurred an era of development, the advent of the railway further helped the region's growth. By the mid-nineteenth
century, Buffalo emerged as a nexus of rail travel. A short tramway connected
Buffalo and Niagara Falls in the 1830s, and by 1842, lines linked the city to
Attica, Corning, and Hornell, New York. A year later, a chain of railroads
stretched across the state from Buffalo to Albany.[8] Eventually, links to New
York City, Toledo, and Chicago, as well as routes into Canada and the coal regions of Pennsylvania, were established. Mark Goldman observes that at the
turn of the century, Buffalo was second only to Chicago as a railroad terminus, with "seven direct lines connecting Buffalo with six different East Coast
cities; six direct lines to Chicago, Kansas City, Omaha, and St. Louis; and two
direct lines between Buffalo and Pittsburgh."[9] Rochester was less of a rail hub,
but lines linked the city with Lockport, Syracuse, and eventually Albany and
Buffalo.[10]

Even in the nineteenth century, Buffalo residents were concerned about becoming a mere satellite of the New York City market. Local business leaders
watched the influx of goods manufactured in New York with a mixture of excitement and alarm. Commerce seemed to be their own city's defining feature,
and at least initially, industries were few. Worried that trade would dominate
all other local endeavors, city politicians and businesspeople "tried desperately
to channel some of Buffalo's commercial vigor into manufacturing."[11] As a result of their initiatives, Buffalo developed a substantial manufacturing sector
and the roots of a highly diversified economy. Among the most significant industries were iron factories (which produced countless items, including stoves
and building materials), furniture manufacturing, brewing, soap making, tanning, and printing. J. D. Larkin built his first soap factory in 1875 in the city.
The company developed an innovative program of direct sales for its soap, perfume, and other toiletries, using premiums to encourage customers to place
orders. The company grew to national fame on its "factory to family" plan,
shipping thousands of household items such as rugs, lamps, and silverware to
Larkin Club members from coast to coast.[12]

After 1896, Buffalo received electrical power from Niagara Falls, and industrial development began in earnest. Because of the area's excellent rail and
canal connections, as well as its access to freshwater, a location in West Seneca,
just outside Buffalo, was chosen as a site for a new mill by the Lackawanna

Iron and Steel Company in 1899. The site at the eastern end of Lake Erie allowed easy shipment of ore from Minnesota and coal from Pennsylvania. The
state-of-the-art plant was another reason for the city to feel confident of its
rising fortunes. Milling continued to be an important industry, with eighteen
grain mills churning out almost thirty thousand barrels of flour daily by the
early 1920s.

Rochester's early history also saw rapid growth. Although contemporaries
often associated Buffalo with electrical power, Rochester had its own claims to
fame with regard to innovative technology. As the telegraph emerged as a key
tool in the development of national markets, Rochester entrepreneurs saw the
advantage of using this system of communication to transmit New York flour
prices as quickly and accurately as possible. A group led by Hiram Sibley in
the 1850s consolidated a number of competing telegraph firms to form Western Union. Throughout the Civil War years and beyond, Sibley and Western
Union pushed for the construction of new telegraph lines across the conti-
nent, simultaneously increasing Rochester's importance as the site of a burgeoning business and linking the city to the rest of the nation.[13] Even more
than the telegraph, the camera transformed the city. As the home of the Eastman Kodak Company, Rochester became synonymous with the production of
cameras and film. George Eastman began his business in the 1880s, and the
first building at the large Kodak Park industrial site opened in 1891. With eight
thousand employees by 1915, the company became the city's largest single employer.[14] The phenomenal success of Eastman Kodak benefited workers for the
company, who enjoyed innovative stock-sharing and bonus plans, and other
businesses in the area as well. Kodak subcontracted to firms such as Bausch
and Lomb for lenses and Wollensak for shutters. Rochester also benefited from
the philanthropic largesse of George Eastman, who made generous bequests to
the city and the University of Rochester and founded the Eastman School of
Music.

Nevertheless, local residents were reluctant to characterize their city as a
mere company town. The "Kodak City" nickname did not seem to fully represent the area's diversified economy. Metalworking and older industries such as
clothing and shoe manufacturing remained vibrant, and they were joined by
cutting-edge producers of new technologies such as the North East Electric
Company (later known as Delco), which produced starters and electrical
equipment for the burgeoning automobile industry. Also located in the city was
the Stromberg-Carlson Telephone Manufacturing Company, which went on to
be a leader in the radio industry.[15] A Rochester architect invented the first mail

chute and built a manufacturing company that supplied chutes to builders around the world. Both the Empire State Building and Radio City Music Hall in New York City featured chutes manufactured in Rochester. There was certainly no shortage of ingenuity within the city: Rochesterians are credited with the invention of the first voting machine, the fountain pen, and the punchable paper transfer for streetcar riders.[16]

Western New York's rapid growth attracted merchants who hoped to profit from the boom. Buffalo's Main Street was (and remains) the line dividing the city's east and west sides. The east side encompassed working-class and ethnic neighborhoods, whereas the city's elite remained on the other side of the divide. Buffalo's first merchants set up stores close to the waterfront area, to take advantage of the canal traffic. Main Street, jutting north from the city's inner harbor, later became home to Buffalo's largest dry goods emporiums. The founders of stores such as Hengerer's, J. N. Adam's, and Adam, Meldrum and Anderson—all establishments that would occupy key positions on Main Street during the 1920s and 1930s—made the decision to invest in the "Queen City" in the nineteenth century. William Hengerer was a clerk in the R. J. Sherman store in 1836 and eventually became a partner at another dry goods outfit, which was renamed Barnes, Hengerer and Company in 1875. The company acted as wholesaler, jobber, and retailer and would do $4 million in business in Buffalo and $1 million at its branch house in Minneapolis. At the time, it was the largest dry goods house between New York and Chicago. Barnes, Hengerer and Company occupied an immense, five-story building that had 125 feet of Main Street frontage. The property was 235 feet in depth, and the entire first floor was devoted to retail operations, with the upper floors dedicated to the wholesale trade. Patrons of the store enjoyed the latest in comfort and convenience—including "toilet and waiting room for the ladies, with female attendant; public drinking fountain; [and] elevators, making access to wholesale departments easy and comfortable."[17] Under the name Hengerer's, the store would remain a fixture on Main Street well into the twentieth century.

Meanwhile, in 1867, Robert B. Adam joined with two partners to open a small dry goods venture that would grow into Adam, Meldrum and Anderson Company, a pioneer in the use of the modern buying office. Another young Scot, named J. N. Adam (no relation to Robert B. Adam), arrived in 1881 to found his own dry goods business. His store occupied the first floor and basement of a seven-story "skyscraper" on Main between Swan and Erie "whose towering height was the pride of Buffalo in those mauve days of the early [18]80's when Delaware Avenue was a speedway for trotting horses."[18] Flint and Kent was another combined retail and wholesale dry goods business located on Main Street. Originally founded in the 1830s, the firm eventually came under the control of two New Hampshire merchants who moved to Buffalo in the 1860s. An observer two decades later proclaimed that Flint and Kent was patronized by "the best class of trade in the city and country, who find here vast stocks, infinite varieties, and the most approved styles, reliable goods, and prices as can be quoted by legitimate merchants anywhere." A fleet of thirty-five clerks and salespeople provided attentive service to customers and visitors.[19]

The downtown stores provided hours of entertainment for area residents. One Buffalo man looked back fondly on the era, remembering how he had excitedly visited department stores on Main Street as a boy, passing the time watching shoppers and poring over displays of toys. Many customers, he recalled, formed personal connections with particular store employees. Mr. Brigham of the toy department at Barnum's on Main Street "knew about every boy in Buffalo," and many local men who ventured into the store to buy fishing equipment "remembered when he sold them ten pins or a rocking horse." At Adam, Meldrum and Anderson, the store manager, Mr. Gibson, dressed in "striped pants and morning coat," greeted female customers by name. The young shopper was impressed not only with the level of service and the goods offered in these establishments but also with the sophisticated equipment that sped the completion of sales. He was fascinated by the elaborate system of pneumatic tubes at Adam, Meldrum and Anderson, which whisked money and sales slips for each transaction away to the cashier and just as quickly brought change back to the appropriate counter.[20] The interiors of these businesses revealed the latest innovations in lighting and communications, and the streets of downtown Buffalo were equally innovative. Easy access to electrical power inspired early attempts to find alternatives to gas and oil lights in the downtown, and in 1886, Buffalo became the first city in the United States to light its streets with electricity.

At the turn of the twentieth century, Buffalo was such a symbol of the nation's progress that it was selected as the site of the 1901 Pan-American Exposition. The building of the Great White Way and a number of pavilions on the fairgrounds led to great excitement, and the visit of President William McKinley seemed to point to glittering new prospects for the city. The exposition celebrated Niagara Falls as the location of the world's largest power station. Two hundred thousand incandescent lights illuminated the fair's Grand Court, dazzling visitors. Buffalo's location was promoted as ideal: using language that would be echoed by area merchants well into the twentieth century, promoters argued that Buffalo was at the center of a "magic circle." Within a radius of five hundred miles and therefore within a day's journey lived half of the population of the United States and three-quarters of the population of Canada—a total of 45 million people, all "within one night's ride." Buffalo was simply the "easiest place to get to from the greatest number of other places in the United States and Canada." Skeptical readers were assured that this claim was "not an advertising superlative but a modest announcement of the truth."[21]

Eight million visitors flocked to the exposition, listening to concerts, observing anthropological exhibits, riding gondolas through waterways separating buildings in one section, marveling at the performers in the Midway, and eating food supplied by numerous concession stands. Along with visitors from across the country (and, indeed, from around the world), area residents were swept up in the excitement. Over 11,000 Buffalo citizens purchased special bond issues to help finance the Pan-American Exposition (pledging more than $1.5 million), and the largest single day's attendance, on "Buffalo Day" (19 October), exceeded 162,000. The myriad displays that awed attendees often seemed guided by competing impulses: the Pan-Am fused the traditional and the modern, elements of fantasy and reality. Buildings designed to evoke the best of older architectural traditions (described in guidebooks as Spanish Renaissance in style) housed demonstrations of the newest manufactured goods. Art and science came together in exhibits such as a fountain designed by Louis Comfort Tiffany, which boasted the artist's world-famous use of colored glass as well as the latest electrical technology to illuminate the design.

Merchants in Buffalo were active in promoting the exposition. William Hengerer served on the standing committee overseeing printing and supplies for the event. The Larkin Company constructed a building where viewers could admire a home furnished, room by room, with items available as premiums in the company's catalog. The H. A. Meldrum department store established a bureau where local residents could list rooms available to rent to Pan-Am visitors. The event seemed to be the culmination of all of the region's aspirations. Unfortunately for the city and for President McKinley, the actions of a gunman at the fair brought Buffalo more infamy than popularity. Anarchist Leon Csolgosz's bullet on 6 September did not end McKinley's life immediately, and many were optimistic about the president's chances for recovery. A week after the attack, however, McKinley succumbed to his injuries; an outraged public blamed the incompetence of the medical team provided by the city to care for the president.[22] Buffalo became the swearing-in place for Vice President

Theodore Roosevelt, and the glories of the exposition were overshadowed by the nation's grief at the loss of a popular leader. Yet despite this tragedy, a sense of prosperity buoyed Buffalonians well into the early decades of the twentieth century.

Merchants saw great potential in Rochester as well. In the nineteenth century, the strip of Main Street on the west side of the Genesee River was the focal point of the city. The intersection of State, Main, Buffalo, and Exchange, known as the Four Corners, was home to the settlement's earliest merchants (the first store, opened by Ira West, appeared in 1812).[23] As early as 1826, the city had forty-two stores, which catered to a population of 7,699.[24] In 1828, the Reynolds Arcade was built, an imposing structure with two rows of stores surrounding a central corridor lit by a skylight, and it was described locally as "Rochester's permanent crystal palace." Over the next few decades, other buildings sprang up to line the north side of Main Street.[25] Rochester's first department store, Burke, FitzSimons and Hone, began operations in the late 1850s. The open appearance of the stores and their prominent display areas encouraged window-shopping along the north side of Buffalo and Main Streets.[26] Older dry goods merchants along State and Exchange faced intense competition from the stores developing along Main and St. Paul.[27] The construction of the Powers Block, an office building near the Four Corners, further added to the sense of Rochester's prosperity in the late 1860s. The multistory building featured the first elevator in western New York. Throughout the 1870s, both the owner of the Powers Block and local retailers invested in a continual expansion of their buildings. By the final decade of the nineteenth century, an extensive network of electric trolley lines connected all sections of the city and facilitated the movement of shoppers and workers to the downtown.[28]

The biggest difference between Buffalo's and Rochester's retailing scenes involved the disproportionate influence exerted by a single store, for in Rochester, one enterprise dominated both the physical and economic landscape. Sibley, Lindsay and Curr was Rochester's largest and most prestigious store, and by the 1920s, it was the largest department store in New York State outside Manhattan. The business was founded by two Scottish retail clerks and a bookkeeper who had worked together in a store in Boston. They initially planned to go to New York City, but on visiting Rochester in 1868, they decided to remain and invest their $5,000 of capital there. They brought with them the then-radical concept of a one-price-for-all policy, which had originated in Boston. Capitalizing on this association, they called their enterprise "The Boston Store." Early on, Sibley, Lindsay and Curr was involved in actually producing many of the items arrayed on its shelves in order to ensure low prices and good quality. By 1873, it had expanded into the manufacture of more than four hundred items, particularly garments (including men's underwear, nightshirts, and eventually business shirts), and four stories of workrooms were occupied by women sewers.[29] The store also acted as a wholesaler, with a fleet of salesmen traveling across New York, Pennsylvania, and Ohio and even as far as Minneapolis and along the Atlantic seaboard.[30] Sibley, Lindsay and Curr was, from an early date, a showplace for the achievements of local businesses. In 1894, it featured the first local viewing of four of Thomas Edison's kinetoscopes, showing motion pictures recorded on film produced by Eastman Kodak.[31]

Retailers in both Buffalo and Rochester became increasingly centered in the downtown areas, primarily along Main Street in each city. Buffalo's downtown did not fully emerge as a central business district until the turn of the twentieth century. In a fairly short period of time, the downtown experienced a rapid expansion, spurred by the building of electric streetcar lines that made the business district much more accessible to residents all over the city. The downtown was first served by a streetcar system in 1861, when three cars and twelve horses carried passengers along Main Street from Exchange to Goodell. By the 1920s, this network was expanded into a combined trolley and motorcar system, powered for the most part by Niagara Falls electricity, that consisted of a fleet of over a thousand cars. As Mark Goldman notes, "Now, for the price of a nickel, anybody, anywhere in the city, could jump on a streetcar and ride downtown."[32] Buffalo residents who had restricted much of their social and cultural lives to their immediate neighborhoods were drawn into the downtown.

In addition to department stores, hotels, theaters, restaurants, and music halls became concentrated in the center of the city. Buffalo was a significant stop for touring productions from Manhattan, and new shows were often tried out in Buffalo before going on to New York. Musicals, dramas, and vaudeville numbers attracted large crowds. Ziegfeld's "Follies" was one of many productions that delighted Buffalo audiences.[33] The concentration of theaters and stores in downtown changed the recreation habits of area residents. Daytime meant strolling the streets, examining the windows at J. N. Adam's or Hengerer's, or eating lunch at the Deco Restaurant (home of the Queen City sandwich—"named after Buffalo, and worth it!"); at night, leisure pursuits such as a trip to the Shea Garden Theater beckoned.[34] Main Street was the prime location for window-shopping and thus a highly desirable location for retailers. By 1920, a glance in the Buffalo city directory would have revealed that seven of the city's largest stores, as well as a number of other smaller retailers, had Main Street frontage. When Sears, Roebuck first arrived in the city in 1929, it, too, would select a Main Street location

The city's silhouette was transformed by the creation of skyscrapers—new office buildings sprang up, many designed by some of the nation's leading architects. Louis Sullivan designed a modern skyscraper for the Guaranty Trust Company in 1896. The same year witnessed the opening of the Ellicott Square office block at 295 Main Street, designed by the Chicago firm responsible for architecture at the World's Columbia Exposition and the Marshall Field Wholesale Store in that city. With adornments of terra-cotta and Italian marble, Ellicott Square was an imposing structure that filled an entire city block and housed shops and offices in the heart of downtown. It was the largest office complex in the country at the time it was built. Farther from downtown, Frank Lloyd Wright contributed the Larkin office building and a number of private residences to the city. Transportation also changed the look of Buffalo. In addition to new streetcar routes, new parking garages were constructed, and at least one park was paved to become a traffic circle. In 1923, E. M. Statler opened a new luxury hotel on Delaware Avenue, which featured a palacelike lobby made of white Botticino marble imported from Italy, a ballroom capable of seating fifteen hundred diners, a fireproof motion picture projection room, private dining rooms decorated in themes (one featuring handmade wallpaper from Alsace-Lorraine, another in Georgian style, and yet another displaying lacquered scenes of China), and a full Turkish bath in the basement with a forty-foot pool. Thirteen floors of the building were devoted to guest rooms (seventy-nine on each floor). These were equally lavish, described as the "last word in luxury and comfort," with "deep, soft carpets, a full length mirror in every room, a reading lamp over every bed, a light over every dresser, handsome furniture."[35]

Retailers kept pace with these developments, expanding and adopting new technologies. Adam, Meldrum and Anderson grew from a small general-goods dealer to a sizable department store, with buying offices in New York City, Germany, Italy, France, and the British Isles. The store first installed electric lighting in 1886.[36] Within ten years of its opening, J. N. Adam and Company had outgrown its original building. Nearby properties were acquired, but as the store continued to grow, it moved to a new location, also on Main Street. By 1891, telephones were installed, and the following year saw the installation of electric lights in the store, making it among the most modern establishments

in the downtown area at the time.[37] Crowds of tourists visited the store's en-
gine room daily to view the dynamos that powered the lights. Hengerer's, too,
expanded. By the time founder William Hengerer retired in 1905, his specialty
shop was the store of choice for fashionable Buffalonians. That same year,
J. N. Adam's and Hengerer's were acquired by Associated Merchants of New
York City, yet management decisions for the two stores remained centered in
Buffalo, and they continued to emphasize their long respective histories in the
city and their role in the development of western New York.[38] Despite the concentration of major retailers on Main Street, other areas of the city also
boasted active shopping districts. There was a cluster of retail activity in the
Broadway-Fillmore district, where slightly more budget-priced variety, furniture, and department stores, including Jahraus-Braun and the Morgan Stores,
were located. Drugstores and grocery stores were scattered throughout the city,
serving local neighborhoods, but the grocery business as late as 1929 was still
concentrated in the downtown district.[39]

Rochester's merchants continued a similar expansion throughout the early
decades of the twentieth century, an era looked back on as the city's golden
age. Sibley, Lindsay and Curr continued to grow despite suffering through a
major fire that destroyed the store's main building. The company already owned
the property on Main Street east of Clinton at the time of the fire, so it ac-
celerated plans to move to the new location. All remaining stock was quickly
relocated, and the new store opened just months after the disaster. One (possibly apocryphal) story told that the fire destroyed all of the store's credit reports yet such was the goodwill of the community toward the business that
every last charge account customer came forward to settle his or her account
in the months after the fire. Whether or not all Rochesterians did, indeed,
honor their debts to the store, the incident was repeated in Sibley's promotional materials for decades as evidence of the close relationship between the
institution and the community.

The year 1906 witnessed the opening of a new grocery and bakery on the
fifth floor of the Sibley building, an "elegant place where the upper bracket
housewife could examine delicacies from around the world."[40] In 1911, the six-
story Tower Building was constructed adjacent to the main selling areas. The
tower held a large clock and bell (weighing thirty-five hundred pounds) and
became a landmark in Rochester. Sibley's grocery department would feature a
line of products under its own "Tower" line. By the time of the store's fiftieth
anniversary in 1918, Sibley, Lindsay and Curr had a main aisle that ran 373 feet
from the entrance on North Street to the exit on Clinton Avenue. The store

had fourteen acres of selling space. In 1926, six more floors were added to the main building, so that the Sibley store and office building now occupied a solid downtown block, the largest business block in the city. During peak times, the store employed twenty-five hundred people, or, as one promotional pamphlet proudly asserted, "almost one out of every 100 people living in the city."[41] A fan system supplied warm air in winter and cooled air in summer, and electric clocks throughout the store were completely synchronized. Thirteen passenger elevators shuttled a steady flow of customers to each of the store's six floors, and modern electric lights replaced old arc lamps to bathe all merchandise in a soft, steady glow.

Other department stores, while not quite as imposing as Sibley, Lindsay and Curr, were still a major presence on Rochester's Main Street. Although the west side had traditionally been populated by retailers, larger stores jockeyed for position on East Main Street beginning in the 1890s. The pioneer in developing this stretch of Main was McCurdy and Company. After an apprenticeship at merchandising in stores in Belfast, Northern Ireland, John Cooke McCurdy emigrated to Philadelphia and eventually made his way to Rochester. He bought out C. H. Carroll to open McCurdy and Norwell east from the Four Corners. Many local merchants doubted his judgment. The store was located at the corner of East Main Street and Elm—supposedly the wrong way from the Four Corners and close to "Hoodoo Corner" (East Avenue and Elm), which was considered bad luck because previous businesses had failed on the spot. An ad for the store explained that "the east end of the city needed a store of its own, so we landed up here, at the corner of Main and Elm."[42] McCurdy and Norwell opened in March 1901, with a staff of seventy-five employees and fifty thousand square feet of selling space. John McCurdy proved his doubters wrong, and in 1910, he built a six-story addition on the west side of the Palmer Block site. The store built a six-floor south wing between 1923 and 1925, and it continued to make improvements such as the installation of elevators.

E. W. Edwards and Son also occupied prime East Main Street frontage. The company was founded in Syracuse, and by the 1920s, it operated stores in that city as well as in Rochester and Buffalo. South of East Main Street on Clinton Avenue, the B. Forman Company was a pioneer, emerging by the 1920s as a leader in women's ready-to-wear clothing. B. Forman boasted that it was the first store to bring the women of western New York "a new method of merchandising, showing the new styles first, cleaning house four times a year to keep the stocks new and fresh at all times, and marking prices always at the lowest level consistent with the quality and the service rendered."[43] Despite this flourishing retail business on East Main, West Main Street was not completely abandoned, as the Duffy-McInnerney (later Duffy-Powers) store grew to occupy six stories at West Main and Fitzhugh. The firm's vice president boasted after a trip to Europe that the store had more floor space than Selfridge's famed store in London.[44] Store founder Walter B. Duffy was also involved in the hotel business in Rochester, helping to build the new Rochester Hotel across West Main Street in the downtown area.[45]

If the downtowns of both cities were transformed into distinct central business districts, so, too, were the residential neighborhoods of Rochester and Buffalo carved into discrete blocks by the 1920s, largely determined by class and ethnicity. The most affluent Buffalonians lived in the wide, tree-lined streets to the north and west of the city's center. Although some realtors tried to encourage the development of downtown apartments, in the style of New York penthouses, most families of means lived in detached houses. Along Elmwood and Delaware, in Wards 18, 19, and 20, large stone and wood single-family homes sat beyond expanses of manicured lawn. The most prestigious streets—those backing onto Delaware Park (designed by Frederick Law Olmsted) and those adjacent to the neoclassical buildings remaining from the Pan-American Exposition—were occupied by Buffalo's older families, some of which had been in the area for generations. Samuel Clemens, before gaining fame as Mark Twain, had lived on Delaware from 1869 to 1871, when he was editor and part owner of the *Buffalo Morning Express*. The descendants of industrialists, the owner of the *Buffalo News*, and the children of politicians lived in Italianate villas, French Second Empire mansions, and Victorian shingle-style homes.

The northern end of Buffalo became an even more desirable address after 1880, with the creation of Olmsted's Parkside community. Parkside was an area of broad, curving streets, served by a parkway system of roads and a trolley line to the business district. It was in this neighborhood that Frank Lloyd Wright built a Prairie Style home for Larkin Company executive Darwin D. Martin. In the early twentieth century, the residents of this area were the lawyers, professors, capitalists, and business owners of the city, and the wives in this community could easily afford to shop in specialty stores and department stores downtown or even travel to New York City occasionally for purchases. These were the families most likely to have standing accounts at the department stores and be on the mailing lists of dress departments.

Ethnic communities made up another vital component of the city. Although not all immigrants lived in ethnic enclaves, there were clusters of settlement, particularly in Ward 5, where Old World traditions and institutions flourished. Buffalo had over 120,000 foreign-born residents, including sizable Polish, German, and Italian communities. In 1920, the foreign-born made up 31.6 percent of the city's population. Of these, a significant number (31,876) came from Canada, Ireland, England, and Scotland and thus did not face the same obstacles in language and custom encountered by other groups that emigrated to America. Just over 15 percent of the foreign-born inhabitants above the age of twenty-one were unable to speak English. Buffalo's civic promoters went to great lengths to stress the high level of assimilation of the city's immigrants. A textbook designed for use in Buffalo schools gave a painstaking breakdown of the population, distinguishing between those who were "Foreign born [but] coming from strictly English speaking countries," those who were "Foreign born coming from non–English speaking countries, but now able to speak English" and those who were "Foreign born and unable to speak English."[46]

Other observers were more appreciative of the strengths of Buffalo's immigrant communities. J. Walter Thompson described the marketing potential of Buffalo's "highly concentrated and well-to-do Polish population," served by its own newspaper. Polish immigrants formed a "remarkably homogenous . . . city within a city with a life of its own."[47] The residents of the ethnic neighborhoods of the city's East Side were also key to Buffalo's success as an industrial center. Polish immigrants, in particular, were likely to find work in the city's factories.[48] Many working-class neighborhoods sprang up within walking distance of the factories located near the waterfront, in the southern and eastern areas of the city. Buffalo's Italian population was concentrated near the southwest corner of Main Street, extending from Niagara Street westward to the waterfront, an area known as Little Italy by the early 1920s. Close proximity to the canal was necessary for the many peddlers, fruit vendors, and seasonal workers among the Italian community.[49] Buffalo also had a black community of over forty-five hundred residents, again concentrated on the East Side in the downtown, primarily in Wards 6 and 7. Some black men found work in the industrial plants, but advancement was difficult because of discrimination from industrial employers and unions, and many worked as Pullman porters, carters, and outside laborers. Black women were almost entirely confined to the field of domestic service.[50]

As consumers, Buffalo's ethnic working class was more likely to patronize small local merchants and only occasionally venture into downtown department stores or chain branches. Immigrants were also less likely to buy branded goods, in comparison with other class groups. Edmund McGarry of the University of Buffalo noted that the "alien populations" of Buffalo were less inclined to patronize chain stores for groceries because they could not secure credit or haggle with merchants in those stores. As a result, they were not as likely to purchase that mainstay of the chain store business, the national brand-name good.[51]

Between the mansions of Delaware and the more crowded neighborhoods of the East Side were the neighborhoods bordering the university and to the east on a larger radius from the downtown, north of Broadway. Wards 16, 19, and 20 were almost entirely populated by white, American citizens. Native white males in Buffalo dominated the positions of factory foremen and highly skilled workers as well as office clerks and professionals. The families living in the North, University, and Malden neighborhoods of the city were less likely to send female members out into the workforce. Women from these areas made frequent trips to the downtown area and were a major target for the advertising and promotions offered by Buffalo department stores.

Rochester had its share of wealthy residents, too. Its blue book was dominated by local figures such as George Eastman, the Bausches and Lombs, and other industrialists. The elite of the city lived in mansions on East Avenue, and wives in this neighborhood sent limousines and carriages to line the curb outside the Sibley, Lindsay and Curr department store. Shaded by "over-arching elms," the homes on East Avenue made up "one of the most beautiful residential streets in America," according to one visitor. Desirable residences included those on Ambassador Drive and along Livingston Park as well.[52] The city's other neighborhoods, though less opulent, tended to be dotted with freestanding homes on treed streets. By 1890, most of the acres within the city limits had been developed for residential purposes, leading observers to christen Rochester the "City of Homes."[53] A guidebook suggested that every residential section, "of whatever economic class," shared a common characteristic: the individually owned home, often surrounded by a "carefully tended lawn or backyard, a continuing expression of the period when the nursery industry prevailed in Rochester."[54]

During the last two decades of the nineteenth century, a steady stream of immigrants transformed the composition of the city. Although residents of Western European origin still comprised the largest segment of Rochester's ethnic minorities, an influx of Eastern and Southern European migrants was significant. In particular, Italian, Polish, and Russian settlers challenged the dominance of the older groups. Rochester's foreign-born residents made up

just over 30 percent of the city's population, with Italians and Germans form-
ing the two largest ethnic groups. Irish, English, and Scottish immigrants, long
a presence in the city, were still sizable in number. Just under 10 percent of
foreign-born residents over twenty-one years of age were unable to speak English. Long-established ethnic communities, such as the Germans, made an
effort to encourage the rapid assimilation of new migrants; among other
things, they offered English language classes.[55]

Ethnic communities in Rochester were less geographically concentrated
than those in Buffalo. Some groups, including the Scottish, Irish, Anglo-
Canadians, and Germans, had deep roots in the city, and over time, many had
become integrated into more traditionally old-stock, "Yankee" neighborhoods.
Newer arrivals, such as the Italians, were more likely to live in separate ethnic
enclaves. Even here, however, there was no single, compact colony. Clusters of
Italian residents could be found in four city wards, primarily in the central
business district and Ward 16. Italians in Rochester were likely to work in construction or as peddlers and small merchants. Only one other group was similarly concentrated: the city's black population, which numbered over fifteen
hundred in 1920.[56] Rochester's tradition as an abolitionist center had attracted
many free blacks earlier in the century. In later years, however, prominent abolitionists such as Frederick Douglass left the city, and Rochester's black population was economically and spatially segregated, primarily concentrated on the
western edge of the Third Ward. Most black residents worked in the service
trades.

Buffalo and Rochester were medium-sized cities in the early decades of the
twentieth century but ones that had been growing steadily. According to the
1920 census, Buffalo ranked eleventh in population nationally, putting it just
after Los Angeles and before San Francisco and Washington, D.C. Local
boosters crowed that the city had passed from "a pioneer hamlet to a place
among the twelve leading cities of the nation."[57] Rochester was twenty-third
on the list, falling between Jersey City, New Jersey, and Portland, Oregon, in
size. Buffalo's population had increased by almost 20 percent between 1910 and
1920 and by a similar amount from 1900 to 1910. Rochester had an even faster
rate of growth, increasing by approximately 34 percent during each of the two
decades.[58] For merchants, estimates of city populations were seen as the starting point, not the limit, of the potential markets open to them.

Advertisers and retail trade writers often referred to a circle around a city
that formed the "metropolitan" or "retail shopping area" of major markets.
This territory included not only direct suburbs but also outlying communities

whose citizens often patronized stores at larger centers. Buffalo drew shoppers from nearby satellites such as Williamsville, Tonawanda, North Tonawanda, Orchard Park, Depew, and Lackawanna, as well as the more distant Lewiston, Youngstown, Niagara Falls, and Lockport. Rochester served the farming communities that ringed it, including Pittsford, Fairport, Greece, Irondequoit, Gates, Webster, Medina, Batavia, Mumford, Palmyra, and North Chili. Promoters of Buffalo's industries stressed the city's location as a key advantage. The authors of a textbook on industry in the city argued, "Within the circle used by economic experts as a means of comparing market territories—with Buffalo as the central point—we find a population larger than that included in the market territory of any other American city. That population will be permanently increased because it occupies land best suited to agriculture and industry. To the east and southeast of Buffalo is one-third of the population of the United States."[59] This tremendous market territory ensured, in their view, easy distribution of the products of Buffalo's factories; it also suggested that the city could act as a magnet, drawing consumers toward its retail center.

In 1925, the J. Walter Thompson Company ranked Buffalo twelfth on a list of "Group I" cities (those having over 500,000 in population). It had a city population of 538,016 and a retail shopping area population of 724,443.[60] The company went even further to suggest that Buffalo was considered the center of a trading zone forty-two miles in area, drawing from thirty-four surrounding towns and bringing its total metropolitan population to 850,000.[61] Rochester, the eighth largest of the "Group II" cities (with populations from 100,000 to 500,000), had a city population of 316,786 and a retail shopping area of 513,935.[62] In 1924, the *Rochester Democrat and Chronicle* acknowledged that downtown merchants served not only those living within the city limits but also those in a wider area beyond: "Every area has its metropolis and the tendency of people within that area [is] to visit the 'metropolis' when they wish to purchase something that cannot be secured in their community stores. . . . There is at present circling Rochester a considerable area, known as the metropolitan area where Rochester has the dominating facilities for retail trade. There are department stores and men's clothing stores, that are held in high esteem among leading retail merchants of cities far larger than Rochester."[63]

To encourage shoppers from the wider area, the Rochester Retail Merchants' Council urged that transportation services be gauged to the needs of visitors, enabling those from outlying districts to "conveniently hop a buss [*sic*] or trolley in the morning, do their shopping in Rochester stores pleasantly and profitably, enjoy an attractive meal and a first-class theater program and return without undue haste or delay."[64] Merchants in Buffalo and Rochester occasionally advertised in the newspapers of surrounding towns, and they ran special promotions to lure out-of-town shoppers. As early as 1909, the McCurdy and Norwell department store courted clientele beyond the city limits, offering free delivery of orders over $5 within two hundred miles of Rochester. Similarly, Duffy-Powers of Rochester regularly ran "Suburban Days" promotions. Newspaper ads featured a drawing of the store building surrounded by over twenty communities, including Webster, Chili, Geneseo, Honeoye Falls, and East Henrietta.

Although retailers and advertisers liked to publicize the largest possible figures in terms of potential shoppers, they acknowledged that not all consumers were created equal: even within a given geographic area, there could be wide fluctuations in income levels. Marketers and advertisers used income tax returns as a rough gauge of the "right sort" of shoppers—those families that had sufficient income to file a tax return presumably had enough to indulge in various consumer goods. The J. Walter Thompson Company's newsletter noted approvingly that nearly 11 percent of the people living in Buffalo in 1925 had sufficient income to file a return, at a time when the average filing rate for the entire country was only 6.3 percent. The individual income tax returns in the area surrounding Buffalo numbered 43,787, or one return for every sixteen residents.[65]

Politicians and business leaders in Buffalo and Rochester during the early twentieth century continually suggested that their cities could become leaders on a national and even an international scale. With the benefit of hindsight, we now know that many of their predictions would not come to fruition. Yet it would be a mistake to dismiss these aspirations as delusions of grandeur or the irrational expressions of boosters who were unable to see the reality of their surroundings. The optimism of Buffalo and Rochester residents was based on a very real history characterized by rapid population growth, economic expansion, and technological ingenuity. Buffalo was a commercial and industrial powerhouse, chosen over all other cities in the nation to symbolize progress as the host of a prestigious exhibition. Its location near the electrical power of Niagara Falls and close to the densely populated East Coast and its positioning as the gateway city to trade with Canada seemed to guarantee future success. Rochester had emerged as a thriving industrial center, whose roster of businesses included the nationally prominent Eastman Kodak. Merchants who located in the area rode this wave of growth and took satisfaction in their contributions to the development of their communities. For retailers and residents alike, the history of the region justified a tremendous sense of pride in the achievements of western New York and a sense of optimism about the future. This understanding of the value of the local would inform the cultural and business life of the region during the 1920s and 1930s.

DOWNTOWN RETAILERS
AND "MAIN STREET TOWNS"

DURING THE 1920S AND 1930S, most large retailers were concentrated in the central business districts of Rochester and Buffalo. Within a few blocks, shoppers in either city could peruse wares at a number of sizable department stores, not to mention countless smaller jewelers, tailors, dressmakers, and other shopkeepers. This chapter explores the active role of retailers in the civic and cultural life of the city during the interwar period. Both literally and figuratively, retailers were at the center of city life—they occupied prime real estate in the downtown, and their stores were a favorite destination for housewives, tourists, children, or anyone else seeking a luncheon spot or pleasurable place to while away an afternoon. Even those who did not actually purchase wares from a department store in Buffalo might excitedly view the Christmas lights strung by the local merchants' association. The clock tower of Sibley, Lindsay and Curr was a landmark for Rochester locals. The parades sponsored by merchants were a highlight on the holiday calendar.

Because Main Street (and, by extension, the stores that lined it) was considered to represent the achievements and aspirations of local residents in many ways, it could also be a source of debate. During the late 1920s, boosters in

Buffalo toyed with the idea of renaming their central thoroughfare to better reflect the city's distinct status. This debate was about more than a simple name change: it tapped into both the pride and the insecurities of a medium-sized city.

Stores were a highly visible component of the downtowns of both Rochester and Buffalo. Indeed, retailers devoted considerable energy to attracting the attention of passersby. Elaborate and ever changing displays of merchandise had become a defining feature of department stores by the early twentieth century, and retailers in both cities paid careful attention to displays. Many merchants subscribed to trade magazines that instructed them on innovative methods in arranging goods. Walking past the Kleinhans Clothing Company store in Buffalo, shoppers could see a range of items such as gloves, handkerchiefs, belts, and men's suits on mannequins, and a price list was prominently displayed.[1] During the 1920s, Sibley's of Rochester used modernist backdrops to highlight women's clothing, employing geographic prints that suggested the art deco trend in decor.[2] Window dressers boasted of their ability to arrange goods in order to attract the most attention and therefore generate the most sales. Efforts to gauge public response to the windows could take on extreme forms: one Buffalo department store eventually installed microphones close to its front windows so that the conversations of spectators on the street could be monitored and their responses to various goods recorded.

The battle to win the public's attention was never won. Stores constantly updated both their windows and their interior display areas. After its renovation in 1926, Sibley, Lindsay and Curr was lauded by a reporter from the *Dry Goods Merchants Trade Journal* (*DGMTJ*) for exemplifying "the last word in store equipment, lighting and fixtures."[3] The trade periodical featured photos of the new fixtures in a special section on store equipment and display. The article included a photo of one of Sibley's windows, which highlighted sportswear by using three panels of graphic, modernist prints. Inside the store, Sibley's had wide aisles and rows of globe lights to illuminate the merchandise. In the bedding section, shoppers could see linens in "homelike surroundings," as blanket-filled cradles and even an actual made-up bed allowed them to imagine the goods in use. The store fixtures were of polished walnut and mahogany. New terrazzo flooring was installed on the main level. Designers paid careful attention to layout and the efficient use of space, with the result that Sibley's merchandise seemed easily accessible and less crowded than that in many competitors' stores, according to the reporter from the trade journal. Even as five-and-dime stores popularized "jumble tables," which allowed customers to feel the merchandise, Sibley's stocked many items such as hosiery and gloves in gleaming glass cases, behind which stood clerks trained in personalized sales. Other retailers were willing to pay for costly renovations in order to maximize both the selling floor and the window area. When McCurdy and Company remodeled in 1923, an entirely new front facade was put on the store, and the show windows on East Main were expanded to create a display space of three hundred square feet.[4]

Even the largest stores were not immune to competitive pressures. During the 1910s and 1920s, Sibley, Lindsay and Curr regularly sent employees to pose as shoppers at other stores and record the number of patrons in each department at specific times. Careful note was made of the numbers of those just looking and those actually buying, not only at other department stores but also in smaller jewelry and specialty shops.[5] A fleet of six "professional shoppers" was also employed by the Comparative Shoppers' Bureaus of two Buffalo department stores to discover the price and quality of items at competitors' stores. These positions had a high rate of turnover, as after about six months salesclerks in the stores would become suspicious of the shoppers and refuse to wait on them. The comparative shoppers also spied on employees at their own stores, reporting poor service to department heads.[6]

Stores were designed with the female shopper in mind. The identification of shopping as "women's work" had most noticeably emerged in North America in the nineteenth century. Where once women and men had worked together in the production of goods at home, the rise of waged labor and, more significantly, a white-collar, salaried workforce increasingly categorized men as breadwinners and women as consumers. Although many women spanned the worlds of production and consumption in their daily lives, the notion that shopping was a female skill—or indulgence—was firmly entrenched by the twentieth century.[7] In response, store management actively cultivated an atmosphere alluring to women shoppers. The very layout of departments within a store encouraged women to linger, and features such as restaurants and tearooms were comfortable spaces for middle-class women to meet and socialize. Western New York retailers were sometimes pioneers in these developments: the original Sibley's tearoom in the Granite Building was built in 1893, six years before Marshall Field's in Chicago opened that city's first large tearoom. The Sibley's tearoom was a popular downtown destination in Rochester, serving tea and lunch to a primarily female clientele and offering discreet entertainment such as bridge lessons and chamber music concerts. The decor was refined and genteel, with white tablecloths and walls tinted in soft colors. The new Main

Street store tearoom (built after the fire) could seat between 350 and 400 patrons, depending on the arrangement of tables. Such facilities were considered a wise use of store space: in 1926, Sibley's opened a restaurant that seated 515 and added a cafeteria and marble soda fountain soon after. In 1934, a main floor buffet became another option for hungry shoppers. To facilitate meetings between women shoppers, the Service Bureau allowed visitors from out of town to register, and a clerk would telephone friends in Rochester and arrange social appointments. Parcels and luggage could also be checked there.[8] Sibley's did not completely ignore its male patrons: in an effort to attract businessmen for lunch, it opened the Pompeian Annex, designed as a café for men. With brick walls, tile floors, and dark paneling, it was a spot where "men friends" could enjoy a cigar or cigarette at the table.[9]

Restaurants were only one part of a dizzying array of merchandise and services offered by department stores across America by the 1920s. Western New York retailers more than kept pace with the newest innovations in merchandising. Sibley's store directory listed over eighty separate departments, carrying everything from draperies, rugs, and leather goods to corsets, toys, and groceries. A branch of the public library was opened on the sixth floor of the store, and customers withdrew over two hundred books per week. New types of services were added to cater to every possible want of the customer. Beauty salons were popular features, allowing female customers a chance to rest and regroup while getting a manicure or permanent wave. One Buffalo store told of the pleasure that a "smart young thing" from western New York enjoyed in the salon. Entering the beauty salon after phoning ahead, the flapper is greeted by a hostess. She then "stretches out in a comfortable chair, breathes a relieved sigh and gives herself up to the luxury of a relaxing interim in a hectic day. Being a modern young thing, she smokes if she wishes. She may enjoy a refreshing cup of tea, without charge. She leaves entirely refreshed, and later finds that her first visit becomes a weekly habit."[10] Services for the home were also offered. Flint and Kent boasted an interior decoration service with experienced advisers who would suggest ideas for furnishing a home; the store offered custom-made draperies, window shades, slipcovers, and furniture. The special training that interior decorators at Sibley's received was considered so valuable that these employees were required to sign a labor contract that prevented their engaging in the same line of work for a competitor in Monroe County for a period of five years after leaving Sibley's.[11] Beyond purchasing new wallpaper and home accessories, patrons could even have rugs cleaned and furniture reupholstered.

Stores offered full delivery services to allow shoppers to purchase more than they could carry. Purchases could be wrapped, sent home, or even shipped abroad at Christmastime by the parcel service. B. Forman featured a bureau in Paris that was able to buy, wrap, and deliver Christmas gifts to "friends in France."[12] Downtown merchants in Buffalo had a coordinated delivery service, which dropped off the purchases of patrons of Adam, Meldrum and Anderson; J. N. Adam; L. L. Berger; E. W. Edwards; Flint and Kent; Wm. Hengerer Company; Hens and Kelly; and Oppenheim, Collins and Company. In Rochester, Sibley's had its own fleet of delivery vehicles. During the 1920s, there were three regular daily deliveries within the city limits, at 8 A.M., 12:15 P.M., and 3:45 P.M. Deliverymen were familiar and enduring features of city life. One Sibley's deliveryman covered his fifteen-mile route three times daily for twenty-five years. Even as Sibley's switched to motorized vehicles after 1920, Ira Perkins continued to rely on his fifteen-year-old brown sorrel. Cy Perkins reported that the use of horse and buggy was, in many ways, more efficient in the downtown—Cy reportedly stopped for red lights and wove through automobiles with "perfect ease"—and his driver contended that the horse knew "a lot more about traffic than most people." When Perkins and Cy made their last rounds in 1938, the *Democrat and Chronicle* covered the story, describing the two as a link to "the days when all Rochester's streets were paved with cobblestones."[13]

Delivery service was an aid not only to shoppers who did not want to carry their purchases but also to those who could not make the trip downtown to shop. All of Buffalo's and Rochester's major department stores had telephone sales departments through which orders could be placed. In promotional materials, Sibley's boasted that its telephone system was unique in the country and used enough miles of telephone wire to reach from Rochester to Albany.[14] The pneumatic tube system through which in-store communications took place (including the sending of sales slips and the retrieval of change for customers) was the second largest in the world, following only Macy's in New York City. Like department stores, the grocery trade worked to streamline communications and improve delivery systems. The Larkin Company Stores of Buffalo, for example, had an extensive system to facilitate grocery orders. Each order was recorded on a "customer card," so that preferences (brand of coffee, cuts of meat, average size of fish order) would be apparent to the operator. Operators could recommend specials in the store or simply fill standing orders each week. Orders received before noon were delivered in time for dinner.[15]

It is worth underscoring the importance of service as part of the shopping experience in department stores during this period. Contact with salesclerks was fundamental not only during the actual exchange of product for cash or credit but also in examining goods. Although some departments by the 1920s were experimenting with ways to increase shoppers' hands-on contact with goods, many types of items were only displayed in glass cases, and customers required sales assistance if they wished to touch or more closely examine gloves, hosiery, accessories, and cosmetics. Shopping for items such as shoes required asking a salesclerk to check the available stock for the correct size. This emphasis on the role of the store's clerk served a number of functions. On the one hand, glass cases and hidden stocks of merchandise behind counters or in back rooms made it easier to control the goods in the store. Clerks had a better sense of which items were popular and could discourage shoplifting (always a concern in department stores). On the other hand, stores hoped that the experience of being waited on by a courteous clerk would enhance the shopping experience, making customers feel indulged and pampered and thus more inclined to spend money.[16]

Careful attention was paid to ensure that salespeople projected professionalism and efficiency. They were formally dressed, making it easy for customers to distinguish between those shopping and those able to offer sales assistance and subtly reinforcing the class distinction between moneyed customers and working clerks. Saleswomen at Sibley's wore all-black dresses until the 1910s, when they were given the privilege of wearing white shirtwaists and black or plain, dark-colored skirts during the summer. Plaid or light-colored skirts were considered too informal, and the company sent memos suggesting that if clerks did not recognize this fact, the store might quickly revert to enforcing a policy of all-black uniforms.[17] An employee handbook from 1926 stressed that the attire of all female workers who came into contact with customers had to fall within acceptable middle-class notions of appropriate business dress. They were to avoid "conspicuous cosmetics, extreme styles of hairdressing, elaborate jewelry or stirring peculiarities in apparel." Men were to forgo "gaudy neck-ties" and were required to wear coats at all times when on the selling floors.[18] By 1937, regulations had softened somewhat (for example, women could wear navy, green, wine, and brown dresses as well as black ones), but employees were still to select garments appropriate for business and would receive a discount on suitable clothes purchased from the store. Store personnel were instructed in the courteous treatment of all shoppers—they were encouraged to think of customers as guests and treat them with the same level of courtesy they would extend to visitors in their own homes.[19]

Members of the sales staff were expected to educate their customers about the benefits of particular lines. Certain departments, especially those selling women's garments, relied on a skilled sales staff to recommend appropriate products for each customer. Saleswomen also aided patrons with the fitting of dresses and corsets, and they entered fitting rooms and even assisted customers in dressing and undressing. The saleswoman offered advice to the customer, often encouraging her to "trade up" to a slightly more expensive version of an item she had chosen. Hens and Kelly boasted that while the store used newspaper ads to draw people in, the sales staff got all the credit for ensuring that women were sold the proper corsets and for suggesting higher-line merchandise. Bernadine Smith, the assistant buyer for the department, commented, "When [shoppers] come to us, we do everything to sell them a good corset. . . . We fit them correctly and send them away so that they'll come back. We sell their minds as much as their bodies. We educate Buffalo women to a new and better estimate of corsets. We sell them the type of garment they need and do everything to give them the best grade possible. We TRADE UP, NOT DOWN."[20] Shoppers were encouraged to put themselves in the hands of the trained sales staff. One Christmas ad campaign for Sibley's spelled out the dire consequences that befell a woman who had refused to follow the advice of clerks in the Men's Store. A disgruntled Rochester man described how his sweetheart's failure to select the proper gift resulted in the termination of their relationship: "Year after year she gave me things I did not want and could never use. Year after year I remained glum and unenthusiastic when she presented me with golf clubs that did not suit me, cigars I would not smoke, and fishing tackle that merely duplicated my equipment." Frustrated that his paramour had overlooked the fine selection of shirts and neckwear available at Sibley's, he left her.[21] Salespeople also offered a range of services to shoppers, not all directly related to the sale of merchandise. On occasion, when local elderly residents or children went missing in Rochester, store management circulated memos with descriptions to the staff at Sibley's and instructed them to report any sightings of the people in question.

The education of shoppers about the advantages of particular products was not limited to informal interaction with members of the sales staff. Retailers in Buffalo and Rochester organized more structured classes and demonstrations, bringing in guest speakers and offering customers a chance to try products before purchasing. The retail outlet of the Rochester Gas and Electric Corporation sold refrigerators, stoves, and small electrical appliances. To encourage the purchase of these goods (and increase power consumption in general), the company offered classes to teach people to craft lamp shades or use new features on stoves. The Home Service Department regularly was filled with housewives registered for half-day sessions. The utility news reported on the cheery atmosphere of one class where women could learn to make Christmas cakes: "Say!" one woman reportedly called across to another, "Do you know that your Elsie and Betty can come in here any Saturday morning and cook, or make a lamp shade, or learn to use the washer and ironer, or how to operate any of these electrical appliances? I'm sending Jenny next Saturday and maybe John will come along, for there are a few boys doing it too." The class's baking was done in an automatic oven with special temperature controls to ensure that the cakes were not burned. The special features of the oven were fully explained to the women, who, to the delight of the instructors, seemed to be "acquiring a fixed, faraway look on their faces portending the acquisition of just such an oven control on their ranges at home."[22] The Gas and Electric Corporation also cooperated with community groups: local Girl Scout troops were given demonstrations in using electric washing machines and irons and could earn badges for bringing in items they had carefully laundered. Beyond offering hands-on classes for small groups in its appliance showroom, the company organized larger demonstrations as well.

These types of classes were very popular with Rochester housewives. During 1929, the store held 59 lamp shade lessons where 254 shades were made. In the baking classes, 443 women did their own work, while 452 others observed them. Over 400 Girl Scouts attended the laundry classes. One Christmas party featured two chefs from the Seneca Hotel, who demonstrated the correct preparation of a suckling pig for roasting (in a modern electric oven, of course). The session was attended by 230 women.[23]

Larger stores often brought in "experts" who promoted specific product lines for the edification of local shoppers. In December 1927, Sibley, Lindsay and Curr boasted that Dorothy Strumph, a skin care expert from New York City, would be available for personal consultation in the Cosmetics Department of the store. In addition, Sibley's had many promotions for the home seamstress, including fashion shows. The store had a dressmaking school, where a skilled seamstress taught cutting, fitting, and sewing and also did alterations for home dressmakers who bought notions and fabric there. In November 1930, Hengerer's sponsored a series of four lectures by Marie L. Fenn, an authority from the International Silver Company who explained proper table settings for various social occasions. McCurdy and Company also used live models to demonstrate permanent waves in a hairstyle fashion show.[24]

The education of shoppers could never begin too soon. Department stores aimed to teach young people to commemorate occasions with the purchase of goods and to take pleasure in the process of shopping. Sibley, Lindsay and Curr produced a special publication, the *Juvenile Magazine,* which was mailed directly to young subscribers (presumably children of charge account holders). It featured puzzles, poems, and fiction that often touched on the theme of consumption. A paper doll on the back of one issue taught young girls that owning a large wardrobe of dresses was desirable and even promoted the store itself in poetry:

> My name is Ruth Sibley:
> I buy all my clothes
> My coats and my dresses,
> My hats and my hose
> —At the nicest big store
> In the city—Yes, Sir!
> You know which it is—
> Sibley, Lindsay and Curr.[25]

In May, young girls were reminded that the Sibley store stocked materials for new frocks, and the different fabrics appropriate for play clothes were carefully listed, including "Fine Tissue Ginghams, Romper Cloth, Crisp Organdies, Dainty Voiles," and a range of other options easily viewable in Aisle H of the store. Special clothing items such as patent-leather pumps from the Second Floor Shoe Shop or two-tone jersey frocks were described in detail.

A recurring column featured the activities of Jane and Billy, two Rochester schoolchildren whose parents were regular Sibley customers. From month to month, the two found new reasons to go to the store and seek out needed items. Billy and Jane were model consumers: always ready to go on a trip to the store, enthusiastic about new purchases, and even active in spreading the news about Sibley's to their friends (and the young readers of the magazine). One story described Billy and Jane putting on an elaborate fashion show for their friends, which naturally highlighted the advantages of Sibley's fashions.[26] The youngsters also often demonstrated the benefits of services provided by the retailer. In August, for instance, Jane and Billy went on a holiday to Albany. Heartbroken over leaving her doll at home, Jane tries to find a replacement at an Albany department store but is disappointed in the lack of selection there. Her aunt kindly contacts Sibley's Mail Order Department, and a replacement is quickly found.[27] Nor was appreciation of Sibley's merchandise a solely feminine pursuit: Billy's trip to camp, he reported, was greatly enhanced by his new swimsuit and hiking boots from Sibley's.[28] When Billy and Jane had visitors (such as Cousin Elizabeth from New Jersey), they showed off the sights of their home city, and the tour would wind up in a visit to the department store, where the children enjoyed lunch in the Sibley's tearoom and were allowed to roam on their own through Toyland, the Book Shop, the Art Department, and the counters of novelties in Housewares while Mother visited the beauty parlor.[29] On another occasion, Billy and Jane got their hair trimmed in the store barber shop, ate ice cream in the restaurant, and arrived home in high sprits, for "[as] everyone knows, it's not hard to be good natured when you've just come home from a shopping trip at the Sibley Store."[30]

At Christmastime, the *Juvenile Magazine* provided explicit instructions for young purchasers of gifts, including lists of appropriate choices for various family members and their locations within the store. "Big Sister" might be pleased with a box of "beaut-i-ful handkerchiefs" from the store's Front Aisle or a bottle of perfume from Aisle C.[31] Billy and Jane also learned the benefits of shopping early for Christmas. On Halloween, they sat down and drew up a list of possible gifts. The following day, after securing permission from their mother, the two children "took their banks to school with them, and opened them up and had their pennies, nickels and dimes changed into dollar bills at a little candy store." The moment that the school bell rang, they jumped on a streetcar to downtown and excitedly hurried to Sibley's, where they spent the afternoon "looking about and buying, and came home just loaded with bundles and packages." After dinner, they carefully gift wrapped and labeled every one of their purchases. The two could breathe a satisfied sigh of relief: "Now they will have no Shopping worries to bother them—and they'll have the rest of the time right up until Christmas to play and be carefree."[32] In the guise of an entertaining story about Billy and Jane, the vignette transmitted a number of messages about appropriate consumer behavior. The children changed their money before entering the store, rather than attempting to purchase a gift for their mother with a stack of coins. They perused aisles of goods and selected appropriate items for family members and avoided the stress that would befall more careless individuals who left their shopping until the last minute. Christmas shopping was presented as a necessary component of the season, a task that simply had to be completed in order to secure the happiness of loved ones.

The store even had suggestions should Christmas come and go without fully satisfying the desires of young *Juvenile Magazine* readers. Although "no good child would ever think of being angry at Santa Claus," one article suggested, it was understandable if girls and boys were disappointed with their gifts. Readers were instructed, "If you asked for skis, or a blackboard, or a baby doll with opening and closing eyes, or skates, or a painting set" or any other particular item and Santa made a mistake by leaving this gift "at the Jones's or Black's instead of your house," a visit to Sibley's Toyland could quickly remedy the situation.[33] The magazine, in this instance, encouraged children to ensure that they were keeping up with their peers in the types of gifts received from Santa—and even "good children" were permitted to cast a critical eye on their December gift haul. While the magazine took pains to maintain Santa Claus as a magical figure and the source of toys during the holiday, it conveniently suggested that through the rest of the year, Sibley's could take on the role of fulfiller of wishes and desires. The *Juvenile Magazine* hoped to forge a lifelong connection with its young readers. Characters such as Billy and Jane routinely addressed the reader directly ("Hello, friend!") and played the part of confidant ("Ssh! Not a word of this to anyone!").[34] Moreover, Rochester children could submit their poems and stories to be published on the magazine's back page, further encouraging a sense of connection with the publication and the store itself.

Special promotions cultivated the notion that the store was a place of excitement and indulgence, a destination where shoppers could forget their everyday concerns and immerse themselves in a fantasy world. The amount of attention devoted to display space became even more pronounced during the Christmas season. November and December were the busiest months of the year for department stores, and elaborate Christmas displays were designed to entice shoppers young and old. On Saturday, 30 October 1920, Sibley's announced the opening of Toyland. In the spirit of Christmas, the store sacrificed some of the floor space from its luggage and housewares sections to the lights and mechanized models that dazzled visiting youngsters. A reporter for the *Democrat and Chronicle* surveyed the scene:

> Wherever you look there is motion. It is one big, joyful, colorful "Land-of-Motion," designed especially for the children's pleasure. . . . As you step from the elevator and enter this Fairyland of Toys you find yourself spellbound gazing at a rapidly revolving and dazzlingly brilliant ball of light—the "Ball of a Thousand Mirrors." Four powerful spotlights playing upon it make it catch the rays of light and reflect them to you. . . . A little further on is a wonderfully interesting mechanical exhibit. The old Flour Mill stands at one end, the mill

wheel moving slowly through the water—and it is real water. There is a long canal with a wide electrically lighted boulevard on one side. Across the canal are high mountains. Along the edge of the canal with the mountains towering above it, is a miniature electric railroad.[35]

Stores experimented with different themes for Christmas displays each year. H. A. Meldrum held four shows for youngsters each Saturday in December 1921, featuring appearances by Santa Claus and Huckleberry Finn.[36] In 1925, Sibley's show windows featured a tableau of carolers making the rounds of a village in "Merrie Old England," while in 1931, the display showed George Washington at Valley Forge on Christmas in 1777. Sibley's spent thousands of dollars in 1927 to create a fairyland within the store, filled with goblins, sprites, and other magical creatures.

The transformation of stores for the Christmas season did not stop with the interiors and the windows. Merchants cooperated in creating lighting displays outdoors, making the local Main Streets a magical experience. The *Buffalo Courier-Express* boasted that Main Street was going to be "brighter than New York's Broadway; Chicago's State Street or London's Piccadilly Circus." Readers were encouraged to bring the whole family to see the lights and the over $10 million in merchandise available in Main Street stores. The article reached high levels of hyperbole, boasting, "No Street Like Main Street within 4000 Miles. No Street So Dramatic—No Street So Thrilling—No Street So Superbly Ready for the Christmas Throng."[37]

At other times of the year, retailers could create special events that commanded public attention. To celebrate the store's nineteenth anniversary, Lewin Brothers Jewelers of Buffalo hired a plane to drop money over the downtown district, as well as a grand prize voucher for a $65 diamond. The Lewin plane dropped "Cash from the Sky," and while no purchase was necessary to win a check for $25 or $5, all prizes were to be awarded in the Lewin store on Main Street, presumably so that winners would be tempted to redeem their rewards in store merchandise.

Beyond the events, displays, and promotions designed specifically to sell store goods, retailers often took it upon themselves to promote the communities in which they were located. Buffalo and Rochester merchants were among the most vocal of their respective city's boosters. During the 1920s and 1930s, retailers used their ad space, their shop windows, and even their selling floors to promote civic pride. It is not surprising that retailers in smaller cities often drew links between their own interests and the interests of their communities.

In one sense, we can view this as a form of long-range business planning: the growth of the city would only mean good things for retailers. Events such as parades and contests, while not explicitly about the sale of goods, nonetheless aimed to raise a retailer's profile in the hopes of increasing sales. And, as will be demonstrated in the following chapters, retailers in smaller cities had good reason to stress their community ties once competition from chain stores and mail-order businesses appeared to threaten their preeminent position.

Newspaper and magazine editorials underscored the civic importance of supporting local retailers, pointing out that money spent in the city was circulated in the form of wages for local workers. An editorial entitled "Buy It in Buffalo" in *Buffalo Saturday Night* magazine argued that this observation was a matter of "cold, hard, business fact," not just noble sentiment. "It is not our purpose," the writer asserted, "to urge upon our readers a narrow provincialism and to criticize milady if she chooses to buy a trinket in Fifth Avenue rather than in Delaware Avenue. At the same time, we would press home so far as is possible, the fact that Buffalo manufacturers cannot employ Buffalo labor unless they get business; and every dollar's worth of trade they get means added work for Buffalo labor; every time a retailer sells a dollar's worth of goods to a consumer, he is able to buy another dollar's worth of "goods from the wholesaler and so on."[38] An accompanying cartoon depicted the network of relationships between "Buffalo citizens who spent their dollars at home" (see Plate 5). The pay packet of a Buffalo worker made the rounds to his wife, a retailer, a local wholesaler, and finally back to the manufacturer who had originally supplied the wages.

Retailers themselves emphasized their own positive place in the community. The rhetoric of "community service" in department store ads could take on almost messianic proportions. Sibley's of Rochester used a fable about a philosopher who asked a number of workmen about their jobs to illustrate the store's commitment to goals beyond simply commerce. While some of the workers felt they were simply "digging a ditch" or "earning five dollars a day," one enthusiast claimed to be "building a cathedral." Sibley's applauded this sense of mission, noting,

> For fifty-nine years, we too have been striving to build a cathedral . . . a House of Service worthy of the good people who expect from us the best. Fathers and sons have contributed their efforts. The lowliest and the highest have added stone on stone to this superstructure. The cathedral is unfinished. It will never be finished for we are restless

people, never content with the efforts of yesterday. Tomorrow brings us new thoughts, new inspirations, bigger ideals. Each day finds us in the travail of growing pains with the goal of perfection still ahead of us, and in its wake the vision of building a better business cathedral most worthy of you.[39]

Sibley's "House of Service" was a secularized church—a cathedral where visitors would go for renewal and rejuvenation, not through prayer but through acquisition of material goods. William Leach dates a new fascination with "service" to the turn of the twentieth century, where retailers such as John Wanamaker promoted a "new kind of store" that stressed the convenience of the customer above all. This new ideology, he argues, was, in part, a response to reformers who equated large businesses of many types with exploitation and unfair practices. Benevolent treatment of workers, new services for customers, and community activism shored up the stores' popularity and conveyed an image of caring responsiveness. Hotel magnates such as Ellsworth Statler, whose hotel in Buffalo was a city landmark, similarly adopted this ideal of service.[40]

The rhetoric of service in smaller cities was more directly linked to local identities. Wanamaker and his competitors in Philadelphia and New York City allied themselves with reformers and cultivated an image of compassion and decency, presenting their operations as stores for "the People." Retailers in smaller centers framed their displays of public service more specifically, in the context of the local community. The extent to which stores in smaller markets clearly and directly linked their own futures with the rising fortunes of the cities in which they were located is striking. For example, on the first day of January each year, the B. Forman Company of Rochester used a large newspaper ad to send out a holiday message recapping not only the store's but also the city's achievements and forecasting great things for the coming year. The 1928 message reflected on the new buildings and apartment houses that were dotting the city and even cited the rising value of local manufacturers' stock and the level of trade in the region as a whole. The ad trumpeted the confidence with which economists were viewing the upcoming year: "They prophecy good business and widespread development, of which we in Rochester should have a full share."[41] B. Forman also used its regular ad space to comment on local developments. When a new theater was built in the downtown, the store proclaimed that this "new enterprise . . . pays additional tribute to Mr. Forman's foresight and judgment" in choosing Rochester as the location for his store.[42] Claims to "local" status proved very pliable, as stores such as Hengerer's and

J. N. Adam's still promoted themselves as local institutions even as they became part of the larger, New York City–based Associated Dry Goods.

Merchants in Buffalo and Rochester further demonstrated their commitment to the community by using store space for civic promotions. During World War I, Sibley's devoted one show window to the display of photographs of local men who were in the service. The "Soldiers' Picture Window" exhibit was so popular that it was expanded to fill another window in order to accommodate the flood of photos that poured in. On Armistice Day in 1921, several retailers held memorials to commemorate the loss of Rochester men in World War I. Hengerer's used a newspaper announcement with no information about sales or promotions, just a simple drawing of a wreath and a notice about the service to be held "IN HONOR OF THOSE WHO HAVE GIVEN THEIR ALL 1918–1921." The activities of "our boys" and "their heroic actions on the fields of France" were given solemn recognition.[43] Hengerer's carried out a program on 11 November 1921, complete with a "patriotic song service" where all store personnel joined in singing hymns and a local reverend delivered an address. Just before noon, a veteran in uniform took his position on the store floor. Promptly at 12 o'clock, the army bugler sounded taps. A *Buffalo Evening News* reporter on the scene described the solemnity of the occasion: "At the first note of the bugle every activity in the store ceased. All but necessary lights were out, the tube and elevator systems ceased to operate. Clerks and customers alike bowed their head in silent meditation for two minutes."[44] A serviceman was stationed on each floor of the store to signal personnel when to stand at attention. J. N Adam and Company and Hens and Kelly carried out similar programs. Other stores closed from eleven o'clock to one or two. J. N. Adam and Adam, Meldrum and Anderson suspended business briefly during the afternoon, as instructed by President Warren Harding. Several stores had flags hanging in their windows, and war pictures and relics were on display.

Retailers in Buffalo thus took the lead in commemorating Armistice Day, a fact that seems even more striking when we realize that there was no other civic ceremony held downtown. Merchants carefully orchestrated much of the public activity in the downtown area, coordinating events that projected a particular image. Using local veterans, religious leaders, and the iconography of the flag gave the stores a certain gravitas. Meanwhile, local citizens who came to participate in this ceremony had a very limited role: observing decorations, listening to sermons, or maintaining silence at the appointed time.

Some retailers took an active part in local politics. In 1935, William A. Morgan (of the Morgan Stores) endorsed Frank Schwab for mayor, buying a quarter page in the *Buffalo Evening News* to write a "letter to voters" explaining his choice.[45] J. N. Adam actually served as mayor of the city. Not surprisingly, many retailers were active in local associations such as the Chamber of Commerce. Gilbert J. C. McCurdy, for example, was selected president of the Rochester Chamber of Commerce in 1930. Merchants also commented on local issues that had little to do with trade. In a roundup of opinions on the issue of adopting daylight saving time, published in the *Democrat and Chronicle*, F. Forman of the B. Forman Company stated, "It seems to me that all Rochester is unanimously in favor of Daylight Saving and you should feel that you are acting for the welfare of the entire community in working for it."[46] While local reformers, doctors, and scientists contributed to the debate with reference to the health and medical advantages for the population, Forman was quoted simply because of his prominence in the community as the representative of an important local institution.

Local merchants also took part in exhibitions that promoted area industries and services. The Rochester Chamber of Commerce and its Retail Merchants' Council sponsored Rochester-Made Products Week in 1927 in order to improve the understanding of regional products and services. A spokesman for the council remarked, "It is not unusual to find manufacturers, retailers and consumers in other sections of the country who know Rochester products better than do the residents of Rochester." The two chamber bureaus hoped that exciting displays in local stores would change that sorry fact.[47] During this week, stores featured the slogan "Rochester Made Means Quality" and ran special promotions of city-made goods (see Plate 1). Sibley, Lindsay and Curr ran ads extolling the virtues of local industries and its own role in promoting these businesses. From the cameras at the Kodak counter to the Monroe County–raised produce in the canned goods section of the grocery department and the Rochester-made shoes and clothing in the men's department, Sibley's boasted in the *Rochester Democrat and Chronicle* that "in both retail and wholesale functions we are a mighty outlet for local products."[48] Sibley's also devoted all forty-five of its store windows to demonstrations of local products. Visitors could witness the construction of neckties, radios, kitchen appliances, spaghetti, spices, cameras, and lenses. Even goods that were not carried in the store, such as a range finder made by the Bausch and Lomb Company for the U.S. Navy, were featured. Sibley's made a tradition of the "What Rochester makes—makes Rochester" theme, promoting local industries yearly. In 1927, its newspaper ad campaign emphasized "Home-made wares." The tradition was continued as late as 1938, when the store used all of its windows for the promotion of local industries.

Merchants also participated in civic promotions outside the store buildings themselves. The Buffalo Centennial in 1932 featured exhibits from regional manufacturers and from stores including Adam, Meldrum and Anderson's; the Wm. Hengerer Company; and the Larkin Company. The program for the centennial explained why citizens should take notice of the event.

> One-hundred-and-twenty important Buffalo industries are exhibiting a host of products that have helped carry the fame of Buffalo around the world on land, sky and sea! The industrial history of Buffalo has been written with the pen that has honored Buffalo products with the signature, MADE IN BUFFALO!
>
> You will see Buffalo products in the making! You will see them in action! You will see their records of thrilling achievement in the affairs of the entire world. You will see how and why and where the quality of the products of Buffalo workers has brought recognition and honor to Buffalo.[49]

Even the local branch of the Sears, Roebuck Company had an exhibit, which suggests that the definition of "Buffalo industries" described by the organizers was flexible.

Department stores also cultivated community goodwill through cooperative events with local clubs and charities. Adam, Meldrum and Anderson regularly sponsored Junior League Day, during which members of the league would act as saleswomen for a day and in return receive a nominal salary and a percentage of the day's sales to put into their organization's general fund. Such events cultivated a positive public image for the store. They may also have been good business: league members encouraged their friends to come shop and be waited on. When B. Forman's announced a benefit project for the unemployment fund of the Rochester Community Chest, the store remained open until 8:30 P.M. so that "men relatives and friends of the women workers may come to buy the gifts they will later make presents of at Christmas time." Similarly, members of the Chatterbox Club, the Junior Workers' Association, and the Twigs volunteered as "storekeepers for a day." The charitable contributions made by the store should not be totally dismissed as a mere publicity ploy, as the donation of a percentage of a day's receipts during the Christmas season would have been a sizable gift.[50] At the same time, however, the opportunity to be shopgirls for a day allowed middle-class women to spend a few hours surrounded by merchandise, perhaps increasing the likelihood that they would make additional purchases when they returned as customers. Other stores claimed to give back to the community through special sales events. Although many stores used the rhetoric of service to suggest that they were helping the city all the time by offering low prices, some went so far as to stage events where they sold merchandise at cost. Jahraus-Braun designated Good-Will, No-Profit Day as a way to show appreciation to "thousands of thrifty housewives for their loyalty to our stores." According to an ad announcing the event, the day would give "the people" a chance to save, while earning the store goodwill.[51]

Stores also publicized their treatment of workers in order to cultivate a positive image. Their paternalistic policies were presented as the "right thing" for local citizens, and workers were depicted not simply as part of the "store family" but as part of the city as a whole. Adam, Meldrum and Anderson used this type of rhetoric in an ad describing curtailed summer hours. According to that ad, the store had always believed in "treating Buffalonians right—whether they happened to be our customers or our co-workers." For this reason, the store was to be closed for six successive Saturdays in July and August, allowing the more than one thousand Buffalonians who worked at Adam, Meldrum and Anderson's to "enjoy six glorious weekends with their families and friends" and return to work refreshed and able to offer the best customer service possible.[52]

By presenting the store closings as necessary for the well-being of a significant number of Buffalo citizens, the store would conveniently deflect any criticism from customers who faced the inconvenience of having to do their shopping on other days. Meanwhile, Danahy-Faxon stores in Buffalo boasted that they brought special advantages to both employees and customers because of their "home-owned and home-operated—100% Buffalonian" status. Every employee was a "partner" in the store, and all profits made by the company were said to be poured back into the community.[53]

The merchants of Buffalo and Rochester framed the services they provided with reference to the local community and stressed their roles as citizens and civic leaders. In 1920, ads informed the unemployed in Buffalo that Bing and Nathan would extend credit: the store managers promised, "We'll carry you along until you're placed. In time of prosperity you made our success possible, in time of adversity we stand ready to help you."[54] The Reliable Furniture Company reported that despite the cost ("thousands of dollars a year"), it offered a special form of security to Rochester patrons. While other insurance brokers offered protection against financial losses resulting from a natural disaster, only "The Reliable" offered the people of Rochester a policy protecting their purchases in furniture. This policy, given free to every buyer, was a "plainly worded, legal document" stipulating that in the event of the death of the head of the family, the balance of money due on any article purchased at the store would be canceled in the company records. There was no price limit placed on this certificate, and it was offered to the customer "without a penny's cost" by the company as a symbol of The Reliable's "25 Years of Faithful Service Throughout Western New York."[55]

This emphasis on the community was not wholly altruistic: as chapters 2 and 3 will demonstrate, the stores' commitment to local causes became an important selling tool in the face of increased competition both from New York City merchants and from chain stores. Yet on another level, these retailers had a genuine interest in the success of their cities, equating the prosperity of the community with their own advancement. Their actions in supporting "local" causes at times went beyond the simple promotion of goods as stores attempted to edify and educate customers about the advantages of the area in which they lived as well as the products they bought.

By the 1920s, any visitor to Buffalo wishing to visit the largest stores in the city would be directed to Main Street. The concentration of retailers in the downtown area also acted as a magnet for residents of the cities themselves. Yet not everyone was contented with the characterization of Buffalo as a "Main Street town." Some felt that the very name *Main Street* had negative connotations. While smaller cities might hope to preserve vestiges of their "village days," Buffalo hoped to assert its position as a leading city. The name of its central street, the focal point for civic identity, became the target of boosters who felt it did not do the city justice.

Town Tidings, a magazine catering to Buffalo's elite, grappled with the dilemma of the city's development. Although Buffalo had grown steadily during the nineteenth century, by 1928 people despaired that it would ever catch up to cities such as New York and Chicago. Writers at the magazine termed the problem one of psychology, which could be solved by the right types of promotion to jolt the city's denizens out of their complacency. At a time when modern advertising was an increasing presence in daily life, it is interesting that many felt that it was not the "product"—Buffalo itself—that needed changing but its "brand name" and associations. A public relations spin might be all that was needed to put the city back on track, not actual, structural changes.

A number of articles in *Town Tidings* explored the topic of Buffalo's future and proposed various remedies. Local writer Tristam Sweet described taking an out-of-town investor named Henry to lunch at the Main Street men's club. Although Henry conceded that the region had advanced transportation and communication facilities to recommend itself, he was not sure about business opportunities on the Niagara frontier. He admonished the local men to "stop bragging and do something about it." Buffalo's natural advantages should have been the envy of all other communities, he argued. "Any other place in America with half the natural endowment of the Niagara Area would be chasing New York for first honors and laughing at the other cities. Look at Cleveland—just a spot on Lake Erie, and not a very good spot, either. Look at Chicago—entirely surrounded by prairie and bossed by bandits—or St. Louis, with nothing from Nature except the stickiest, muggiest climate this side of Sheol."[56] Yet despite their inferior locations and other attributes, these cities were outpacing Buffalo in growth. Henry concluded that it was psychology, not material factors, that was causing this lag. Buffalo remained an "overgrown village" whose citizens paid little heed to "metropolitan" issues such as street widening, traffic regulations, and downtown parking. Henry linked an active downtown with metropolitan status: world-class cities facilitated the flow of people into the downtown, particularly into retail areas.

A listener at the table, identified as lawyer Matt W—, accepted Henry's indictment and provided a diagnosis: "We are all suffering from a bad case of inferiority complex! . . . a panicky hesitancy in taking the initiative, an excessive fear of failure based on emotion rather than logic."[57] This collective condition was preventing Buffalonians from taking advantage of opportunities, while at the same time giving them "delusions of grandeur." Matt went so far as to identify the root cause of the psychological trauma afflicting the city. He diagnosed an inferiority complex, which "is usually implanted in early youth as a result of rigid repression or of a failure so overwhelming as to sap the victim's courage and spirit of adventure. The Niagara Area has experienced just such a calamity. . . . From 1888 to 1893 we had a time of exceptional expansion, together with a fever of speculation. . . . When the bottom fell out in 1893, the reaction was a terrible thing to behold."[58] The people who lived through this time of crisis became inhibited and unable to shake off feelings of worry and insecurity. Fortunately, Matt argued, a new generation of business leaders, unscarred by the legacy of the past, was rising up to take full advantage of all Buffalo had to offer. While Cleveland or Detroit might be at the high point of their expansion, he contended, Buffalo stood poised on the brink of rejuvenation. By the end of the lunch, Henry declared that he was going to stick around to witness Buffalo's imminent boom.

In an article entitled "The Superiority of Feeling Inferior," *Town Tidings* writer Joseph Leeming returned to the issue of Buffalo's inferiority complex. He described an encounter between a group of businessmen in the men's steam room at the local club. During the encounter, an argument broke out over the feelings of inferiority suffered by many Buffalonians. While one man identified only as "The Optimist" pointed to the high output of Buffalo's factories as evidence of its economic and, in turn, psychological health, another known as "The Pessimist" countered that he was mistaken. He argued, "This town is all wrong, too, and all that tommy rot about industry and production won't make it right." Local people were so wrapped up in their own petty affairs—"the men with their business and their golf, and the women with their everlasting parties"—that they had turned Buffalo into "just the kind of a hole in the ground that an ostrich would want to put his head into, to get away from what was going on outside."[59] He recounted that on returning to Buffalo after a recent trip to New York, he faced residents who tried to cut him off before he even said hello in order to prevent him from "high-hatting" like the New Yorkers did.

Restrained appreciation for the city's attributes seemed to best indicate the maturity and healthy adjustment of its citizens. The steam room's "Philosopher" posited that it was preferable to have an inferiority complex if that spurred one on to great accomplishments. Without an inferiority complex, he argued, Benito Mussolini would still have been an underpaid newspaper reporter. The town struck with an inferiority complex was fortunate, for "from it springs the Will of Power" that would help to put it on the map.[60] The trick was to recognize one's shortcomings with dignity and resolve—this was half the battle. Perhaps Buffalo did not suffer from a sense of inferiority as much as some towns out west. Unlike the reserved Buffalonians, for example, Californians were relentless in their boosterism: "Their bumptious shouting, while no doubt partly due to the *jejeune* enthusiasm of youth, the zeal of the pioneer,—also show unmistakably the consciousness of inferiority. We handle our complex, if, as I hope, we have one, with greater dignity and restraint. Urged on by it, we get results. My only fear is lest we do not feel quite inferior enough."[61] An older statesman overhearing the conversation suggested yet another possibility. While cities such as Detroit and Cleveland took "bustling, noisy, head-achey New York as their ideal," Buffalo modeled itself after London and other English cities. Established of blue-blood New England stock, well past its pioneer phase, and similar in climate, Buffalo and London shared many parallels. The two cities enjoyed a sense of leisure and culture not easily reproduced in a "thoroughly industrialized, mechanized bee hive" like New York.[62] Buffalo's diversification of industry allowed it to progress with quiet confidence, unlike rival cities that depended on a single industry. They "vacillate[d] between a state of hysterical enthusiasm and depressing panic," while Buffalo moved quietly ahead.[63]

The solution *Town Tidings* proposed to counter Buffalo's supposed inferiority complex involved changing the name of its principal street and thus changing its image. Articles asked if Buffalo really was a Main Street town, filled with narrow-minded, corncob pipe–smoking inhabitants.

The animosity toward Main Street no doubt stemmed, in some part, from Sinclair Lewis's novel of the same name, first published in 1920 and excerpted in the *Buffalo Evening News* in December 1921. After her marriage, Lewis's heroine, Carol Kennicott, finds herself trapped in Gopher Prairie, Minnesota. Carol has lived in Chicago and St. Paul and is not impressed by the Main Street of her new town. She is dismayed by the plain storefronts, the mud-filled street, the single movie theater. The street seems to symbolize the limitations of the town and its inhabitants. Carol is overwhelmed by the street's almost hostile atmosphere: "Oozing from every drab wall, she felt a forbidding spirit which she could never conquer." After a brief walking tour, she "escaped from Main Street, fled home." All of her dreams of quaint village life were destroyed in a single afternoon.[64]

The writers of *Town Tidings* hoped that a name change would distance Buffalo from the Gopher Prairies of America. Lewis's novel brought new attention to the provincialism and narrowness of small-town life, and Buffalo's writers and civic leaders wanted their home to be seen as "big-city" rather than "small-town" in all respects. But some of this angst over the name Main Street predated Lewis's novel. In fact, this was not the first time that a name change had been proposed: there had been a similar movement in Buffalo after the 1901 Pan-American Exposition, when area residents had similarly become preoccupied with the city's status and image.

By changing the name of Main Street, it was hoped that Buffalo would shed its provincial inhibitions and achieve true metropolitan status. Again, the language of psychology was appropriated to explain the city's situation.

> "Main Street" has had an insidious psychological effect on our leading citizens, when the best reason they can advance for not giving the

thoroughfare a truly metropolitan name, is the cost of new stationery and stationery dies! We may next expect that young ladies will refuse to be married because they could no longer use their maiden name calling cards. . . . Buffalo must overcome some of the provincial inhibitions that are strangling it, or the city deserves to be considered a "small town" forever. If we hesitate to change the name of Main Street because of such minutiae as stationery dies, an inferiority complex is obviously rampant.[65]

Buffalo claimed to be the "Queen City of the Lakes" or the "Metropolis of Western New York," yet the mere existence of Main Street was thought to detract from the city's image. Buffalo needed a name for its main thoroughfare that was not "shared by every hamlet in the country."[66] By holding on to the name, the city was relegating itself to second-class status. Only communities such as "Henpeck Corners, O'Flaherty's Flats, and Podunk," with their "whisker and corncob pipe inhabitants" would "christen their avenue of monumental watering troughs and mud ruts" Main Street.[67] Buffalo's central business street deserved more.

The major cities of the world had distinctive names for major streets. A writer from *Town Tidings* exclaimed, "No one needs to ask what cities are referred to when you speak of Bond Street, Rue de la Paix, Unter den Linden, Fifth Avenue and Michigan Boulevard." The names of these famous thoroughfares immediately summoned up their respective cities, representing the "distinctive spirit" of the place in which they were located, "the essence of the city itself." To truly arrive on the international scene, Buffalo needed to rethink the name of its principal street, finding a new moniker so suitable that "the mere mention of its name will be synonymous with Buffalo, whether the street be spoken of in Rangoon or Helsinfors." The existing name was harsh to the sophisticated ear, sounding like "one of Edison's early experiments on a wax cylinder," and should be relegated to "a remote corner of your attic" with the other remnants of the "gaudy parlors of the last century."[68]

If Main Street was key to the city's identity, then the retailers who located there had a special responsibility. Nothing could make a town appear more backward than the existence of "old-fashioned" stores. An anonymous editorial writer for *Town Tidings* derided the name *Main Street* and criticized such stores at the same time, sneering, "The name recalls the days when the two-step was *risqué*. Sidewalks were made of planks, and a single 'horseless carriage,' in a cloud of dust, could paralyze traffic with its dizzy eight miles an hour. The name suggests a scattered sprinkling of stores with 'false fronts' à la Charles Burchfield: stores with dingy interiors, redolent of kerosene, potent cheese, herring in open tubs and sawdust on the floor."[69] Given that Buffalo was now home to a number of leading merchants who employed the latest in display, merchandising, and distribution techniques, a new name was in order if Buffalo was ever to escape the stigma of being "an over-grown, Main Street town."[70] A new name with "advertising value" would benefit the merchants on the street and the city as a whole. S. A. Stephens, owner of a local business, complained that the impression of visitors to Buffalo regarding Main Street was surely negative. He protested that the city was too large and prosperous to be joked about over the name of its most important thoroughfare, especially since the appearance of "Sinclair Lewis' famous book, several years ago, which seems to have characterized 'Main Street' along with a small community." Not only did the name lack individuality, he argued, it had contributed to keeping "most of our business activity in a retail way, on one street," as merchants jealously held onto any Main Street frontage and resisted efforts to build away from the central artery.[71]

By June 1929, the magazine's campaign to change the name of Buffalo's major thoroughfare had attracted correspondence from a host of other cities. Not everyone was enthusiastic about the proposal. The editor of the *Houston Gargoyle* felt no need to change the name (Houston also has a Main Street), despite "the assaults on its good name by Messrs. Lewis, Mencken et al." A writer from Denver pointed out that a group of merchants in his town had actually tried to change one of the downtown streets *to* Main Street, with no success. A member of the Memphis Chamber of Commerce cautioned that the surest way to advertise a city as a "hick town" was to change the name of Main Street. By contrast, the editor of the *Times-Picayune* declared, "We have no Main Street in New Orleans. We feel sorry for you!" The secretary of Indianapolis's Chamber of Commerce congratulated the magazine's editor on his progressive work, arguing that "Buffalo is too big, too great to be handicapped with a 'Main Street'!" For his part, Ralph Webster, the chief editorial writer of the Gannett Newspapers (which included both the *Democrat and Chronicle* and the *Times-Union*), said that few Rochesterians showed much interest in changing the name of their own Main Street. Perhaps, he contended, city residents feared the possibility of changing the name for the worse: "Suppose the old Republican machine had wished 'Harding Street' on us!"[72]

Local observers were also divided. Buffalo's mayor, Frank Schwab, refused to give an opinion, and another writer simply asked, "What the Hell differ-

ence does it make? Some people make much ado about nothing." Retailers
seemed to favor the idea. The controller of L. L. Berger wrote to say that most
of the store executives agreed that the name "marks the city with too provincial a flavor." He suggested Iroquois Avenue as a possible alternative, which
would acknowledge New York State as the home of the Iroquois Indians, or
McKinley Avenue (although one might argue that the name would only serve
as a reminder of a painful incident in Buffalo's past). The chairman of the Liberty Bank humbly suggested Liberty Street or Liberty Avenue as "glorious" suggestions. Another observer suggested that retention of the old name had
helped to concentrate retail activity along one street only in Buffalo.[73]

Yet some merchants were members of the Main Street Improvement Association, which only two years previously had reported excitedly on a proposal
in Manhattan to change the name of Eighth Avenue, Central Park West,
Jerome Avenue, West Broadway, Hudson Street, and parts of Greenwich Street
to Main Street. If New York City merchants had considered adopting a Main
Street, some wondered whether a name change might not be necessary for
Buffalo. Despite the feeling that the name implied "the sleepy little road of
the backwoods four corners," an impression encouraged by Sinclair Lewis,
"the fact that a group of business men in our largest city propose to adopt this
name for their street shows that they realize its established value as a distinctive, short, easily remembered name which can be replaced by no other
title."[74] The association counted among its members representatives from
some of the city's larger stores, including Paul C. Fleer, president of J. N.
Adam and Company; E. L. Kleinhans, president of the Kleinhans Clothing
Company; and R. H. Shone, advertising manager of Adam, Meldrum and Anderson Company. Others worried that a name change would cause confusion
and entail financial costs in reprinting maps, promotional materials, and stationery.

In the end, most felt that changing the name of the street was too drastic a
step. Unless Buffalonians let the current name "reflect a state of mind" and
hinder their ambitions, many felt that the name alone should not be blamed
for any failure to grow.[75] As local observer Frank S. Sidway succinctly put it,
perhaps citizens were currently caught up in a wave of interest in the issue, but
the long-standing tradition of the name (and simple inertia) would win out.
After the publication of the book *Main Street* by "a man from the middle west,"
a few people in Buffalo wanted to change the name of their street, but the
people who owned property on Main Street were satisfied with the name. Sidway argued, "Main Street has been Main Street in fact and name for about one

hundred years. It probably will be Main Street for the next one hundred years."[76] Sidway's instincts proved correct: the campaign to change the name of the street faltered, and Main Street still runs through Buffalo's downtown to this day. Despite this failed initiative, the very nature of the controversy reveals a great deal about the position of merchants in the city.

Main Street was the symbolic and geographic center of Buffalo, and as the major "residents" of the thoroughfare, merchants were inextricably linked to the image of the city. Changing the name of the primary retailing street was proposed as a way to revamp Buffalo's image. Few suggested that the city's merchants themselves were not modern or forward-looking—if anything, it was thought that the name *Main Street* did not do justice to Buffalo's actual institutions and businesses. At a time when Americans were increasingly aware of the power of the brand name to convey a certain image to the public, the community's boosters felt that renaming the city's major street would firmly entrench their home in the pantheon of the big cities of the world.

The tensions over Main Street reflect both the successes and the limitations of midsized cities in America in the 1920s. Main Street was the focal point of both Buffalo and Rochester. On the one hand, local residents were proud of the accomplishments of their cities. They celebrated the rapid expansion of area industries and had reason to believe that their communities would continue to grow. On the other hand, they were keenly aware that their communities did not necessarily "measure up" in the eyes of outside observers. In the case of Buffalo, writers at a local magazine teamed up with business and civic leaders to suggest that perhaps a name change would be all that was necessary to create a new, more dynamic image of the city.

The debate over what constituted a modern city and how to define a cosmopolitan perspective would continue throughout this time period. Merchants were central to this discussion because of their active participation in the civic and cultural life of their communities. Retailers in both Buffalo and Rochester performed a number of functions that went beyond the sale of goods. As cultural brokers in their cities, they brought in entertainments, hosted concerts and lectures, and provided a wide range of services to their patrons. Department stores were an imposing physical presence in the center of the city. They invested in new technologies and experimented with the latest innovations in display and lighting. Visitors to the downtown marveled at innovative shop windows and elaborate Christmas decorations. Retailers helped to shape the cultural life of the city, and they were vociferous in their defense of their communities.

SELLING IN HUB AND HINTERLAND

FACED WITH INCREASING COMPETITION from big-city retailers, merchants in Buffalo and Rochester experimented with a number of strategies and often played on local loyalties in an attempt to retain customers. For retailers in smaller centers, new innovations in distribution, marketing, media, and transportation made satisfying local customers more and more of a challenge. Magazine advertising and movies made Americans in all regions of the country more aware of national brands and changing styles; trains and automobiles made it easier than ever for shoppers to leave their hometowns to check out merchandise in the metropolis. In one sense, retailers in western New York lay in Manhattan's sphere of influence: indeed, they kept a careful eye on the stores in the big city. At the same time, however, they were not willing to concede the superiority of retailing in the state's main hub of economic activity. They used a number of strategies to assure their clientele that Buffalo and Rochester stores offered the same brand names, the same new fashions, and the same level of service as their New York City counterparts.

The development of the American mass market can be understood on one level as the process of bringing the advancements of industry to consumers living farther and farther away from the city. Throughout the nineteenth century, urbanites had enjoyed goods produced in British or New England factories, but it was not until the turn of the twentieth century that a multitude of manufactured products became readily available to individuals in all states of the Union, in city and hinterland. Companies such as Gillette, National Biscuit, and Singer Sewing Machine rapidly established chains of distribution, which snaked out from key cities to touch the rest of the nation. Merchants, too, played a key role in the development of the new national market. In the years leading up to World War I, mass marketers such as the department store, the mail-order company, and the chain store were transforming the practice of selling.

By the 1920s, consumers in western New York State and in communities throughout the nation were able to purchase many of the same name-brand goods as big-city dwellers on the East Coast did, often from the same general-merchandise retailer. James C. Penney was operating more than a thousand stores across America by 1928, and Sears, Roebuck was entering the retail field after much success in the mail-order business. National manufacturers, advertisers, and mail-order houses were based in cities such as New York and Chicago, and even manufacturers of national brands with roots in other areas came to realize that these hubs of distribution were crucial to their success. Yet there was no simple, one-way movement of goods and ideas from metropolis to hinterland. On the eastern seaboard, patterns of settlement were complicated, with numerous smaller towns and cities in New York's radius jockeying for advantage in the late nineteenth century. Boosters in cities such as Buffalo and Rochester were aware that their communities lay in the shadow of New York City, yet they were convinced that a time would come when their cities would rise to greatness. The ability of local merchants and manufacturers to compete with the best New York City had to offer became a major component of this civic pride.

The trade papers of the retail industry reveal how store owners and managers in hundreds of smaller American centers relied on New York City for supplies and ideas yet simultaneously resented the city's influence. The *Dry Goods Merchants Trade Journal*, later known simply as the *Dry Goods Journal*, was a major periodical for owners and managers of dry goods and department stores from the late nineteenth century onward. The *DGMTJ* aimed for a truly national perspective on the retailing industry, employing itinerant writers to visit stores in every state. This editorial decision certainly reflected the fact that most of the periodical's subscribers were the proprietors and buyers of independently owned stores in cities and towns across the country. These small retailers were

likely to enjoy reading stories about their own stores or ones in cities of similar sizes and proportions. Broader coverage no doubt helped to boost the circulation of the magazine. Yet at the same time, this practice reveals a level of
interplay between smaller stores and larger ones and between the small city and
the metropolis. Bigger stores were not assumed to be the only ones worth
watching.

Writers went to great lengths to report on developments in all regions of
the United States. Articles featured sales ideas from every part of the nation.
In 1923, the *DGMTJ*'s editorial staff shared business ideas from 416 stores, representing each of the forty-eight states.[1] The magazine consciously kept track
of its coverage nationwide: it conducted a survey of over a thousand articles
from the first seven months of 1928 to evaluate the breadth of the *DGMTJ*'s
coverage. The survey revealed stories from 340 cities and towns, located throughout the East, Midwest, South, and West. New York State was the subject of
seventy pieces, and every state except New Mexico and Nevada was represented
by at least one article.[2] Although retail centers such as Chicago and New York
City received consistent coverage, there was a conscious effort to go further in
presenting a more fully representative, national view. Moreover, the existence
of separate sections devoted to cities with populations of 10,000 or less and
10,000 to 50,000 suggested that the concerns of merchants in smaller towns
could not always be solved by copying the merchandising strategies of larger
firms. In some cases, smaller stores were urged to adapt these ideas to the scale
of their organizations; at other times, they were shown ideas that had originated in small stores. A typical story described how a small store located only
thirty miles from a major center was "whipping big city competition" through
its selling of known lines.[3] According to the *DGMTJ*, one store in a small Minnesota town carried seventy-five nationally advertised brands, including a number featured in fashion magazines such as *Vogue* and the *Ladies' Home Journal*. It
could thus boast to customers that it provided a considerable range of the
same brands that would be carried by stores in nearby St. Paul (the closest
major city) and would therefore save them a trip there.

While stores in New York, Philadelphia, Boston, or Chicago were larger in
terms of both volume of goods and customer base, the *Dry Goods Merchants Trade
Journal* did not depict stores in the metropolis as the unquestioned leaders in
"the new retailing." Policies such as standard pricing, departmental separation,
and money-back guarantees for consumers were key to the successes of the early
mass marketers. Industry observers at the time did not, however, assume that
Macy's, Marshall Field's, and other big-city retailers had a monopoly on such

strategies. Innovations adopted by stores in Buffalo or in Waukesha, Wisconsin, or in Alden, Iowa, were judged to be as worthy of detailed description as were the latest fashions and window displays on Fifth Avenue. Journalists for the *DGMTJ* did not presume that merchandising experiments carried out by larger stores in major cities could or even should be mirrored throughout the country. Editorials admonished department managers and buyers to keep in mind the peculiarities and tastes of their own markets.

Indeed, the activities of the big department stores in New York City and later those of chain stores were faithfully reported in the *DGMTJ*. But throughout the 1920s at least, smaller stores constantly boasted of their ability to "compete with the best of them." Specific departments or individual buyers in stores in smaller cities and towns were singled out for praise. Western New York retailers were among those recognized for their achievements. In December 1922, Clem Kieffer Jr., the display manager of the Kleinhans Clothing Company of Buffalo, was commended for devoting a window display to bridegrooms, complete with dress suits and accessories. The *DGMTJ* claimed that this was "probably the first [window display] devoted to the groom in any store anywhere" and went on to draw the reader's attention to the low prices in the display.[4] Sibley's department store of Rochester was featured for its success in promoting women's lingerie. Newspaper ads were reproduced for interested readers to inspect, and an effective saleswoman from the corset department was interviewed about her techniques in selecting the proper corset for each customer.[5]

Smaller stores were particularly encouraged to follow the lead of their larger brethren in adopting modern management techniques. Like other sectors of the American economy during the late nineteenth and early twentieth centuries, merchandising was becoming a corporate enterprise, employing a new breed of specially trained managers. In line with this shift, the *DGMTJ* adopted a much more professional tone by the 1930s, in contrast with the folksy charm it had emphasized in previous decades. The proprietors of stores in markets of all sizes were counseled to streamline and systematize their businesses as much as possible. Articles were accompanied by estimates of the reading time they required, presumably to allow the busy store executive to maximize his or her time. For similar reasons, the table of contents of the magazine was divided into specific areas for different department store professionals: articles targeted for the proprietor–general manager and merchandise manager were separate from those written for the display director, the salespeople, and the personnel department.

Though competition from chains and business fluctuations had a disproportionate impact on smaller businesses, stores in small towns were described
as efficient, modern operations employing the same up-to-the-minute merchandising methods as their larger counterparts. Beir Brothers of Niagara Falls, New
York, was the subject of a study of budget control in smaller stores. Despite
being in a city of fifty-eight thousand and competing with retailers in Buffalo
(less than twenty-five miles away), Beir's had relied on haphazard budgeting systems until 1925. According to the *DGMTJ*, adopting a new, more scientific system had taken the guesswork out of merchandise selection in each department.
A new system of sensible buying resulted in an upswing in "the morale of its
force of buyers." The article boasted that this attention to budgeting in each department allowed Beir's to increase sales and profits "in the face of active competition from large cities, syndicates and mail order houses."[6] This emphasis on
rationalization and systematization was heralded as the solution for shopkeepers who suddenly found themselves in a defensive position. Significantly, retailers such as Beir's saw the department stores of Buffalo as their "metropolitan"
competition. While Buffalo might have been the hinterland to Manhattan, it, in
turn, acted as a hub of retailing and marketing activity for the satellite towns
that surrounded it. Sibley, Lindsay and Curr of Rochester considered a range of
fifteen counties part of its trade area, and it placed advertisements in some twenty
weekly newspapers in adjacent counties.[7] Beir's hoped that modern management
techniques would allow it to keep up with Buffalo competitors, just as Buffalo
stores adopted this strategy to keep up with the big stores of New York City.

Not everyone was enthusiastic about the changes in store culture as departments were systematized and skills were professionalized. A satirical piece
of correspondence that circulated in the offices of Buffalo's Flint and Kent
store contrasted sales fifty years previously and "today." Despite the fact that
the older store "carried everything from a needle to a plow," gave credit freely,
did not bother with inventory, and placed orders for goods a year in advance,
it "ALWAYS MADE MONEY." In contrast, stores that had modernized "have electric lights, cash registers, elevators, escalators and air cooling systems, never
have what the customer wants—trust nobody—take inventory daily—never
buy in advance—have overhead, mark-up and mark-down, quota—budget—
advertising—stock control—annual and semi-annual, end-of-the-month, dollar day, founder's day, rummage economy day sales . . . AND NEVER MAKE ANY
MONEY."[8] The article romanticized the "old days" when retailers could "trust
everybody," yet few retailers at the time felt they could realistically hope to turn
back the clock.

The *DGMTJ* was not the only retail trade periodical that acknowledged the achievements of stores outside Manhattan. The 1930s witnessed the birth of a new magazine for department store management. *The Merchandise Manager* described itself as a "Magazine for Major Executives in Department Stores." Although the periodical was more focused on New York than the *DGMTJ* was, the *Manager's* second issue, in July 1931, featured a photo of Buffalo department store J. N. Adam's merchandise manager, who urged that store merchandising be backed by intensive research on consumer demand. Stories about the concerns of merchants in smaller cities remained a mainstay of the periodical. Editorials at times consciously advised smaller stores not to follow blindly the lead of big-city precedents. In "The Macy Complex," writer Don Herold argued that both big department stores and "little hole-in-the-wall emporiums" watched Macy's like hawks, but often they did not recognize that the big store was just as capable of mistakes. Herold noted that the successful merchant did not imitate but ran his store his own way: "Stores ought to ape Macy's in the one, but fundamental idea that has made Macy's Macy's, and that is that Macy's is Macy's." All truly successful stores did not simply imitate: they were true to their own character. The quality that ensured success for both large and small retailers came from "following some inner light, and not from following some other fellow." The most successful store in the author's hometown of Bloomfield, Indiana, was able to attract people from other towns by following the same principle. Herold could not describe the secret of the store's owner but simply stated that "he bought his own way and sold his own way." In the end, the writer's advice to store executives in smaller outfits was to carve out their own style, even if they were less than successful: "It's even better to fail, being yourself, than it is to fail, aping Macy's."[9]

This celebration of American self-reliance sheds some light on notions of individualism during the interwar period (Herold went so far as to instruct his readers to take a look at Ralph Waldo Emerson's essays once a year until they "[got] the idea"), but it also illustrates the changing relationship between smaller stores and larger ones. Whereas once the independents had been proud to develop their own styles, Herold argued, by the 1930s they were too reliant on the initiatives of the big stores and, accordingly, were too defensive in their approaches. The notion that smaller stores should follow their own instincts persisted in the retail trade press. The *Department Store Buyer* cautioned its readers that they could not use the same formulas for success across the nation, for "New York ways do not fit the merchandise routine of thousands of stores in every part of the country." Retailers in smaller communities would make a serious mistake if they copied the store operations of merchants in Chicago, San Francisco, or Philadelphia.[10]

Evidence suggests that despite their expressions of pride and satisfaction with local initiatives, some store owners were still looking to experts in larger centers for guidance. In 1934, Buffalo department store Adam, Meldrum and Anderson sought advice from an advertising firm based in Long Island. Adman Thomas Robb reported to Adam, Meldrum and Anderson that the store's newspaper advertisements in the *Buffalo Evening News* and the *Courier-Express* suffered in comparison to those of J. N. Adam's, Hengerer's, E. W. Edwards and Son, and Hens and Kelly. He attached a sheet of ads from New York firms including Macy's, Best and Company, Gimbel's, and Lord and Taylor. A follow-up letter in May of the same year claimed that Adam, Meldrum and Anderson's print advertising lacked "a real selling urge"—that ads only presented merchandise, without actually selling it. Robb recommended getting tie-in cooperation from leading women's magazines to stage special promotions, as well as the development of private brands within the store.[11] While Adam, Meldrum and Anderson relied on a big-city consultant, other Buffalo and Rochester stores benefited from personnel who had trained at larger stores elsewhere. Harold Hecht, president of the Wm. Hengerer Company in the late 1930s, had entered the executive training group at Gimbel's in Philadelphia before settling in Buffalo.

Another force, the university business school, worked in tandem with the trade press to encourage stores across the nation to adopt modern retailing methods. Hecht himself had attended the Wharton School of the University of Pennsylvania. Sibley's routinely recruited graduates from Harvard Business School to enter the store's management. Yet even stores whose personnel did not attend business school might be transformed by contact with the university. As universities developed new curricula that focused on the actual workings of American business, they found it necessary to collect detailed information about business operations for study by their students. The case study approach to business education was pioneered by Harvard and adopted by other schools across the nation. In 1911, Harvard Business School formed a separate entity to compile data about a range of industries. At its inception, the Bureau of Business Research (BBR) had two main objectives: to compile statistics in the study of operating expenses on an industry-wide basis and to collect specific cases, or profiles, of individual companies. These two types of information could be used together in training students.

The bureau sent out field agents to collect information from a host of businesses, ranging in size from large steel manufacturers to small neighborhood grocers. As the operation grew, the surveys were sent out by mail. In return for their completed surveys, participants would receive copies of the school's findings. By 1920, approximately five thousand cases were collected for use in twenty-one courses in Harvard Business School and in one undergraduate course at Harvard College. In the retail field, the BBR conducted separate studies of the operating costs of department stores, jewelers, drugstores, grocers, chain stores, shoe stores, and specialty shops. Some of these surveys tracked business changes for over a decade. The findings of the BBR were described in 1929 as "yardsticks by means of which business men could determine whether or not they were operating as economically and as wisely as others in their field."[12]

That retailers were hungry for this information is indicated not only by the increasing number of businesses participating in the surveys but also by the fact that the costs of many of the studies were covered by national trade organizations. The National Retail Dry Goods Association published the findings of the BBR in its trade publication and funded the lion's share of the cost of collecting the data. Other smaller organizations encouraged their members to participate in the surveys. The *New England Grocer and Tradesman,* for example, roundly endorsed the project in 1925, noting, "Many merchants have been able to reduce their expenses and place their businesses on a firmer basis by comparing their operating expense figures with the common figures for all firms reporting to the Bureau and then taking steps to remedy their weak points."[13] Even stores that did not participate in the studies could purchase copies of the results from the BBR, and national publications such as *Women's Wear Daily* often quoted from completed bureau studies.

A number of western New York retailers—including McCurdy's, J. N. Adam's, the Wm. Hengerer Company, Duffy-Powers, and over thirty shoe stores, twenty drugstores, and dozens of grocers and jewelers—participated in the Harvard surveys during the 1920s and 1930s. During its meetings, the Operating Committee of Sibley, Lindsay and Curr referred to the "Harvard goal" in order to evaluate store sales.[14] Buffalo stores also were also scrutinized by the University of Buffalo's own Bureau of Business and Social Research (BBSR), which charted changing business conditions on a monthly basis in Buffalo and did occasional in-depth studies of local groceries and department stores. Buffalo's BBSR published the monthly *Statistical Survey,* which promised to present information "in a detached and scientific spirit," leaving it up to local citizens to draw conclusions and take action. A 1926 mission statement in the first issue of the publication declared, "It is the hope of the University that business men, citizens interested in social problems, and thinking Buffalonians generally will recognize the *Statistical Survey* as an important addition to the work the University is doing in service of its city."[15] Like the Harvard BBR, the University of Buffalo bureau also embarked on extensive studies of retailers, surveying various operational methods in department stores, groceries, and drugstores. By reading the findings of both institutions, Buffalo retailers could compare their operations with those of their counterparts across the country as well as next door.

The Harvard and University of Buffalo statistical reports show that stores did, indeed, use the surveys as yardsticks of operational effectiveness and also that many stores had to adopt more up-to-date record-keeping practices to simply report their operating expenses. To have figures that formed the basis of comparison, Harvard had to make sure that responses to the survey were uniform—to be sure, for example, "that the expense item of A, in New York, could be compared with the expense item of B, in Chicago."[16] Harvard was instrumental in having stores adopt a uniform system of record keeping, in order to ensure that the figures being compared were truly comparable. The initial surveys collected in the summer of 1911 revealed that even within the same industry, "hardly two firms in one trade used the same terms in the same sense." The bureau subsequently developed standard classifications of accounts to overcome this confusion. In addition, some types of stores developed their own forms. For example, the Controller's Congress of the National Retail Dry Goods Association developed the standard accounting format used in bureau reports. No matter the origin of the forms, the fact that Harvard encouraged their widespread use had a profound effect. As one 1920s historian of the bureau noted, the new definitions quickly became more popular, leading to increased uniformity of accounting practices within specific sectors. He noted with approval that more and more stores had adopted the standard classification of accounts for general use, and he remarked, "Even many firms that have not adopted the complete classification are using some of its provisions."[17] A growing number of stores adopted the standard classification of accounts for general use. This increased uniformity in accounting practices enhanced the bureau's ability to collect more reliable data.

The Harvard bureau sent out simple work sheets to assist stores that did not use double-entry bookkeeping. Many promotional pamphlets for the BBR and articles in various trade journals repeated the apocryphal story of a retailer who used outdated methods and as a result did not even realize that his business was losing money. The retailer owned his own store and ran it himself, mistakenly figuring that this meant that it "didn't cost anything" to run the business. He failed to take into consideration depreciation and shrinkage in inventory, did not even pay himself a salary, and as a result calculated that he was making a net profit of 6 percent when his store was actually running at a loss of 4 percent.

The studies compared everything from overhead costs, fixtures, stock turnover, and wages to the amount of floor space leased to other companies. Some of these categories required a complete rethinking of the way a good number of the stores kept their accounts. For many retailers, keeping abreast of these changes would have been an uphill battle. Yet those that did take advantage of the latest innovations in accounting or inventory could assure themselves that they *were* doing all they could to remain competitive and assert themselves in the face of competition from larger stores in bigger cities. This desire to remain competitive had the effect of reducing the differences between outfits of all sizes as even small stores adopted more standardized bookkeeping practices. In the words of David Monod, "'Modernization' involved a kind of homogenization of twentieth-century business."[18]

At the same time, larger stores in Chicago and Manhattan were not simply dictating to the rest of the nation. Just as the *Dry Goods Merchants Trade Journal* aimed for broad coverage, the BBR tried to include as many stores as possible in its statistics. The BBR's emphasis on collecting returns from numerous retailers meant that as early as 1923, the bureau had gathered reports from over 2,000 retail shoe stores, 1,800 grocery stores, 300 drugstores, and 500 hardware stores.[19] In 1930, 768 department stores in forty-five states were regular contributors of returns.[20] Indeed, the BBR often classified stores according to net sales, so that those operating in smaller markets or only ringing up a few hundred thousand dollars in sales a year were assessed separately from retail giants such as Macy's. Insofar as overall statistics for the industry were derived by putting all stores on an equal footing, even small shopkeepers were assured that their input mattered.

The bureau took great pains to ensure the anonymity of all participants in the studies. Each store was assigned a confidential file number that would be used on all correspondence, and business students or BBR staffers working on the reports had no idea which particular stores they were studying, beyond the general geographic region and the size of sales indicated on a given store's questionnaire. Nevertheless, stores in smaller markets were interested in what was going on in the metropolis, and some went so far as to request the names of New York and Philadelphia merchants who used the Harvard system of stockkeeping. While the bureau would decline such requests, the Harvard reports allowed stores to compare themselves with others in similar-sized markets or with competitors who had roughly the same amount of net sales. Yet more significantly, Harvard's findings gave the shopkeeper a sense of what was going on across the whole industry. The very methodology of the BBR suggested that it was worth keeping track of developments throughout the nation, rather than simply following the lead of the big stores in New York City.

In-house management was not the only area where stores took pains to keep up with the latest national trends. For department stores, the issue of style was as important as price in competing with national chains and stores based in larger cities. In particular, the selling of fashion was the source of tensions between the hub and hinterland. On the one hand, stores in smaller centers made an effort to keep track of the latest styles displayed in New York and, by extension, in the fashion magazines that reached across the country. Just as the owners of smaller stores were aware of new business practices adopted by their competitors, they followed the latest styles being offered in Manhattan. Yet on the other hand, these merchants maintained that they had a special understanding of the needs and wants of their clientele and provided an edited version of styles that they believed would suit local tastes.

It was not that an entirely new emphasis on fashion took over the department stores during the early twentieth century. Fashion had been a concern of dry goods merchants decades earlier. In the 1880s, for example, Flint and Kent in Buffalo had gained a reputation for carrying the latest laces, ribbons, velvets, and ginghams for seamstresses, as well as imported accessories and some ready-made items. Rather, by the 1920s, there was a perception that the pace of style changes was accelerating. Retail industry observers acknowledged that merchants in smaller centers faced increasing pressure to constantly update their inventory to reflect the latest styles. Many looked back fondly to the days when store owners rarely had to modify the selection of goods they kept in stock. *Dry Goods Merchants Trade Journal* writer H. L. Post stated in 1934 that in an earlier period, "the wants of the people were simple. . . . Demands changed slowly." In this idyllic past, he claimed, merchants had intimate contact with their customers and thus an almost intuitive sense of the types of goods in demand. Post also described a localized market, where consumers were less influenced by national trends: "Because of the slow change of fashion and lack of means for travel, the consumer was more or less isolated from other towns and was forced to buy in his local trade center."[21] This slow rate of change allowed retailers to pack away goods left over from one season to be sold at regular prices later on—"markdowns were nil." In contrast, Post presented a view of fashion in which the modern customer was more fickle and the merchant was less able to know the patrons and keep their needs in mind. According to Post, the fact that ready-to-wear apparel was becoming increasingly important (Post dated this development from 1914 onward) placed even more pressure on merchants to keep the latest goods in stock.

The shift from the "good old days" of slow change to the rapid pace of trend-driven "modern times" was not as clear-cut as Post described. Certain lines of merchandise, including millinery and dress goods, had been suscepti-ble to changes in fashion even in the nineteenth century. Yet this *DGMTJ* edi-torial touched on some real changes that were affecting relationships between the small-town retailer and the fashion-conscious consumer in the early twen-tieth century. As consumers gained easier access to images of fashion from magazines, movies, and advertising, as well as to metropolitan shopping dis-tricts, smaller retailers developed a number of strategies to remain competitive. None were willing to concede the superiority of style retailers in New York City and Chicago. Instead, they aimed to demonstrate how they, too, were "up on fashion."

Some merchants in outlying areas recognized that their customers might take fashion cues from the big city: one store owner in a small town outside Chicago argued in the *DGMTJ* in 1924 that the big-city stores actually educated his trade to buy more at home. A woman traveling to a larger city saw the beau-tiful dresses in department store windows and well-dressed women in the street. She might then decide that she needed a few new items for herself. But she did not necessarily go to the bigger stores to buy: the store owner noted, "She can be persuaded to go to her own store in her own home town and buy the best they have there, which is in reach of her pocketbook."[22] His observa-tion suggests that while many women in smaller centers desired big-city style, they were less willing to pay the prices associated with designer wares. More-over, the store owner claimed to encourage his sales staff to write to Chicago retailers regularly for items requested by customers that he did not have in stock. Although many women were astonished that he would provide this service, he estimated that this prevented his clientele from going to the city themselves and buying many more items there.

The trade press cautioned retailers to recognize the fashion consciousness of their patrons. Modern mass communication was bringing the world right to the doorstep of the customer; the retailer who talked down to the rural or small-town customer did so at his or her own peril. Customers, even those in smaller centers, were becoming increasingly savvy about style. In the *DGMTJ*'s view, it was a mistake to assume that a woman living in a smaller city knew nothing of Fifth Avenue: "That would be as much as to say that she has never seen a moving picture, or the *Saturday Evening Post*, or a Montgomery Ward catalogue, or the Sunday newspapers, or been in an automobile, or listened in on the radio. The achievements in publicity, in advertising of all kinds, even during the last decade, have put the same information before us all. In these days, wherever she is, a woman knows about the length of skirts and the style in hats."[23] Customers, then, had an increased understanding of the newest styles and presumably would select the stores they patronized according to their ability to deliver these wares.

Yet while this increase in communication might produce more demanding shoppers in one sense, stores could also profit from the flood of information. Even stores in towns much smaller than Buffalo and Rochester could claim to be in step with current fashion if they relied on magazines to determine their stock. In smaller stores, in particular, name brands were thought to serve as proof of the store's style currency. Lolliner's of Stillwater, Minnesota, a town with a population of less than ten thousand, boasted in the pages of the *Dry Goods Merchants Trade Journal* in 1936 that the store carried fifteen lines advertised in *Vogue* and a similar number of those advertised in magazines such as *McCall's*, *Good Housekeeping*, *Ladies' Home Journal*, *American Magazine*, and national weeklies.[24]

Department store buyers could use the national media to stay up to date. Magazines provided an easy way for stores to assert that they, too, were aware of current fashion. In Buffalo, J. N. Adam and Company's success in selling notions was, in part, attributed to the "fashion knowledge" of Assistant Buyer Miss Cummings, which she gained through reading magazines. Although the store had carried a large stock of buttons, a large proportion of this merchandise was not fast-selling. Miss Cummings "watched the fashion magazines. She knew at all times what buttons were right in style" and gradually built up a new stock of buttons that were "fashion-right" and consequently became best-sellers.[25]

These types of decisions were being made from Buffalo and from inside the store. J. N. Adam's presents an interesting example of locally based style knowledge. Although the company had ties to other stores in New York and was a member of Manhattan-based Associated Merchants, it rested with local buyers to use the tools at hand to determine what was fashionable. There was no direct dictation from New York, not even within one particular organization. At a time when ready-to-wear clothing was becoming more of a mainstay of department stores, even buyers for departments such as notions (aimed at women who sewed clothes for themselves) kept close track of mass-market fashion magazines. J. N. Adam's buyers assumed their clients were well aware of fashion trends and turned to magazines themselves to attract these customers.

National advertising campaigns provided rich opportunities for cross-promotion. In 1920, the *Dry Goods Merchants Trade Journal* reported on the successful "Nationally Advertised Goods Week" promotional campaign of a St. Paul, Minnesota, store. The store devoted all of its window and display space to the selling of brand names that were promoted nationally.[26] Sibley, Lindsay and Curr of Rochester used images from national advertising campaigns in direct-mail circulars promoting fabric and notions. According to a 1929 *DGMTJ* article, Sibley's staff would select a photo of an attractive style of dress from a "fashion book which is widely read," and the image would then be reproduced and attached to a swatch of material. This circular was mailed to women who often bought sewing materials. Sibley's assumed that customers were well acquainted with fashion magazines. The buyer of wash goods (washable fabrics like rayon) argued that this familiarity would encourage a woman seeing one of the circulars to come in and buy: "The recipient immediately realizes where she has seen the picture . . . and often looks it up to be sure. Then she reads the description and our advertising takes a stronger hold in her mind."[27]

On other occasions, stores tied selling to specific magazines. The *Dry Goods Merchants Trade Journal* noted with approval that a Utica, New York, department store had decided to highlight selected goods that were advertised in the March 1929 issue of the *Ladies' Home Journal.* The trade periodical advised display managers that they should take advantage of the promotional work being done for them by national advertisers, stating, "Manufacturers are planting some excellent seed in these magazines, seed which begins to grow almost as soon as the cover pages are opened. Are retailers taking advantage of this, cultivating it, and harvesting it?"[28]

Every reader of a fashion magazine was confronted by a number of advertisements—sometimes over half of the total pages of any issue—featuring goods that ranged from cosmetics to home appliances to clothing. These ads, according to the *DGMTJ*, were skillfully laid out to present a compelling message of "health, beauty, economy and utility" to the consumer. "With such a tremendous influence constantly bearing on her," store managers were advised, "it is only natural that the reader absorb some of these points and desire some of the products so fully described."[29] Smaller stores could thus view advertising in two ways. On the one hand, advertising was one of the forces reaching out to consumers to educate them about the latest styles, products, and trends. According to this perspective, merchants might hurry to keep up with the changing demands of consumers in their area. On the other hand, both advertisers and retail industry commentators encouraged store managers and buyers to take a different, more positive perspective. Stores could choose to work in tandem with magazine editorial content writers and advertisers, letting magazines do some of the selling for them.

Manufacturers often communicated directly with retailers, describing upcoming newspaper and magazine ad campaigns so that stores could coordinate their promotional efforts. Cannon, a major towel manufacturer, bought space in the November 1924 *Dry Goods Merchants Trade Journal* to show merchants the layout of its Christmas ads for towel gift sets.[30] The Kleinert's Rubber Company used a striking visual display to demonstrate to retailers the company's "Spring Campaign to increase *your* sales." It bought a two-page spread in the *DGMTJ* to show the various media it used to advertise. The left-hand side of the ad consisted of a photograph of the December issues of nineteen national magazines (including *Charm, Harper's Bazaar, Vogue,* and the *Ladies' Home Journal*) that featured Kleinert's ads. The right-hand page was a jumble of over seventy newspaper mastheads. Among those visible were the *Rochester Times-Union* and the *Buffalo Evening News.*[31] Along similar lines, the American Viscose Corporation, makers of rayon fabrics, boasted to merchants that "wherever you live, East or West, North or South," the company's national advertising in eleven national magazines was "working for YOU." The company asserted that "National Advertising Does a Local Job," doing the selling for merchants in communities across the country.[32]

In addition to the advance notice and assistance provided by manufacturers, trade papers provided help for retailers that wished to capitalize on magazine promotion. The *Merchandise Manager* went so far as to give an "advance picture" of the editorial content of some leading publications a month before they went to press to help stores coordinate their merchandising activities with the anticipated demand. Starting in the fall of 1933, they made a digest of the nonfictional content of six major women's magazines with an aggregate monthly circulation of 13,374,922.[33] Department stores were advised to tap into this valuable source of influence, since magazines provided suggestions that were "carefully heeded" by women buying for their personal wardrobes, their families, and their homes.[34] Stores that carried American designers, for example, were likely pleased to learn that *Good Housekeeping* was instructing its readers to ask for particular dresses "by the names of the designers," and they were told to use window and interior displays to tie in with the magazine article. Others could tap into more general trends outlined in the magazines. To capitalize on a *Woman's Home Companion* piece on fall coats with decorative trim on the shoulders, the *Merchandise Manager* instructed stores to develop window displays comparing shoulder treatments for women of various ages. In addition, the new fall colors described by the *Ladies' Home Journal* could be highlighted in in-store promotions.

Response to this new service was enthusiastic. One store president wrote that he had struggled to read all of the women's magazines "in order to dig out the new trends."[35] The *Merchandise Manager* saved him the trouble of sifting through these issues each month, providing the main points of articles on fashion, housekeeping, home decorating, and beauty a month before the magazines hit the newsstands. By the mid-1930s, *Life* magazine took the initiative to set up an entire merchandising department to encourage retailers to use tie-ins in their window and counter displays. The magazine sent reprints of ads, posters, arrows, "advertised-in-*Life*" stickers, and blowups of covers to interested retailers. *Vogue* magazine provided similar services to retailers as well.[36]

Even without this type of coordinated advice and advance notice of advertising campaigns, magazines provided a valuable tool for buyers, display designers, and window dressers. This use of magazines as a "measuring stick" of style can be read as evidence of the homogenizing effect of the national media. If stores jumped to show the current styles or color outlined in magazines, they were, in one sense, forfeiting their own ability to make decisions in merchandise selection and display. Across the nation, perhaps, we can imagine store after store featuring similar window displays with the latest shade of hat or length of skirt as depicted in the *Ladies' Home Journal* or *Good Housekeeping*.

Yet in the context of competition between smaller cities and the influence of the large metropolis, magazines can also be seen as a welcome means for smaller stores to assert their own ability to stay up-to-date. The national media leveled the playing field for merchants in smaller centers in this regard. National fashion magazines tended to exclude residents of smaller cities from the limelight, for not all places were equally visible to readers of periodicals. As Richard Ohmann has argued, "People read the magazines in homes all around the nation, but the magazines did not consider all parts of the nation as places worth representing."[37] In particular, New York City and, to a lesser extent, Boston, Philadelphia, and Chicago were *the* places to be, and readers who did not live in these centers were left with only the vicarious thrill of following the exploits of high society on the eastern seaboard and in the Windy City.

At the same time, however, we can think of these readers as measuring their own experiences against those described in the stories and articles of the magazine. Readers and retailers in smaller towns may, indeed, have felt like outsiders peering into the prime social space of the nation. But local merchants turned this equation around to assert their own participation in the national scene. Stores used magazines to advance the claim that although they were not located in New York City, they were just as good as New York stores in providing key styles or brands. Readers might never hobnob with the elite in the Hamptons or eat at the latest Manhattan hot spot described in *Cosmopolitan*, but they could wear clothes that fit the descriptions in national magazines or buy the branded goods advertised there. Local merchants maintained that there was no reason to look elsewhere for style goods: magazines were offered as proof that the stores in smaller cities were keeping up with national trends.

Newspapers also acted as boosters for stores, underscoring the ability of local merchants to provide the latest styles. The *Rochester Democrat and Chronicle* had a fashion bureau that provided many services to local women, including selling sewing patterns and directing shoppers in search of particular items to specific stores. The bureau relayed style news provided by the newspaper's wire service but remained committed to promoting (according to its official motto) "AUTHENTIC FASHIONS . . . FOR ROCHESTER WOMEN . . . FROM ROCHESTER STORES." Bureau writers reported on the availability of the latest styles in the departments of Rochester stores. One of the bureau's female "shoppers" gleefully confided to readers, "I have seen the smartest coats in our own stores this week. . . . Aren't we lucky that we don't have to rush down to New York to find the things we want?"[38] There were, of course, good economic reasons for the papers to promote local retailers as centers of style: Rochester's department stores were the ones buying ad space in the *Democrat and Chronicle*. Yet it is significant that the paper explicitly rejected the idea that New York stores might offer more variety in style merchandise. Local stores were rated just as good at providing the fashionable wares described in newspapers and magazines.

The print medium was not the only force spreading style knowledge. By 1920, the automobile made travel to large cities much more of a possibility for the rural or small-town consumer. Rochester's Retail Merchants' Council directly linked the car with the changing appearance of customers who lived far from centers of style: cars blurred the boundaries of the metropolitan areas, allowing shoppers to travel a hundred miles to a particular downtown store if they so desired. A 1928 council report noted, "Not many years ago the inhabitants of the small town could be recognized easily in the city because of the difference in dress; city styles had not penetrated even to near-by towns. The town merchant, therefore, had no demand for the variety of style or quality of merchandise which he recognizes as a necessary part of his stock. But there has grown up a competition between metropolitan areas which formerly was un-known, and Rochester is in competition as a shopping center, not merely with Buffalo and Syracuse, but also, in a very real way, with New York and Chicago."[39] This new competition, of course, meant not that Chicago or New York risked losing customers to Rochester but that Rochester would have to take action to keep trade at home. In a similar vein, a speaker at the National Retail Dry Goods Association's annual convention argued that cars had increased compe-tition between the small town and the big city. In his view, there were no small towns left in America: "What used to be known as small towns are in reality suburbs of larger cities. Distance has been annihilated."[40]

While cars thus created new challenges for Buffalo and Rochester mer-chants, they also created new opportunities. Cars enabled more shoppers to go to the downtown area to buy. Initially, the automobile was heralded by urban merchants, for it allowed easier access for customers wanting to shop down-town. Although problems of traffic congestion and other factors would lead to the demise of the downtowns in the postwar era, for a brief period many smaller cities envisioned their downtowns rising to compete with the best that New York and Chicago had to offer. And Main Street retailers were considered the heart of the dynamic downtown core.

For the areas around cities such as Buffalo and Rochester, the downtown acted as a magnet for shoppers. Just as the elite of Buffalo saw shopping in New York as an entertaining excursion, many wives in the small towns that ringed Buffalo looked forward to going downtown on shopping trips. Trolley lines connected the outlying areas with the downtown, but automobile own-ership often made the difference in terms of a family's decision to shop down-town. One survey by the University of Buffalo's Bureau of Business and Social Research indicated that almost 60 percent of the housewives who shopped in Buffalo once a week or more traveled by car.[41]

Respondents to the survey had a variety of reasons for traveling to Buffalo to shop. Over 50 percent cited wider selection as their main incentive for mak-ing the trip, with price ranking second as an influential factor. Others simply enjoyed the experience of a shopping visit. One woman made clear that it was not just a matter of better selection: she remarked that the stores in her town were "just as good as Buffalo's" but claimed, "I like to drive to Buffalo just for the enjoyment of shopping in different stores." Some made an effort to shop in the outlying towns because their husbands owned businesses there. The wife of a Tonawanda merchant asserted, "I do all my shopping right here at home because my husband is in business here himself." But many others happily made the trip to Buffalo's downtown, particularly to purchase shoes and clothing. A map produced by the Buffalo Chamber of Commerce highlighted the role of the city as the center of a wider circle of trade (see Plate 11). It boasted that 60 percent of the population of the United States and 80 percent of the population of Canada lived within five hundred miles of the Niagara area, just one night's ride away.[42]

Rochester also boasted of being the "hub of a great agricultural, industrial and trading area." Sibley, Lindsay and Curr claimed to cover a territory with a "radius of many miles" and often featured maps of "Sibleyland" in its promotions. One Christmas promotion in 1927 displayed the store as the heart of "Santa's Charted Territory." A map of western New York extended to communities as far as Scranton, Pennsylvania, to the south, Utica to the east, and Hamilton, Ontario, to the west.[43] A network of state and county highways linked the six counties around the city, and as one Rochester newspaper promotion boasted in the 1930s, the 139,619 automobiles owned in the area could bring "families from its farthest towns to Rochester in an hour's easy drive." This ease of transportation made shopping "a matter of minutes, rather than miles" for residents of the area.[44] According to a 1936 Rochester newspaper ad, it also bound the sizable suburban population of the city into one market, a "compact, closely-knit community, with similar habits, tastes, and wants." The ad, which promoted the city for investment, proclaimed that "from every doorstep in this area, roads lead to the downtown shopping district of Rochester."[45] Buffalo and Rochester thus enjoyed new status as hubs in their own retailing regions, their downtown stores acting as magnets for shoppers in the outlying areas.

The stores' ability to respond to the changing demands of patrons depended on the success of their buyers in bringing home the goods featured in magazines and national advertisements. By the 1920s, most department store buyers in smaller cities such as Rochester and Buffalo made seasonal pilgrimages to New York City and Europe to select merchandise. In their ad copy, they stressed how consumers in the local market could rest assured that they were receiving the latest from the runways of the world's fashion capitals. Sibley's newspaper ads featured "letters" from Madame Paulet, one of their Paris representatives. She promised Rochesterians that the store's Paris office provided daily updates on fashion items in the city, receiving the newest styles the moment they were launched. Readers were told that Sibley's departments would stock the items Madame Paulet discovered—or "clever copies of them"—for their buying pleasure. The B. Forman Company informed Rochester customers that their "style-scouts" had offices in Brussels, Paris, Lyons, Berlin, Chemnitz, London, Belfast, Vienna, Gablonz, Florence, and Zurich. B. Forman's promised to keep its clientele up-to-date on the absolute latest fashions through its foreign buying offices, European buying trips, systems of direct importation, and "constant use of post, cable, and even trans-Atlantic telephone."[46]

Hengerer's of Buffalo similarly stressed the store's connections in Europe, publishing a pamphlet that referred to buying operations in Paris, Florence, Vienna, and England. Ad copy boasted of the superior service the store was performing "in bringing to this community the markets of Europe."[47] Berger's specialty shop made a tongue-in-cheek observation that the store's ability to provide up-to-the-minute French fashion might lead to some confusion. A female shopper was described as exclaiming, "So This is Paris!" to which Berger's replied, "No, *Madame*, it is Buffalo. But the mistake is easily explained. . . . Berger's since 1905 have always been just a little more like the Rue de la Paix than Main Street."[48] Having buyers in the centers of fashion could ensure that the right goods were brought home, eliminating the need for customers to look elsewhere.

The notion that Paris was the world's fashion capital was still firmly entrenched in the 1930s. Although New York designers were gaining recognition, Parisian trends still had a certain cachet that elevated them in the minds of many department store buyers and customers. The *Merchandise Manager* ran an article urging Americans to "throw off the Paris fashion yoke" and instead embrace "American styling for American women."[49] The writer bemoaned the fact that while U.S. designers were coming into their own, they suffered a tremendous "commercial inferiority complex." All too often, he argued, Parisian designs were embraced simply because they came from Europe, and American designers of merit were ignored purely because of their country of origin.[50] The highly defensive tone of the article suggests that Paris was still the undisputed center of the style world at that time—in this case, New York found itself relegated to the role of hinterland to Paris's hub. In bypassing New York entirely, buyers for Rochester and Buffalo stores asserted that they were going to the source of fashion.

A Buffalo magazine article highlighted the way in which the city's department stores culled the finest fashion goods from Europe. The writer noted, "It's awfully easy to feel that New York is the only place to shop, but you're wrong. We've tons of irresistible treasures right here in town."[51] The decision to shop at home could thus be made without fear of being limited in the array of items and styles available to the consumer. Buffalo merchants could use improved technology to keep up with fashion in Europe just like their Fifth Avenue rivals, as one editorial observed: "If we were living in an age devoid of transportation and communication, clothes in New York would be better. But look in the shops there. Ninety-five per cent of the dresses are merely copies of French models. These copies, quite as beautiful, every bit as good in quality, also come to Buffalo."[52] If Parisian fashion was the object, both Buffalo and New York City could offer copies.

The ability to provide world-class fashion items and other style goods remained important even during hard times. During the Depression, as a later chapter will explore, newspaper editorials encouraged shoppers to spend their dollars at home, arguing that spending money in the area would boost the region's economy and help provide jobs for local people. Yet it is interesting to note that buying at home did not mean giving up on fashion. As one writer contended, "It's all right, Madam, to go to New York, or Paris, for something you cannot buy here in town. But the chances are that it's already on sale for less money in Rochester. . . . There isn't much in New York, anyway, which cannot be found in Rochester."[53] Women were not the only ones reprimanded for going to New York in search of fashionable clothes that they could just as easily get at home. A magazine editorial took issue with "prominent citizens" who made their fortunes in Buffalo but went to New York City tailors. It admonished that these men need not go elsewhere and "watch our money slip into other markets. Our tailors will stand your closest inspection."[54]

Use of New York interior decorators came under similar fire, for services of equal caliber were available at home and had the additional advantage of helping the local economy. Patronage of local stores might even result in unexpected bargains. Some Buffalo stores actually acted as importers, selling goods to New York merchants who, in turn, charged higher prices for the same goods. B. Forman's of Rochester boasted that it had exclusive selling privileges on many of the items in its store that came "from across the Atlantic and the Pacific" and were "not to be duplicated, not just in any other store in this city, but in any store in any other American city."[55]

Although ready-to-wear collections were most often associated with being on the cutting edge of fashion, department stores acknowledged that women who sewed their own garments were also very conscious of changes in fashion. In

1929, Sibley, Lindsay and Curr ran monthly promotions during which "fashion artists" spoke about new style trends and demonstrated techniques in cutting and fitting. Display tables of fabrics were arranged in a square to create a runway for the demonstrations. The fashion artist wore a dress or suit made of featured fabric and spoke about the pattern number required, the type of material, and notions. To complement her dress, she drew from other departments in the store, selecting suitable jewelry, hosiery, and shoes that were also readily available for purchase. Hats, gloves, and bags might all be featured in the fashion show, a tactic designed to make onlookers "ensemble conscious" and likely to buy many different items to create a complete outfit.[56]

The department stocked paper dress patterns that were quick knockoffs of European designs. Sibley, Lindsay and Curr endorsed McCall Printed Patterns with the comment, "The promptness with which the latest Paris designs are duplicated in your paper patterns has encouraged us to add them to our other pattern services."[57] Women who sewed their own clothes had a variety of reasons for doing so: some were motivated by saving money, others enjoyed sewing, and still others might have had trouble buying clothes off the rack that fit. Sibley, Lindsay and Curr recognized that interest in Parisian lines and pulled-together ensembles was not limited to customers of haute couture or even ready-to-wear. Its promotions in dress goods used style as a selling point.

Beyond claiming to be up-to-the-minute in terms of European or New York styles, stores in upstate New York often tried to put a local spin on fashion. Buffalo's severe winters inspired the manufacturers and retailers of outerwear to claim a special understanding of the needs of local customers. For many years, the Kleinhans Clothing Company offered the "Buffalonian fleece overcoat," arguing that it was an ideal coat for "our variable Buffalo climate." The company promoted its new union suit (long underwear) with the warning, "You know how cold it gets in Buffalo in November." Kleinhans stressed that upstate residents had to pay particular attention in choosing the right winter apparel, as "in Buffalo we wear an overcoat right through November, December, January, February, March. Five long months." The Mt. Rock Fleece coat promised to make it seem like "Palm Beach in Buffalo," even at times "when Buffalo streets resemble the Antarctic." Hengerer's similarly boasted "coats Designed with You in Mind . . . and Buffalo's Icy winters!" Hens and Kelly offered a velvet-and-beaver combination hat christened "Miss Buffalo," and department store buyers claimed a special insight in selecting appropriate merchandise because they lived in the area and experienced the cold. Rochester merchants, too, made appeals based on local weather. Sibley, Lindsay and Curr boasted that it had snapped up some special suits in New York City with local needs in mind: the suits were "warmly interlined—suits made to stand the Rochester kind of winter."[58]

Stores claimed that by selling to a specifically local market, they could better gauge the tastes of local shoppers. The B. Forman Company prided itself on being especially responsive to the needs of local shoppers. It claimed a special advantage in merchandising because it took extra steps to find out "the wants of its public." In June 1920, it sent out questionnaires to several thousand randomly selected individuals who had charge accounts with the store and used the information gathered through this process to inform its fall buying for October. Typical questions asked the female patron if she expected to buy an evening gown the following season and how much she would be willing to pay. B. Forman's boasted that the information would directly shape its fall buying plans. Every order was confirmed by "the expressed wishes of our public." The customer surveys enabled B. Forman's to place the largest order for fall fashions in its history—buyers knew "not only what would be wanted but the prices at which these things would be wantable!"[59]

Retail industry observers claimed that this increased responsiveness was easier to accomplish in one particular community. The *Department Store Buyer* argued that the characteristic intimacy of the small-city store with its customers "simplifie[d] its buying problems." Stores in smaller centers could achieve a "more complete grasp of the buying preferences of the consumer populace" because their customers were more likely to be a homogeneous group. Stores in different regions had very different needs, depending on whether they were located in a company town, a resort area, a university town, or some other type of city. The successful store was the one able to "find an individualized approach keyed to the character of its community" to attain a level of responsiveness to clients' needs not achievable in the big city.[60]

Stores claimed they served the community both by responding to their customers' needs and by supporting local manufacturers. Many shops stressed that they stocked goods that had been made in the area. Rochester's status as the site of a number of national clothing manufacturers was translated into special bargains for the home market. McFarlin's Clothiers boasted that it had a long-standing policy "to give the lion's share of space to merchandise bearing Rochester labels. Imports are featured only in certain specialities which can only be secured abroad." Purchases would give local residents the added satisfaction of "knowing that you are helping Rochester business by wearing clothes created by Rochester labor."[61] Some of these companies were, in fact, manufacturing-retailing hybrids that shipped to merchants across the country but had single retail outlets in their home locations.

Rochester's status as a center for clothing manufacture, in particular men's clothing, persisted into the 1920s and 1930s.[62] The National Clothing Company, despite its "national" name, emphasized its roots in the area and in 1926 devoted a full-page ad to thanking Rochesterians for their business. The company recapped its history, emphasizing that each innovation adopted by the business only helped to better serve the local market. The ad described the company as

> not the only men's store in Rochester, but one that has endeavored to render service with courtesy, with intelligence and with profit to him who buys here. Pioneers in Rochester in the making of clothes we sell in order to give Rochester better values; Pioneers in maintaining our own representatives in foreign and domestic markets, in order that the city we serve might get the best they can produce; Pioneers here in group purchasing through association with leading stores in other cities, so that you and Rochester might share the advantages of volume buying, and have the values that cannot be secured in any other way.[63]

The ad described the National's evolution in terms of the company's desire to provide Rochester with "better values." The firm explained innovations in distribution or manufacture in the context of serving the community, not increasing profits.

Advertising suggested that a product's origin in one's hometown might be a special source of pride. The story of the spread of national brands to ubiquity often emphasizes the "placelessness" of these products: by definition, success for these early mass marketers meant having the ability to be sold *everywhere*, without appearing to favor one part of the nation over another. However, unless one hails from Atlanta or Battle Creek, it is sometimes easy to forget that a brand name such as Coca-Cola or Kellogg's originated in one specific community and thus had a special place in the hearts of local residents, even those not directly involved in the product's manufacture. The extent to which localness remained a strong selling point into the 1920s and 1930s is striking. Even giants of mass-market magazine advertising such as Eastman Kodak made clear their geographic roots. Well into the 1930s, the company prominently identified itself at the bottom of national ads as being located in "Rochester, N.Y., the Kodak City."

Newspaper ads, with their concentrated local exposure, could take this suggestion of place a step further. When retailers were selling to the home market, locally produced items had a special cachet, both in terms of support for the local economy and, more intrinsically, in the nature of the goods themselves. One 1923 ad described how locally produced fashion items could serve as a point of reunion between western New Yorkers. It described two passengers sitting in adjacent deck chairs on a steamer heading out of Hong Kong. "You must come from western New York," one woman said to the other, "for you are wearing the Eastwood pedestrian boot like mine. I bought this pair at the Eastwood store in Buffalo. My home is in Erie." Her newfound friend replied, "And I bought mine in the Eastwood store in Rochester." These shoes immediately identified their wearers with the region, a trait that Eastwood presumably felt would appeal to local readers of the ad. The company touted its "worldly" connections forged by patrons who wore their shoes far beyond the upstate region: "We have touched Asia, seen strange sights in Korea, visited a half dozen provinces in China, sauntered among the bazaars of Bombay, shivered with memories of rebellious deeds at Luchnow, heard the roar of the lion and recoiled from the snarling attack of the bengal tiger. Without moving, we have circumnavigated the globe."[64] Yet while these goods were circling the globe, they were also bringing local wearers together, allowing them to reconnect in a world of exotic sights and strangers. Eastwood boots were not just American mass-produced goods; they were particular to the western New York region and could connect their wearers with home, no matter how far abroad they wandered.

On one level, then, certain "upstate styles" or locally made goods served as a means of selling specifically to the region. Conversely, not every New York City style would make a successful transition to the smaller city or town. National trade magazines also recognized regional fashion tastes. The *Department Store Buyer* ran an editorial about the differences between New York stores and their brethren in smaller cities. Entitled "New York is not America," the article outlined the different fashion priorities for women in smaller cities. It argued that a woman in a smaller city might actually need more garments than a big-city dweller: "Fashionists find that, unlike women in New York and other large cities, the matron in the small city needs many costumes because her circle is limited and she is constantly with the same people. In New York, circles of acquaintance are likely to be so large that fewer costumes are required for the adequate wardrobe. This tendency of itself means that the few costumes of the New York woman will necessarily be better wearing and higher priced than the more numerous garments suited to the needs of the small town woman."[65] This condescending depiction of small-town life as an endless round of parties involving the same limited number of friends over and over recalls Sinclair Lewis's *Main Street,* where the heroine tries in vain to break free of her limited social circle. Nonetheless, the *Department Store Buyer* acknowledged that women in smaller cities were interested in fashion and had certain special demands because of their distinctive social engagements.

An ongoing feature in the same periodical reveals that even the makers of fashion in New York City admitted some limits in their efforts to dictate to the hinterland. During the late 1930s and early 1940s, *Department Store Buyer* ran "In the Marts of Trade," a column of humorous fiction describing encounters between a model in a chic New York City dress house and a buyer from upstate. Marge, the fashion model, aims to show the hapless buyer the latest lines from the runways of the city. Mr. Adelstein, a buyer from a nameless Buffalo department store, tries his best to select dresses he feels will move back home. It is not surprising that the *Department Store Buyer* would feature articles relating to Manhattan: most buyers from around the country made the trip to New York once a year, if not once a season. The choice of Buffalo as the fictional character's home may also suggest how the city could easily represent the home of the "typical" buyer, from a medium-sized center, in the reader's imagination. The interaction between buyers and New York dress houses would have been familiar ground for the journal's readers and, as such, would provide a rich source of material. One might imagine many scenarios where the hick from out of town becomes the object of ridicule as he clashes with a modern woman from the metropolis.

The humor of the feature does not, however, derive from Mr. Adelstein's lack of sophistication or inability to cope with haute couture. Rather, the two players often manipulate each other and enter into complicated negotiations before Adelstein finalizes his dress orders. And it is often Adelstein who prevails in these vignettes, due to his knowledge of his community and what will be practical to keep in stock in his store. He may defer to Marge in some matters of style, but in the end, he is the one being courted by the dress house to purchase its new line. Marge's willingness to follow any trend, no matter how ridiculous, is as much a source of amusement for the reader as is Mr. Adelstein's tendency to pick more conservative fashions for his customers. The two characters act as stereotypes not only of the metropolis and the hinterland but also of gender roles. Marge is flighty and emotional, concerned with fashion and frivolity; Adelstein is practical and rational, concerned only with the bottom line. The choice of the name *Adelstein* for the buyer further fit the stereotype of the Jewish businessman involved in the rag trade and retail industry.

In a typical encounter, Adelstein arrives in New York in May, seeking washable pastels and other sensible wares. Marge, in contrast, is already anticipating the fall season, and she offers him black broadcloth dresses more suitable for November.[66] In January, Marge proffers sheer dresses, causing Adelstein to sputter, "Of course, it wouldn't interest you, but we're having a blizzard up in Buffalo."[67] On another occasion, Adelstein complains when Marge shows him the newest fashion—somber dresses with no trimmings that look like uniforms. Marge placates him by modifying the severe new dresses she is showing with white lace collars, pleats, and belts, and Adelstein happily orders fifty dresses in a full range of colors and sizes.[68] Each player in the drama feels smug about manipulating the other. Marge is happy to secure a large order of dresses, and Adelstein is pleased to have obtained the more conservative styles, which he feels will better satisfy his customers.

Adelstein appears in September with an eye toward dresses for the Christmas season. Marge attempts to sell him a ludicrous red sequined ski suit with a suede seat and is insulted when he suggests that she provide him with his usual order of sequined dresses with jeweled belts. Adelstein shocks Marge by telling her that he modified the red chiffon evening dresses she had sold him last year, adding ostrich feathers and sashes.

> *Marge* (tartly)—How were the markdowns?
>
> *Mr. A.* (gleefully)—Didn't take any! Sold two dresses and put the other eighty-eight in the store-room and now they're all ready for this Christmas.[69]

At this, Marge faints, and Adelstein claims victory. This scenario would have been perceived as even more absurd by an audience of buyers who faced tremendous pressure to move goods quickly. It would be highly unlikely that Adelstein's real-life counterparts could devote storage space for a year to a rack of dresses; nevertheless, his character could present a fantasy for readers, triumphing over suppliers and customers alike by presenting last year's goods as current. Besides squabbling over the appropriate attire for the season, Adelstein and Marge clash over sizing. Marge presses Adelstein to buy smaller sizes, to which he snorts, "Buffalo's not the corn belt, miss, but it's not a city of midgets either."[70] Her protests that lots of stores are selling size tens are met with the observation that lots of stores are going out of business as well.

Although Adelstein dutifully checks out the newest styles on his trips to New York, he edits his choices to suit the body types and the tastes of his clientele. While some of the styles shown by Marge might be appropriate for young women, Adelstein knows his business depends on pleasing older matrons. When Marge pitches a particularly youthful style, Adelstein rebels:

> *Mr. A*—Who cares about the young crowd, Miss? My customers are all middle-aged married women and they want . . .
>
> *Marge*—Don't tell me! I know! Black dinner dresses! Then they'll love our new strapless black chiffon.
>
> *Mr. A*—Strapless! (Ed. note: The poor guy practically swoons . . .)
>
> *Marge*—Look, Mr. Adelstein. Nothing above the bust-line!
>
> *Mr. A.* (livid)—No, and nothing above the eyebrows, either! Now, listen, Miss. I've wasted enough time here. If this house isn't smart enough to know that conservative women still want black dinner dresses, I'll take my business elsewhere.[71]

Adelstein knows the preferences and the limits of his customers and will not risk spending his entire budget on styles that will not sell at home. When Marge tries to get him to be a little more daring in his ordering, he protests piteously, "But Marge, every time you make me buy imagination, I gotta take mark-downs."[72]

This process of negotiation is a recurring motif in the serial. One encounter has Marge wearing a party dress shaped like a Christmas tree—complete with flashing lights and jingling bells. An alarmed Adelstein persuades her to sell him some plain black and white dresses, asserting that Buffalo loves simpler styles. He is willing to indulge Marge to a point, allowing her to show him outrageous styles as long as she eventually provides tamer versions, or, in his words, "dresses to sell." In exasperation, Marge agrees to give him what he wants, acknowledging that all her other customers also favored plain woolens.[73] In the summer, Marge tries to sell Adelstein some extreme evening dresses with an outlandish stars-and-stripes motif, calling this the "American Way line." When Adelstein rejects the dresses outright, she grouses, "I can see there's no point in wasting our masterpieces on you. However, we've developed some *modified* American Way for the volume trade." The buyer is delighted, for these dresses are so modified that they are exactly what he is looking for.[74]

The timing of orders is another issue that causes continual conflict between the two characters. During a February buying trip, Adelstein makes the mistake of hoping to reorder a style of navy blue dress that is currently popular. He tries to convince Marge that despite her assertion that "navy's through," he has constantly been getting requests in the store for more. Marge is unable to think of current sales, only future seasons:

> *Marge* (genuinely baffled)—I can't understand you, Mr. Adelstein. You're always asking for the things women are wearing now.
>
> *Mr. A.* (choking but accustomed to frustration)—Did you ever hear of the law of supply and demand?[75]

The joke here, of course, is that demand in the fashion business is highly unpredictable and always based on the next new thing. Marge claims to be able to predict what outrageous styles will be popular in the coming months, but she is bewildered when Adelstein wants to obtain more of a style he has already ordered. And no matter how early Adelstein appears in the Seventh Avenue showroom, it is never early enough. In September, the traditional time for Christmas orders, he is frustrated, as Marge has already moved on to the spring season.

> *Marge* (unheeding)—It's the melting season, Mr. A! You've completely melted me. I *will* show you our new spring line and yours will be the first eyes to feast on it. Won't Buffalo be thrilled?
>
> *Mr. A.* (frantically)—But, Marge! For Spring thrills Buffalo can wait. Right now . . .
>
> *Marge* (gaily)—Thrills wait for no one, Mr. A. Open your arms to Spring!
>
> *Mr. A.* (sobbing)—But I want Christmas! Here it is only September and I haven't had Christmas yet.

Part of the humor in the interactions between Marge and Adelstein lies in the fact that he is constantly behind the times, trying in vain to keep up with the young and flighty woman. This could, in one sense, be seen as a comment on the fashion tastes of his clientele, always just a step behind New York. Yet for the readers of *Department Store Buyer*, many of them out-of-town buyers themselves, the satire also touched on the failure by big-city manufacturers to adapt to the actual needs of local markets and, by extension, of the buyers for stores there.

Readers of the trade journal would also have recognized Adelstein's frustration with the acceleration of the calendar urged by Marge. Buyers faced continual pressure from manufacturers to place orders as early as possible. A poem in another section of the *Department Store Buyer* suggested that buyers viewed the hurried schedule for orders with a mixture of amusement and resignation. As they began their all-important round of Christmas ordering, the poem acknowledged,

> September may seem early to
> Begin the round-up, but the fact is
> We all must follow standard practice,
> And brood on skates and skis, although
> It will be months before there's snow.
> Come heat, come drought, we dare not pause . . .
> Them's orders, straight from Santa Claus.[76]

Complaints about the four-month frenzy of preparation that went into each successful Christmas sales season peppered the articles in the *Department Store Buyer* every September.

The high jinks of Marge and Adelstein would only have been funny to buyers reading the magazine if the power struggle between them contained a kernel of truth. The outrageous items offered by Marge are amusing because they would be immediately rejected by the average consumer upstate. The readers of *Department Store Buyer* might have seen themselves in Mr. Adelstein, forced to deal with New York houses that pushed styles that might be briefly popular but would not translate into solid sales in smaller towns and cities. Adelstein's frustration with Marge underscores how buyers and, by extension, department stores in smaller cities negotiated to bring the "big city" home to their clients while maintaining a distinct sensibility.

Stores in cities such as Buffalo and Rochester tried to walk the line between cosmopolitan and provincial, taking the best of what the mass market had to offer but presenting themselves as the old-fashioned remnants of a bygone retail era. Stores systematized their operations and followed the latest business practices described in the trade press and by university business schools. They carried a host of national brands and watched trends in national magazines. Simultaneously, they asserted their distinct ability to respond to the needs of their local markets. The more fashion-conscious department stores assured consumers that they were being kept abreast of the latest style trends, carefully selected by the caring local merchant. With buyers around the globe, stores such as Hengerer's in Buffalo or Sibley's in Rochester declared that they were presenting an edited version of "Parisian fashion" or "New York style" for their clients.

This push-and-pull relationship between the hub and hinterland complicates our understanding of the evolution of a national market in America. The changes in retailing and marketing that are associated with the growth of a consumer culture in the United States in the late nineteenth century are often viewed as a homogenizing force, uprooting Americans from their local identities. Even as areas across the nation were flooded with the same goods, sellers took pains to differentiate themselves. Local pride and traditions were modified, not eliminated, in the spread of modern retailing and marketing during the 1920s and 1930s.

A regional perspective reveals that local loyalties died hard. Consumers were encouraged to take pride in products made in their own communities; merchants in smaller cities forcefully resisted the suggestion that any store could serve their particular market as well. Examination of these changes "on the ground" reveals that the spread of national phenomena such as the mass-market magazine and nationally branded goods could have a distinct meaning from the perspective of the smaller retailer outside of New York City. Eager to demonstrate their ability to keep up with national trends, shopkeepers in smaller cities measured themselves against reports in trade magazines and national magazine advertising. At the same time, they used a language of localism to differentiate themselves from metropolitan competitors.

THE "CHAIN STORE QUESTION"
AND THE INDEPENDENT RETAILER

IN THE FIRST TWO DECADES of the twentieth century, independent merchants in Rochester and Buffalo looked to the big stores of New York City as
competitors for local dollars. The cachet of Fifth Avenue, the increased ease
of transportation, and the coverage such stores received in national media
prompted smaller merchants to fight back, stressing their ability to provide
competitive goods while paying special attention to local needs. As time wore
on, however, it was the chain store, not Macy's, that loomed larger and larger
in the imagination of the independent merchant. Department stores themselves had faced opposition from small retailers during the late nineteenth century. Smaller merchants had viewed the newly arrived "Boston stores" such as
Sibley, Lindsay and Curr as dangerous new hybrids. Carrying a number of
lines under one roof and offering one price for all, these stores were thought
to undermine the traditional relationship between store owner and patron,
gaining unfair advantage because their sales volumes encouraged manufacturers to offer them better deals.

By the 1920s, Rochester and Buffalo's department stores had assumed the
position of business leaders in their communities. No longer frightening new

forms of operation, they were now familiar and seen as committed to the area. Moreover, institutions such as Sibley, Lindsay and Curr were anything but small businesses, having grown over the years into considerable operations with international buying offices set up in other cities. Sibley's attained the $10 million mark in annual sales by 1920. At the peak of that decade's prosperity in 1927, it rang up $13,107,305 in net sales. This figure would drop dramatically in the early 1930s but still remain around the $8 million range.[1] Yet in terms of their images within their communities, the department stores were unassailable. As so-called independents, often owned by the same families who had founded them years earlier, these stores asserted their place as part of the local fabric, with a stake in the success of the small and midsized cities in which they were located.

Chain stores were not new in the western New York region during the interwar period, but they became a much more visible presence at this time, particularly during the Depression. Hard times pushed some independent retailers out of business, as consumers who had once been willing to pay a little extra for service were attracted by the minimal frills and low prices that characterized many chain operations. The chains put locally based department stores on the defensive in much the same way that department stores had put small retailers on the spot decades earlier. At first, these new retailers were thought of as insignificant for merchants who had built up a loyal local clientele. With time, however, local merchants began to pay attention, first copying the chains' management and buying techniques. Later, independent stores emphasized their local roots and community spirit to fight the encroachment of this new form of merchandiser, discrediting interloping chains for their ties to other areas and their perceived lack of commitment to the cities in which their branches were located.

Hindsight suggests that independent merchants had a lot to lose with the coming of chain groceries, drugstores, five-and-dimes, and department stores. Yet local retailers, particularly independent department stores, did not immediately perceive the chains as a threat, initially viewing their new rivals as a possible source of renewed vigor and fresh retailing ideas. As late as January 1928, the *Dry Goods Merchants Trade Journal* could put a positive spin on the increased competition brought by chain stores. One article, entitled "Why These Independents Do Not Fear Chain Stores," trumpeted the "good fight" put up by intelligent and aggressive merchants. According to this article, some independents tried to match the chains on advertised items, while others relied on service to persuade customers of the value of buying "quality" rather than "discount" merchandise. One department store owner from Wisconsin went so far as to announce that the arrival of the chains was good for business, for it shook the independent merchant out of a stupor of complacency. Chain store expansion was valuable to the independent, he argued, as it forced many stores to become more systematized. And systematization, not volume, was deemed the key to the chains' success, a tactic that could be easily imitated by the independent. He had little sympathy for store owners who felt threatened by the chains, stating, "If many of the independent merchants would give more time and attention to increasing the efficiency of their own business and a little less to 'crabbing' about conditions there would be fewer chain stores and more individual retailers making a regular yearly net profit."[2]

This emphasis on store systematization was echoed throughout retailing industry literature. "Scientific training of managers and other personnel" was ranked number one in a list of seven "common elements of success" for all retailers, chain or independent, in a 1929 *DGMTJ* article.[3] Even partisan observers such as Godfrey Lebhar, editor of *Chain Store Age* and outspoken advocate of the advantages of chain retailing, conceded that chain stores enjoyed little advantage over retailers who had modernized their operations. Lebhar argued that there was no indication that the chain store would ever be able to drive the "really efficient independent" out of business. "Even those who protest most against the growth of the chains," he noted, "are constantly pointing out that the independent who is efficient, the independent who adopts modern methods, both in his buying and in his selling, has nothing whatever to fear from chain store competition," an observation that he felt was also made by operators of chain stores themselves.[4] In his view, systematization and streamlining could usher in a new era of retailing populated by both chains and small retailers. Those who did not adopt up-to-date methods would become extinct. There was no question about the value of embracing the modern.

The chains themselves argued that it was no fault of theirs if independent retailers could not keep up. As one editorialist noted indignantly in 1926, if a grocer continued to use 1776 methods while other merchants operated on a twentieth-century basis, he would be "criticized, outlawed, reviled and . . . destroyed."[5] Store owners who did not adapt, in this view, deserved to go out of business. The *Chain Store Manager* sketched the transformation of the chain of distribution, noting its advancement with satisfaction. Humanity had made tremendous progress in the work of distributing the necessities of life: a single trapper might once have handed a skin overcoat to the ultimate "consumer," but now "a thousand laborers produce sugar at the opposite side of the globe and a thousand grocery clerks hand it over the counter to a million people." Given these changes in distribution, the single-store merchant should expect to adapt in order to survive. Every retailer had to become "a marcher in this parade of progress."[6] From the perspective of the chains, the independent who failed to get in step with this parade was perversely committed to outdated practices.

The debate over chain stores was thus not about whether their "professional" methods of operation were superior. Because the debate was framed by a Darwinian understanding of the evolution of business, the only question was whether these methods gave an *unfair* advantage to the chains. Independents with the proper initiative could adopt strategies such as departmentalization and scientific training of personnel, so these kinds of tactics were not seen as problematic. Other advantages enjoyed by the chains, including special deals from suppliers, were attacked as not falling within the parameters of square dealing, in part because they could not be easily copied by independent stores.

In one sense, this emphasis on "progressive retailing" led to a homogenization of stores and business practices. By following the advice of suppliers and retail experts, as David Monod contends, "retailers were being encouraged to think of themselves as on a par with big businesses, and in so doing they were being led to conform to the demands of the great transformation that had accompanied mass production."[7] Yet evidence suggests that while merchants did, indeed, look to both manufacturers and industry experts for suggestions, not all of the advice proffered was accepted without question: this was not a dictatorial process, with statisticians and retail giants prescribing universal formulas to be adopted immediately by all merchants across America. Even as they were being encouraged to embrace new retailing methods, local merchants were urged to adapt this advice to the particular circumstances of their stores and their communities. And they often came up with their own innovations, taking part in a dialogue (although admittedly an imbalanced one). The successful independent appropriated the best of the "new retailing" methods, while trying to maintain those practices that gave the store its distinct character.

Group buying was another example of a strategy adopted from the chains to make the independent retailers more profitable. By banding together to make purchases, independent stores from smaller centers hoped to attain the same purchasing clout as their national competitors. A new regular feature in the *Dry*

Goods Merchants Trade Journal, entitled "Meeting Chain Store Competition," explored group buying as an option for independent retailers. The pooling of resources among the independents was declared the "way out" for stores, "the Moses which [would] lead them out of the wilderness of chain store and mail order store competition."[8] The Pelletier Company of Sioux City, Iowa, made group buying the focus of an ad campaign, noting that chain stores often emphasized the advantages that came from cooperative buying. Pelletier's argued that it had joined with sixty-five of America's great independent stores to enjoy the strength of group buying yet carefully adapted its business to remain in touch with local conditions. The *DGMTJ* contended that a "voluntary chain" of independents retained the "personal touch with the local community."[9]

Options such as systematization and group buying were most feasible for medium- to large-size independent merchants. Department stores were most likely to adopt at least some aspects of chain store operation. Local newspaper advertisements carefully positioned the retailers involved in group buying as "community stores" that offered the advantages of the chain store (cheap prices, scale in buying) while remaining "able to select style merchandise to fit the individual needs of the community which they serve, something the chains are handicapped in doing."[10] Retail pioneer Edward A. Filene, of Filene's department store in Boston, predicted that buying pools and associations of retailers in groups would "give the independents buying power as strong as that of the chains."[11]

Buffalo and Rochester stores experimented with various forms of group buying. As early as 1905, the Wm. Hengerer Company of Buffalo had become part of a buying group, although its ads continued to present the store as an independent with local roots and traditions.[12] The Duffy-Powers store ran an ad in 1931 explaining that the store was and would continue to be "owned and operated exclusively by Rochesterians—for Rochesterians" but that their participation in a joint-buying agreement would benefit the local community on a whole new level. Ad copy stressed that the store was "controlled by the same families as always" and that the president of the company was the son of the founder of the business. The agreement with 106 other stores would allow them to bring new values to their home market. Joining the organization meant that manufacturers made concessions to ensure orders, and Duffy-Powers would pass on the savings to the shoppers of Rochester. The start of the group-buying venture also coincided with the beginning of a new cash-only policy, suggesting that at least some of the older traditions of trust between merchant and customer were to be jettisoned in the pursuit of large-scale efficiency. In

1937, Sibley's of Rochester stopped supporting its own buying office in New York City and became a member of the Frederick Atkins Buying Office. The organization, a group of "30 independently-owned, non-competitive, department stores throughout the nation," hoped to use the combined buying power of thirty large stores to get low prices for Rochester consumers.[13]

Joining these types of organizations raised some questions about who actually was setting store policy. In 1929, the New York representative of a group-buying organization reported to the *Dry Goods Merchants Trade Journal* that buyers from other communities often resisted the influence of the central buying office, not wanting to completely centralize buying (and possibly limit their own influence).[14] Stores were also careful to counter the suggestion that joining a buying group meant that distant bureaucrats had control of a local institution. In 1929, E. W. Edwards and Son of Buffalo, Rochester, and Syracuse used ads in the *Buffalo Evening News* to explain how store policies were set from within. The company claimed that it was able to act as a "new kind of Santa Claus for Buffalo people." The store was a family company, "now in the hands of its third generation of founders," and officials boasted that decisions were made with the welfare of the local community in mind. While chain stores might have to adopt policies to please executives in other cities, Edwards was different: "Because of its independent ownership, entirely apart from any national chain organization, its policies as to prices are entirely its own." As an example of this independence, the store announced a new selling strategy for Christmas 1929. Instead of featuring a special gift department with marked-down prices, all merchandise would remain the same price all year.[15] Shoppers could buy with confidence, knowing that they were paying the absolute lowest price for gift items. This experiment was unique to the store.

Chain Christmas marketing seemed particularly ripe for attack from independents stressing their fine-tuned local sense. W. Bruce Philip, secretary of the Alameda County Pharmaceutical Association in California, wrote a spirited defense of the independent retailer in 1931 in which he drew a line between the local merchant's sincere Christmas window and the opportunistic displays of his chain competitor. Because chain stores had their policies and windows directed from afar, displays were designed solely for profit and failed to "show or feel any local enthusiasm." While all stores in December used holiday themes, he stated, only the independent store could capture "the real enthusiasm of the holiday" with local or personal decorations, even as the chain store made Christmas displays "from only a mercenary standpoint, that of more dollars per holiday."[16] Philip drew a clear distinction between the mercenary chain and the spiritual and civic-minded independent, dismissing the notion that the independent might also design its windows for profit as well as Christmas sentiment. In his view, if independents prospered, it was not because they were stooping to the calculating levels of the chains but because they were intrinsically more adaptable. The independent merchant, he noted, was more flexible and open to change, for he was able to "accept at once the best that any group or independent offers," unlike the slow-moving bureaucracies that dominated chain stores.[17]

Philip was not alone in his characterization of chain bureaucracies as problematic. Some industry observers suggested that independents might do best to wait and see just how successful certain chain policies actually were before adopting them. As late as 1929, Harvard's Bureau of Business Research suggested that independent department stores were tending to show lower operating costs than chain department stores. According to a report in *Business Week*, chain bureaucracies did not always earn their keep: too many chain stores were "paying for central organizations not yet organized to save more than they cost."[18] Higher advertising, purchasing, and "professional service" costs, including the maintenance of central offices, were thought to inflate chain expenses.

Chain stores themselves recognized that the independent merchants in particular markets enjoyed certain advantages. Speaking to a convention of domestic science teachers in Des Moines, Iowa, a representative of the J. C. Penney Company spoke frankly of trying to build up community goodwill for Penney stores by visiting state, county, and district fairs throughout the Midwest and Far West, in order to make the company known to farmers and residents of smaller towns. Penney's set its sights on the trade that went to local merchants simply by "right of heritage."[19] The S. S. Kresge Company and Montgomery Ward took a more proactive stance in cultivating local goodwill, realizing that "they had a public relations problem to solve."[20] Charity work and local involvement became matters of corporate policy, not something to be left to the whim of the individual manager. In this sense, we can think of new chain store branches as imitating the established merchant in allying themselves with local causes and concerns.

Chain stores worked hard to get a feel for the various communities where stores were located. The director of personnel for Penney's in the early 1930s stipulated that the manager of a new store should have lived in a city the same size as the one where the store was to be located. The new manager would arrive in town at least a month before the store opened for business in order to talk to people and to peruse the windows of other retailers, "trying to analyze the type of merchandise that appeals to that community and the kind of store that will be especially liked. He [would begin] to sense the special needs of that town."[21] Although the layout of each Penney's store was set out by the company, the manager had discretion in buying stock and arranging departments depending on the needs of the city. The general manager of a small chain of drugstores in Colorado argued that there should be a certain level of individualism, even among chain branches in the same town: "We cannot switch managers easily, for we must have managers whose personalities fit in well with the personalities of the people in their communities. For example, the man in charge of our store located in the railroad district must be able to handle railroad men and their families. I manage the main store myself because it is located in the foreign section and it is difficult to find a man who knows the people and their languages as well as I do."[22] This emphasis on the fit between the store and its surroundings was recognized as an important trait of the successful independent, one that the chains were wise to copy.

Trade publications acknowledged that chain store managers often kept an eye on the activities of the independent merchant. The *Dry Goods Merchants Trade Journal* noted that in addition to exchanging management ideas internally within their organizations, chain stores also adopted ideas from their independent counterparts. One editorial argued that the management of chain stores such as Penney's should constantly read trade papers and profit from the "interchange of ideas" that the *DGMTJ* and other publications provided.[23] Penney's not only subscribed to that magazine, it also ran ads in the periodical for personnel, highlighting the training offered by the company and the opportunities for advancement within the organization. In advertising in a medium aimed at independent merchants, Penney's appropriated the language of self-sufficiency to override any qualms readers might have about working for a chain organization. One 1929 testimonial from a happy Penney's employee described how he had enjoyed a good salary in his previous position but had "little hope of self-betterment or of even gaining financial independence."[24] Now, working for Penney's, he felt assured of a successful future. Another ad asked, "Are you a *Partner* in the business?" and offered young men "without any capital" the chance to become partners in a progressive business. It exhorted the reader, "Measure yourself against our requirements! Are you well educated; have you a thorough grounding in the dry goods, clothing or shoe business; are you between the ages of 21 and 35; have you lived cleanly?"[25]

By listing a certain moral standard for prospective employees as well as a level of business experience, Penney's attempted to undercut the suggestion that chains were run by unscrupulous managers. In line with this, the company used a certain definition of manliness to attract potential employees: it only wanted "men who can look us straight in the eye," "red-blooded men" who recognized that a partnership was more valuable than a mere job.[26] Implicit in the Penney recruitment campaign was the need to overcome any sense that chain store employees were less autonomous and thus less manly than their independent counterparts. Emphasizing the masculinity of financial independence, the company offered the chance of a "partnership" to clerks, assistant buyers, or lower-level managers who presently worked for independent merchants and thus read the *DGMTJ* but might consider jumping ship to join the chains. The interchange of ideas between the chains and independents thus could also lead to a swapping of personnel.

In addition to their close relationship with the towns they served, the independents were thought to have another weapon in their corner: their ability to provide specialized service could not be duplicated by the chains. In a 1938 study of chain store competition, Theodore Beckman and Herman Nolen, professors at Ohio State University, argued that the very structure of the chain operation made personalized service less of a priority. While independent merchants usually realized that they had to serve their individual customers well (or risk their entire business), the chain store manager could feel that "even though the success of his particular store may be of considerable importance to his own career, the success or failure of the chain is not dependent on the accomplishments of this one single unit."[27] Customers could sense this difference, Beckman and Nolen contended, and they appreciated the personalized service often offered by the independents.

For working-class consumers, the personal relationship between the smaller merchant and the surrounding community was particularly important. University of Buffalo economist Edmund McGarry observed in 1923 that Buffalo's immigrant population had more immediate reasons for avoiding chain stores. In an article published by the Bureau of Business and Social Research's *Statistical Survey*, he noted that these largely working-class consumers realized "their language handicaps in buying from American stores" and often had few options but "to purchase their goods from merchants of their own race or those who can speak their language."[28]

In her study of Chicago's working class during the same period, Lizabeth Cohen describes a similar tendency for ethnic workers to favor neighborhood independents over chain stores.[29] Working-class consumers would forgo any price savings in order to patronize stores that had staff who spoke their language and that offered more flexible credit and services such as check cashing. Cohen contends that although Chicago's neighborhood ethnic grocers were successful in staving off the influence of the chains and supermarkets during the 1920s, their situation was precarious: as chain stores became more aggressive, these small merchants lost out.[30] Cohen dates this change to the mid-1930s in Chicago, but the time line for the change seems to be slightly later in Buffalo; as late as 1939, McGarry contended that chain competition had not threatened the livelihood of most small grocers in the working-class neighborhoods of Buffalo:

> It would seem more reasonable that these stores, scattered throughout the area and catering to a population which, though price-conscious, have little opportunity to compare prices, enjoy a monopolistic position which enables them to charge somewhat higher prices than are charged elsewhere. Furthermore, it is significant that stores of this character have been little affected by the development of voluntary chains since their volume of sales and methods of doing business seldom approach the standards set by these organizations.[31]

McGarry argued that these smaller stores provided a valuable service to their clientele, selling smaller quantities than large grocers, remaining open longer hours, and even providing extra services such as check cashing. He cautioned, however, against seeing these small stores as beneficent members of the working-class community. To remain profitable, they had to charge much more than large stores or chains with superior buying power. As a result, he noted, "it may mean that the less fortunate parts of the population, those having least with which to pay, in turn pay most for what they get."[32] While Cohen has stressed the solidarity between the small grocer and the community being served, this relationship was also exploitative to some extent. In working-class neighborhoods, geography prevented consumers from comparison shopping. McGarry explored the behavior of grocery shoppers by income group across the city and noted that while housewives from high-income neighborhoods preferred to drive to what he termed "shopping sub-centers," to compare prices and look at a wide variety of goods, those in poorer sections often did not have access to cars and might find even streetcar fares too expensive. These patrons frequented corner grocery stores "as their needs [arose], buying from meal to meal."[33]

Yet there was no simple equation relating income and level of chain patronage. Working-class consumers might feel more comfortable patronizing neighborhood grocers, but those facing hard times could find the lower prices of a chain store worth a special trip. On the other end of the spectrum, families with high incomes were often more sympathetic to the notion of the independent merchant and more able to spend money according to principle, rather than price. A study of attitudes toward chains in Urbana-Champaign, Illinois, in 1931 indicated that people of very different income levels might share antichain sentiment, although for different reasons. Paul D. Converse of the National Association of Teachers of Marketing and Advertising identified two groups of occupations that were "particularly hostile" to chain stores: local businessmen and workers in the building trades. Among respondents to Converse's survey who belonged to these two groups, 60 percent were opposed to chains. Opposition to chains thus might have made strange bedfellows, including business owners who feared chain competition and unionized workers who viewed chain labor policies with mistrust. In contrast, "non-union labor, executives, and salesmen show the most friendliness for the chains," Converse reported, revealing that income level alone was not enough to determine one's position on the issue.[34] There was also often a gap between respondents' stated attitudes toward chain stores or independents and their actual buying behavior. Thus, 36.9 percent of families from the lowest income bracket (earning $1,500 or less per year) claimed to favor chains, but only 16.1 percent actually bought from them, suggesting that perhaps geography played a great role in determining their patronage. For families on the other end of the financial spectrum, the idea of patronizing chains was less attractive in sectors such as clothing, where the appeal of buying from an independent outweighed any possible cost savings of chain patronage.

Not all retailers were willing to leave it to the consumer to select which type of store organization was preferable. Some smaller shopkeepers argued that the way to compete would be to educate the public about the cost to local institutions if people patronized chains. Although they might enjoy lower prices in the short term by patronizing the chains, they contended, consumers would ultimately contribute to the demise of their own communities. The editor of the *Michigan Tradesman* argued that while the independent kept bank deposits in the community and invested locally, "the chain store, on the contrary, sends the entire receipts of the store (less rent and wages paid the store manager and his clerk) to the headquarters of the chain system in Detroit or elsewhere, to be immediately transferred to New York, where they are absorbed by high priced executives and clerks and divided among the greedy stockholders of the organization. This steady stream of money, constantly flowing out of town every

week, never to return, must ultimately result in the complete impoverishment
of the community. It is a process of slow but sure starvation." This stream of
money was understood to flow only one way; it was assumed that the absentee
executives and rapacious stockholders had little incentive to reinvest in the
towns and smaller cities that were home to chain branches. Any consumer who
patronized the chain store instead of the regular merchant was thus "placing
an embargo on the further progress of his community" by contributing to
business stagnation and lowered property values. By making the public aware
of the consequences of their buying habits, the editor argued, merchants could
encourage civic-minded consumers to avoid chain stores and waive any personal, short-term savings that might have negative, long-term consequences
for their hometowns.[35]

In a full-page ad in the *Rochester Democrat and Chronicle*, Butterick (publishers of
national magazines including *The Delineator* and *Everybody's Magazine*) offered another way for independents to fight fire with fire: by selling national brands.[36]
Historians of marketing have often described the emergence of national brands
as part of a transformation that stripped small retailers of their power. In this
view, independent merchants were under siege from both chain stores and national manufacturers who wanted to erode their power in the local market.
Brand names undermined the discretionary power of the small retailer at the
point of sale. While small stores could attempt to respond to the mass merchandisers' low prices by substituting private labels for brand names, Susan
Strasser notes that "more and more of their customers asked for Ivory soap and
Baker's cocoa; national advertisers were training them to 'refuse all substi-
tutes.'"[37] David Monod similarly argues that retailers lost influence in the minds
of consumers when goods became associated with the manufacturer, not the
seller. Larger stores and chains became "models to be emulated" because they
knew how to promote the type of image desired by national brands.[38]

Nationally branded goods, according to this interpretation, worked to the
advantage of chain stores, whose bulk buying power allowed them to undercut
the independents. For observers at the time, however, the relationship between
independent stores and branded goods was not so clearly antithetical. Instead
of seeing national brands as part of a revolution in distribution that would
spell the demise of the small store, independent merchants were encouraged
by manufacturers to view national brands as their *allies* in the battle against
chains. Because small retailers could not afford the large advertising budgets of
the large chains, they should look to national manufacturers to do their advertising for them. Butterick argued that stocking national brands gave the

small retailer support from these national enterprises: "By selling trade-marked, standardized, nationally advertised goods, a merchant can ally himself with enormous aggregate manufacturing capital." A moderately stocked grocery store could thus benefit from national advertising campaigns with budgets totaling $50 million. Butterick appropriated the chain-link metaphor and applied it to the independent merchant, stating, "Even the smallest store may thus become one of a chain protected by this national barrage of fire."[39]

Butterick clearly had its own reasons to encourage merchants to stock brand-name goods: national manufacturers bought sizable ad space in the company's mass-market periodicals. Further, there was no love lost between chains such as A&P and some national brands, for in the 1910s, a series of lawsuits had pitted grocery chains that sold items for less than their nationally advertised prices against manufacturers who refused to sell to them. Butterick may have thought it had found a solution that pleased manufacturers and independents alike: manufacturers would be happy to sell to independents who could not afford to price-cut, and smaller stores would appreciate the ad expenditures for goods they kept in stock.

Department stores, as well, were encouraged to capitalize on the power of the national advertiser. In 1936, the *Dry Goods Journal* touted the sale of "known lines" and nationally advertised brands as one strategy for smaller stores facing competition from chains and mail-order merchants.[40] By 1940, the relationship between retailing chains and national brands would shift: new-style supermarkets came to rely exclusively on branded and nationally advertised goods. It is important to note, however, that smaller merchants in the 1920s and 1930s did not automatically see the national brands as harbingers of a new era in retailing that would erode their power. They instead envisioned branded goods as possible allies and hoped to harness the clout of national manufacturers for their own benefit. That this development made the store into "a kind of promotional mechanism, a sort of free-standing corollary to the newspaper ad and the sales catalogue," as Monod notes, may have, indeed, been the case.[41] Yet perhaps small store owners at the time envisioned this as a new alliance, one that would give them access to a level of public attention they had not previously enjoyed. A shopkeeper who tapped into, say, a national campaign for Aunt Jemima pancake mix by using a promotional card in the shop window may have been relinquishing the ability to substitute other brands for that particular product. But the merchant was also identifying himself or herself as a reputable dealer of the product and might even be featured in local advertisements by the manufacturer.

Although they were initially optimistic about their ability to compete with the chains, many independent merchants were less sure of their place in the retailing pecking order by the mid-1930s. Articles in the *Dry Goods Merchants Trade Journal* about chain stores took on a decidedly more pessimistic tone. A series of pieces in 1934, entitled "The Independent Does Not Need to Surrender," highlighted the ways in which the independents should study the factors that led to chain store success. The headline suggested the siege mentality of many independents. Standardization of price lines, studies of local and community buying, and the lowering of markups allowed chain stores to take customers away from department stores. In departments such as notions, shoes, hosiery, and lingerie, chain stores managed to suck away business.[42] In 1934, author H. L. Post warned beleaguered merchants that the "Whoopee Era" of 1914 to 1929 had lulled them into a false sense of security. During the boom times, an orgy of consumer spending had encouraged merchants to expand or to specialize in higher-priced goods because the middle and upper classes were spending freely. The next phase of this boom was a migration of shoppers to other cities: "The upper middle and rich consumer in village, town, and city began to migrate to the next larger center to buy. No longer was he or she satisfied with the assortments offered in home-town stores." In Post's view, stores in towns and medium-sized cities stocked higher-priced goods in an effort to hold onto the trade and "forgot all about the old staple profit producers." New buyers had become accustomed to shopping for the wealthy, not the always elusive "average consumer."[43]

The key to the chains' success, in his view, was their ability to recognize both the needs of the rich and those of the broader masses. Undercutting the independents in price in key departments (notions, hosiery), the chains lured customers away. Efforts to combat the trend through special sales events often backfired, as "Mrs. Consumer . . . soon discovered that many of these sales items were the same values she could get all the time at the chains." Superficial remedies such as the installation of new store fixtures or the creation of new departments often failed to stop the slippage. Again, systematization seemed the answer. With this in mind, Post argued that perhaps intense competition would, in the end, benefit the small stores. Only those that adapted would survive. He argued, "I am of the opinion that all will be forced to recognize the simplicity of chain store operation and cut many wasteful services and do more efficient merchandising and promotion." Post advised merchants in smaller stores to think long and hard about the remaining buying power in their communities. Were there enough people with money left in the community to support both a main floor and an upstairs floor, stocked with merchandise in the higher quality ranges? Or would it be better to include average or lower-priced lines?[44]

Still, Post pointed out, independent merchants did enjoy some advantages even at the height of competition with the chains. The fact that these stores were run by hometown merchants not only pleased local customers but also allowed managers of independent stores to have a much better sense of local demand than a chain store manager who relied on marketing information supplied by the chain's headquarters. Post also believed that the personnel at the independent store were of higher quality than in the chain, as workers were "treated more fairly and will work harder for a comeback." He prescribed a complete rethinking of the store policies, with advertisements geared to tell the public that this was a "reorganization" rather than simply another liquidation. Stores had to keep up with the newest innovations to beat the chains at their own game while still retaining the elusive status of the independent.[45]

Part of the confusion over the appropriate response of independent merchants to the "chain store problem" lay in the very definition of the chain. The National Association of Teachers of Marketing and Advertising had an ongoing debate in the pages of their *Bulletin* over whether voluntary chain stores—that is, stores that came together with a wholesaler to enjoy chainlike benefits such as group buying—could still be considered independent merchants. A "committee on definitions" was struck in the early 1930s to discuss how members of a voluntary chain differed from branches in a chain store and reported an even division of opinion on the matter.[46] Edmund McGarry, an economist at Buffalo's Bureau of Business and Social Research, also explored the issue. The U.S. Bureau of the Census collected data on retail chains in 1929, 1933, and 1935 and designated any organization with four or more units to be a chain. In contrast, the Federal Trade Commission used two units as the point of demarcation between independents and chains, provided that both were centrally owned and carried substantially similar lines of merchandise. This lack of clarity allowed some stores to stress chain store attributes when advertising low prices, for example, while maintaining the positive moral connotations of independent status.

The Independent Grocer's Alliance (IGA) was one such organization. The hundreds of IGA stores that dotted cities across the nation, including upstate New York, based their very name on the concept of the independent merchant. The alliance was first formed in Poughkeepsie, New York, in August 1926, when seventy-six retailers joined with a wholesaler to form a cooperative group. Their purpose was to eliminate price competition with chain stores and maximize collective buying power. IGA founder J. Frank Grimes was an outspoken critic of the chain store movement and defended the rights of the independent merchant in almost mystical terms. At an address to the Advertising-Selling League of Omaha, Nebraska, Grimes played up the specter of faceless, absentee bureaucrats associated with the chains. "I say to you," he roared, "if the chain stores start in the state of Nebraska until they cover every avenue of retail endeavor, I say to you that Omaha will suffer, and it will suffer severely." Only the smaller merchant was responsive to the needs of consumers in smaller cities such as Omaha. Big business and chain stores were too detached from the area and made no effort to get to know the community. Grimes echoed generations of populist protestors who saw the world as a conflict between eastern capital and western consumers. "Men, sitting back, managing these big corporations in the eastern states, with no intimate knowledge of what this territory needs, send out their stores here to break down the individual in business; they don't understand what the west or any other part of the country needs, or how it really lives or how it exists." He admonished his audience that the nation was at a crossroads in retailing history. The time was at hand to answer a pivotal question: "Shall America cease to be a country of proprietors, or shall it become a country of clerks?"[47] In his view, the chains were commercial despots with little stake in the communities in which stores were located. Although the chain organizations were technically legal, he argued, their natural tendency was to encourage the concentration of wealth, and as such, they threatened American traditions of initiative and self-reliance.[48] Newspaper ads in Buffalo presented the IGA proprietor as responsible to the customer alone and thus "free to select the foods you wish." The customer was his "one and only boss."[49]

Yet in some ways, the proprietors of Grimes's own IGA branches were more like franchise managers than independent merchants. IGA store proprietors, or members, shared a common logo to reinforce customer identification and make possible group advertising by the wholesaler for the retailers. By 1929, the IGA had developed its own label for goods. Members paid a weekly charge (about $3.50 during the 1930s) for advertising and store management advice. New recruits were advised of ways to renovate or modernize their stores, and they began subscribing to the company's monthly house organ and weekly merchandising bulletin. All promotional materials were coordinated by the head office, including window displays, newspaper ads, and direct-mail flyers.

All stores, of course, carried the IGA brand label, and some IGA wholesalers required quotas for the amount of merchandise to be purchased each month by a particular store. All stores were to be self-service operations (a relatively new phenomenon in the 1920s), in order to maintain the organization's image of modernity and efficiency. One of the few services not provided by national headquarters was the negotiation of orders for manufacturers' nationally advertised brands. While the branches could enjoy special deals on IGA-brand goods, they had to negotiate with the wholesalers of other national labels on their own.[50]

A similar type of alliance of independent retailers was the linking of independent druggists under the McKesson Service symbol. In a large 1929 ad in the *Buffalo Evening News*, McKesson listed "10 reasons why millions of people prefer to buy at the *Independent Druggist's*," including not only competitive prices, extended operating hours, and delivery service but also factors that called into question the character of the chain drugstore. By declaring that the independent drugstore "gives that special service which is obtainable only from men who own their own store," the ad invoked Grimes's prophecy of a "country of clerks" who did not control their own destinies and were thus less motivated to please the customer. Another reason for patronizing the independent druggist was that "you can send your children shopping there with perfect peace of mind," suggesting that the friendly local druggist would look out for children in a way that the faceless, bureaucratic chain could not. Finally, the McKesson ad boasted that most independent stores offered charge account service, implying that chains were not willing to extend the same sort of trust to the consumer.[51]

For their part, owners of bona fide chain operations looked on the voluntary organizations with skepticism. Godfrey Lebhar, editor of *Chain Store Age*, compared the voluntary chain where unit stores had "the right to do as they like" to a military operation that lacked discipline. In his view, one of the big challenges of the regular chain operation was to get its managers to follow all directions from the head office without fail. Lebhar assumed that owner-managers might prove even more resistant to directives from on high. Voluntary chains often lacked any sort of discipline structure to enforce prices, for example. Only when the owner-managers of branch units were convinced to "surrender their independence *entirely* so far as the operation of their stores went" did Lebhar feel that the voluntary chain stood a chance in competition with more centralized business organizations.[52]

Another wrinkle in the definition of chain stores was the existence of regional chains, often concentrated in one city. Wegmans grocery stores in Rochester made their connections to the local community a selling point in promotional materials. A typical newspaper ad for the chain emphasized,

> Wegmans serve Rochester trading area EXCLUSIVELY. Being in close touch with each store, and with the wants of each customer assures a higher order of service. No red-tape and chain-store detail at Wegmans. No long-distance arm-chair executives to support in other cities. . . . Every Rochester family benefits from Wegman home-ownership. . . . Your own comparison will show you the benefits of shopping at Wegman home-owned food markets—where your dollars come back home to you, because Wegmans in turn, spend them right here in Rochester.[53]

At what point did the successful independent merchant who was able to open up a few more branches in the hometown become part of the "chain store menace," usually associated with faceless bureaucrats located in distant centers? The answer, of course, is that few stores could be neatly classified as purely independent or chain, and no store was—or would want to be—completely local. Defenders of the chains pointed out that the owner of a chain store was simply a businessperson who had started off small and, through hard work and perseverance, had developed a large, successful enterprise. Instead of regarding chains as an aberration, they urged consumers to recognize these stores as part of the natural evolution of American business. In 1926, the *Chain Store Manager* argued, "THIS IS THE REAL CHAIN STORE GIANT as he actually lives and works. He started out in life as a small merchant with one store. Every chain of grocery stores now in existence commenced with one store and from the original store the progressive merchant enlarged his field of activities to serve more people. So the chain store giant is HUMAN. He is not a born monstrosity, but has naturally developed into his present size."[54] In a similar vein in a 1931 issue of the *Rotarian,* one chain store defender presented the fable of John Jones, a hardworking grocery store operator who finds that he cannot enlarge his present store in his hometown. Instead, John buys out the store of his neighbor Jim Smith in the next town, puts his best assistant in charge to run it, and finds himself suddenly the owner of a chain store system.[55] To castigate him for being a "chain store dealer," it was implied, was to punish him for working hard and succeeding. The alternative was to reward the unindustrious and unscientific. Sure enough, the founder of the Hart grocery chain took this line of attack in an article in *Chain Store Age.* He argued that many grocery businesses were started by the type of individual who had "failed to make good as a railroad man or a farmer or a bookkeeper or a carpenter" and so had little ability or knowledge in the grocery business. Thankfully, in his view, this was changing so that stores were no longer inefficiently run and badly stocked.[56]

In an address about the social and economic aspects of chain stores, James L. Palmer, a professor in the Marketing Department at the University of Chicago, rejected the notion that any retailer could be purely locally based and still remain competitive. He argued that it was unrealistic for consumers to think that they could find a way to spend money that kept it in the community. Even if they patronized local merchants, consumers inevitably would buy products manufactured in other cities. He contended, "The Battle Creek cereal manufacturer and Detroit automobile manufacturer take money out of the community just as does the chain store organization."[57] A car from Detroit could be sold much more inexpensively than one from a small local company; consumers who did not take advantage of this fact were simply being foolish. Palmer also discounted much of the criticism that chain stores undermined local civic spirit. Because they originally developed in larger cities that lacked "the community life which characterizes the small town," the notion that the chains negatively affected social organization was, in his view, doubtful. He felt that trading relationships in larger cities had already become "depersonalized" before the advent of the chains.[58] Finally, Palmer contended that although chain stores might drive some local independents out of business, their presence would ultimately result in a stabilization of the retail trade structure and the reduction of risk, for only competent stores would survive. This increased competition would benefit local consumers.

Chain branches, although certainly controlled from without, tried to cultivate local community goodwill through charity gestures. They also emphasized how chain stores could bring employment and other benefits to the community. When Walgreens opened its first branch in Rochester in 1936, the newspaper ad copy was headlined "LABOR OF CITY BUILT STORE," and it included a list of the local concerns that had been involved in the building's construction.[59] While their management might be parachuted in from elsewhere, chains often employed local workers and thus could lay claim to some community feeling. Sears, Roebuck boasted that it was company policy to hire area people to work in its retail stores. This approach was good for business, a store executive argued, for two reasons. First, the company hoped to aid in the development of the communities in which its stores were established, going so far as to stock the individual retail store with merchandise purchased from manufacturing sources within the same community. Second, the company believed that a local person could "do a much better job in a Sears store in Buffalo than a clerk of equal ability from outside. No one else could possibly know the folks of this community better; could understand their needs so readily."[60] In ads and statements to the press on the opening of a new store in Buffalo, Sears, Roebuck went to great lengths to emphasize its commitment to "hiring local."

In one sense, however, this emphasis on local pride was perhaps disingenuous: it made financial sense for Walgreens or Sears, Roebuck to use local labor in the building and staffing of their stores. It would have been a sizable and unnecessary expense to move workers into the area. Although a few management positions might have required extensive company training, many local people would already have possessed the skills required for jobs in construction or sales. But by claiming to have "chosen" local workers, these concerns could make a play for community goodwill. It is debatable whether there really was a choice to be made.

A similar use of the idea of choice framed the discussion of the new stores opened by Loblaws grocery chain. Loblaws originated in Canada and first expanded across the border to Niagara Falls and then to the Buffalo area by 1925. Newspaper ad copy regularly emphasized the investment that Loblaws was making in the community. A 1931 Buffalo spread proclaimed that "Loblaws believe [*sic*] in Buffalo" and thus earned and spent money in the community.

> It is a constant endeavor of Loblaw groceterias, to share with their customers in Buffalo and the municipalities in which they operate, the profits accruing from their business. Loblaws take pride in the fact that they are contributing to the success of Buffalo as a city, by the very substantial investment represented in the new Loblaw warehouse. In addition to this, many thousands of dollars have been spent with Buffalo workmen, in the erection of stores. Thousands of dollars are paid out monthly in Taxes and Store Rentals.[61]

By suggesting that Loblaws stores were choosing to spend money in Buffalo and disregarding the fact that taxes and rent were not choices to be made but simply the cost of doing business for both independents and chains, the campaign subtly counteracted criticism that the chain stores did nothing but siphon money away from the community.

The W. T. Grant company, which originated in Lynn, Massachusetts, in 1906 and operated almost five hundred stores coast to coast by 1939, drew attention to its use of steel from the Buffalo and Lackawanna plants of Bethlehem Steel in the construction of its newest Buffalo store. A 1939 newspaper article about the store opening highlighted the advantages that the company was bringing to the community. In the previous year, the company had purchased $200,000 worth of merchandise made in the city of Buffalo. This merchandise was sold not only in Grant's stores in Buffalo but also in other Grant's stores throughout the country. The W. T. Grant organization paid a further $200,000 to Buffalo people in the form of employee salaries, $50,000 for local and state taxes, and $266,000 for rent and miscellaneous expenses.[62] Again, any money spent by the company was held up as proof of local feeling—even expenditures such as rent, salaries, and taxes, which, one could argue, were by definition local expenses and could not be spent in any other way.

For their part, independent stores, while strenuously asserting their "mom-and-pop" nature during the interwar years, were changing to remain competitive. Rochester consumers enjoyed the buying power of a number of area-based grocery operations. The Hart chain stands as a good example of the local chain phenomenon. Founded in 1917, the organization operated close to a hundred stores in the Rochester area by the late 1920s, while maintaining in promotional materials that it "served Rochesterians" in a way that other groceries such as the A&P did not.[63] On the one hand, the Hart stores seemed to embody the new trends in chain merchandising: large-scale buying, centralized distribution, coordinated weekly specials, and self-service convenience. But on the other hand, the Hart chains took pains to emphasize their local character and the fact that they had adopted these innovations only to better serve the Rochester customer. Hart's ad copy boasted, "We have forced competitive chain organizations to sell their products cheaper in Rochester than in any city in the country. Our success is a triumph for the housewives of Rochester."[64] The ad also pointed out that customers in Buffalo, a larger city, actually paid higher grocery prices than their Rochester counterparts. Elimination of overhead costs such as expensive fixtures and delivery service allowed Hart's to keep prices competitive. The stores also had their own premium system of coupons to encourage customer loyalty, not to one particular branch but to the Hart organization itself.

The Hart chain also based its success on its ability to provide branded goods. The founder of the company argued that it was against store policy to offer private-label items. He contended that substitution of private labels for requested brand-name items did little except annoy customers and eventually drive them away. Alfred Hart argued, "We still stick to standard, nationally-advertised brands. We have never handled a product bearing an exclusively

Hart label and probably never will. I believe that the slight extra profit to be had on most private brands is much more than offset by the sales assistance and by the irritation to customers in having something sold to them which they do not know about but which is represented as being 'just as good.'"[65]

The stores were therefore local successes at handling nationally advertised goods. They saw no apparent contradiction in claiming home-operated status while simultaneously selling branded items that were anything but local goods. The store's ownership was what qualified it for home status.

The Wegman grocery stores also drew this distinction between the locally owned chain and the branches of a national outfit. Declaring that its outlets served the Rochester trading area exclusively, the company ran ads that trumpeted the close attention it paid to local needs. The customer enjoyed lower prices, for there was "no red-tape and chain-store detail at Wegmans. No long-distance arm-chair executives to support in other cities."[66] Advertising for Wegmans emphasized its supposed home-operated status, arguing that the stores' use of strictly local personnel eliminated "costly district supervisors and a wide variety of executives and other 'long-distance' expenses" passed on to the consumer by national chains.[67] Instead, dollars spent at the stores "come back home to you, because Wegmans, in turn, spend them right here in Rochester."[68]

The S. M. Flickinger organization, with grocery stores covering western New York and northwestern Pennsylvania, was another regional chain that claimed to provide the benefits of cooperative operation while clinging to independent status. Company founder S. M. Flickinger proclaimed a "revolution" in chain grocery store merchandising. He noted that the Flickinger manager was required to invest capital in his store and thus became a part owner and received a majority of the store's net profits. This qualification made the manager "in fact, a real merchant, instead of an employee." His personal stake in the company would make a difference for consumers: the independent grocer had a natural community interest that was not easy for chain stores to replicate. The average paid employee of the chains became "more or less of an automaton" who simply followed company instructions, without allowing his own personality to emerge. In this manner, Flickinger was "humanizing the chain store." With mass buying power, uniform standards, and a high turnover of merchandise, Flickinger stores combined "modern" selling with the charm of the "old-time" grocer.[69]

The Flickinger organization also developed a new hybrid of subsidiary stores. In addition to operating 310 stores under the Flickinger name, it was in charge of the Red and White grocery chain, which was intended to be "a cross between the chain store merchant and the independent grocer."[70] The 250 Red and White grocers were former independents who had once been wholesale customers of the Flickinger company. Red and White grocers sold the same private-label goods as the Flickinger stores, bought dry groceries from a Flickinger distributor, and painted their stores in standard colors. They received advice on layout, shelving, and fixtures; monthly advice on bookkeeping and other management ideas; and an annual audit that allowed each store owner access to "full information as to prices charged by the Flickinger company to its chain stores." All stores were to operate on a cash-and-carry plan, eliminating the discretion of the individual merchant in offering credit. By becoming part of the Red and White plan, the grocers gained a guarantee that they would receive all merchandise carried in stock at the same price as the Flickinger company charged its own chain stores. The company boasted that it avoided problems finding good personnel because its managers each had a personal investment in their stores, having formerly owned them.

Red and White cut costs by eliminating the need for many jobbers. It struck deals with a few manufacturers and ordered in large quantities. Producers of name-brand products were contracted to make similar lines under the "Serv-us" name. A price per unit under the cost of the name-brand good was determined, and all units of the Red and White organization would stock the goods. In this way, the organization "controlled its own brands" and was not at the mercy of the manufacturers of advertised brands. Instead of sending salespeople to each individual merchant to bargain, the Red and White plan enabled a few jobbers to cover large amounts of territory. Manufacturers, in turn, agreed to this plan because their selling expenses were eliminated, except for a small brokerage fee that went to the Red and White corporation. Eventually, another line of in-house brands was adopted: "Serv-us" remained the line of high quality, comparable to advertised brands, while the "Red and White Brand" represented "good wholesome food at popular prices."[71]

Flickinger took pains to earn goodwill from the patrons of independent grocers and also from the merchants themselves. The company offered to buy out independent grocers who were its wholesale customers; if refused, Flickinger agreed not to locate one of its chain stores within two blocks of the independent's location (this was opposite to the strategy of most chains, which opened up in direct competition with neighborhood grocers). As a result, the company boasted, "this brought us good will and left a good impression in the mind of the retail trade." Store managers who did join the Red and White or-

ganization gained a promise that Flickinger's would not operate another grocery branch in direct competition, and they might even be given the edge over
a particular trading area. President S. M. Flickinger noted, "For instance, in a
village of a few hundred, the grocer is given a monopoly." By creating the Red
and White chain, the Flickinger company was "taking the independent into the
fold," organizing separate grocers under centralized control and converting
"troublesome competition into helpful co-operation."[72]

Despite this language of harmony and altruism, the Flickinger company had
good economic reasons for getting the independent merchants on its side. The
Red and White plan offered Flickinger's an increased number of retail outlets
for wholesaling, even in territories that seemed to have reached the saturation
point in terms of Flickinger store locations. Red and White stores were typically located in smaller cities and towns in western New York and northern
Pennsylvania. The subsidiary chain also increased exposure for Flickinger
private-label goods. The company was thus able to capitalize on the benefits
of supposedly independent status while running a highly centralized business
organization. The Red and White was not the only hybrid organization of grocers in operation in the United States in the late 1920s. *Chain Store Age* described
the Chicago-area Royal Blue Stores as another "so-called independent chain,"
a loose organization where participating stores paid a membership fee and
gained consolidated buying power.[73] Both the Royal Blue and Red and White
chains were initially centered in a specific region, although by 1928, the Red and
White had successfully expanded not only outside New York and Pennsylvania but into Canada as well.

The advantages of independent proprietorship were also outlined in ad
campaigns for the Danahy-Faxon chain of "Home Operated Stores." By drawing an implicit comparison with chain store managers who had no personal
investment in their business, Danahy-Faxon personnel were said to serve in the
"spirit of, and for the rewards of 'PROPRIETORSHIP.'" Every store manager and
many assistants were partners in the business, and Danahy-Faxon suggested
that this associated ownership encouraged "a more sincere desire to please
you."[74] Other types of businesses besides traditional merchants also used the
language of the independent proprietor. In 1931, the Texaco gasoline corporation placed an ad in the *Buffalo Evening News* encouraging motorists to "Spend
Your Money With The Man Who Spends His Here." Describing all dealers of
Texaco gasoline as independents who "spend their money in the community
where they earn it," the ad suggested that patronizing a Texaco dealer was a way
of doing a "good turn" for the local area.[75]

The amount of energy used by retailers and industry observers in studying the chain store phenomenon during the 1920s and 1930s suggests that the chains touched a nerve for many merchants fearful of new forms of competition. Did the chains warrant this attention? Were they becoming a threat in this period? Even within the grocery industry, the sector most inundated with chain competition, chain branches did not form the majority of stores. By 1927, only about 15 percent (or 376) of Buffalo's 2,673 grocery stores were chain branches. Of these, 295 were part of six local chains. Only two national chains operated in the area. Chain stores made up 19 percent of the 1,549 grocery stores in Rochester. The city had three local chains, operating a total of 131 stores. Other chains operated an additional 163 stores.[76]

These figures do not tell the whole story, however, for it was not the number of stores that mattered but the share of the market they were gaining. Chain branches tended to be larger and to dominate a trading area. In terms of market share, their impact was much greater. The grocery trade in Buffalo exemplified this tendency. In 1929, chain stores numbered only 355 but made 42.8 percent of the total grocery sales in the city, averaging $54,259.96 in annual sales. Independents were far more numerous with 1,609 stores, but they averaged just $15,975.27 in annual sales. The total sales figure for independents in 1929 was $25,704,206, compared with $19,262,287 for chain branches.[77]

In the period from 1929 to 1933, chain store business dropped by 15 percent, but independents suffered even more dramatically. Chains took in 53 percent of the city's total sales. By 1933, the independents had made something of a comeback, and chain store sales went back down to 48 percent of the total sales in the city. Still, total chain store sales during this period remained virtually unchanged, despite the fact that the actual number of chain units decreased. In 1935, 320 chain store branches averaged $51,338, while independents averaged $10,600. Total grocery sales for chain stores in the city in 1933 were $16,325,311 in 357 chain store branches, compared with $16,428,193 in 1935 for 320 chain store branches. The total sales for independent stores went from $14,470,205 in 1933 to $17,638,561 in 1935. There were 1,449 independent grocers in Buffalo in 1933, compared with 1,664 in 1935. Clearly, each chain store branch could do a volume of business equal to that of a number of independent stores.[78]

The impact of chain branches on department stores is somewhat harder to gauge. While departments that featured lower-cost merchandise (for example, hosiery or nail polish) might face stiff competition from five-and-dime chain branches, others were, for the most part, able to retain customers, particularly in selling goods where style or quality was emphasized more than price (shoes, women's clothing, men's suits). An observer in the *Dry Goods Merchants Trade Journal* asserted that certain departments were put in jeopardy by chain variety stores such as Kresge's and Woolworth's. Chain variety stores managed to steal away the notions business from many department stores, and they took a bite out of shoe, hosiery, and lingerie sales.[79] Other types of purchases, however, were less susceptible to chain competition. A 1931 survey conducted by the National Association of Teachers of Marketing and Advertising tried to determine which products consumers would purchase from chains and why. Families in higher income brackets (those making over $5,000) reported that 100 percent of their purchases of men's and women's clothing were made at independent stores, no doubt reflecting the fact that most chains handled lower-priced goods. Despite the fact that 39.6 percent of lower-income families (those with incomes under $1,500) reported that they "favored chains" for men's clothing, over 82 percent of the purchases of men's suits came from independents.[80] The survey reached the general conclusion that "the percentages of the consumers favoring and buying from the chains decrease as their incomes increase," yet even within the poorer income classes, independent clothing retailers enjoyed the advantage. Further, a sizable percentage of the middle-income groups reported shopping at *both* independents and chains, suggesting that for some items, chains offered better prices but that consumers still patronized independents for certain types of purchases.

In the late 1920s, independents tried new means to sway public opinion against the chain stores.[81] In radio broadcasts, pamphlets, and editorials, antichain activists used the power of the mass media to spread the view that the chains posed a threat to traditional values and the American way of life. Sentiment against chains ran so high that fraudulent antichain associations were able to solicit donations from small retailers "ostensibly to go into a fighting fund against chain stores but in reality used to enrich the promoters."[82] Defenders of the chains warned of "Anti-Chain Bolsheviks," whose propaganda was breaking out like a "severe rash in every part of the country."[83] By the mid-1930s, the chain store problem would be a source of heated debate in trade publications and legislatures across the nation. States experimented with special chain store tax legislation, which steeply increased taxes for every additional unit beyond a retailer's initial store. Not only states but even municipalities passed antichain legislation. Portland, Oregon, initiated the first city tax on chain stores and enforced the law until 1942. This practice was duplicated in other cities, including Milwaukee, Knoxville, Louisville, Phoenix, and

Cleveland. The federal government also got involved in legislation to aid the independent merchant, in the form of the Robinson-Patman Bill. The bill prohibited manufacturers from discriminating in price between different purchasers of goods. In other words, it was supposed to prevent chains from enjoying special discounts from manufacturers—not eliminating the chains but leveling the playing field for smaller businesses.[84]

Despite these aims, many retailers viewed the legislation with skepticism. Arthur Boreman, publisher of the *Dry Goods Journal,* included the full text of the Robinson-Patman Bill for his readers and provided his own analysis. He argued that loopholes in the bill would allow chains to evade its provisions by buying factories and added that "if this happens the independent merchant may be much worse off than he is now."[85] Boreman had little faith in the ability of the government to enforce the legislation and predicted that as soon as the chains protested that the new law was causing them to raise prices, consumers would revolt. He also criticized the diffuse language of the bill, noting that in his opinion that "almost any group of high school students could and would have prepared a more intelligently drawn, less inconsistent, less confusing piece of legislation."[86]

In the end, many of Boreman's fears proved well founded. Historian Ellis Hawley concludes that despite the good intentions of the bill's sponsors, Robinson-Patman was largely ineffective. Like other initial attempts at regulation in this area, it "tended to restrict production, prevent change, hold up prices, and bilk the consumer."[87] Part of the reason that the bill appeared inconsistent was that it included a number of amendments from different groups, which added various qualifications to the prohibition of price discrimination in the act. The Federal Trade Commission's enforcement of Robinson-Patman was not overly harsh toward big business or the chains; instead, officials decided to accept "all good-faith efforts" by manufacturers to meet the law's requirements. Far from acting as "The Magna Carta of Small Business," as it was intended, Robinson-Patman ended up both hurting small business and irritating consumers.[88]

Whatever the actual impact of chain stores on local business, evidence suggests that the rise of chain stores certainly captured the imaginations of western New York retailers. Although the emergence of chain stores is often described from a national perspective, the battle between chains and independents was waged at a local level. A national perspective has caused many historians of retailing and marketing to assume a seamless progression from small, backward-looking independents to centrally organized, national chains.

A closer look at changes "on the ground" reveals a much more complex story. The very definition of terms such as *independent* and *chain* proved highly malleable in the hands of retail trade activists and store owners themselves.

Just as Buffalo and Rochester stores attempted to draw a distinction between local interests and metropolitan competition, they drew on the same language of localism to suggest that chains run by far-off bureaucracies were foreign interlopers into the community. Yet at the same time, many of these businesses were adopting some of the strategies of the chains, including group buying, systemization, and other modern management techniques. In the face of this new form of competition, independent merchants strenuously resisted the encroachment of chain retailers and asserted their own place in the communities they served.

THE DEPRESSION AND LOCAL SPENDING

IN LATE SUMMER 1931, nearly two years into the Depression, store owners and business leaders in Buffalo decided that hard times had gone on long enough. Something had to be done to improve economic conditions in their city. Despite its diversified economy, Buffalo had experienced rising unemployment and stagnant retail sales. Merchants felt they had the solution: they declared Buffalo Day, a special occasion when retailers would offer drastic savings and hire six thousand unemployed persons to serve the needs of shoppers. The idea behind the plan was to have a huge day of sales that would pump more money into the local economy and overcome the psychological barrier to spending that many felt was the main thing keeping America in an economic slump. The day would have a carnival atmosphere, with a band concert, automobile parade, baby beauty contest, dog show, and doll display. Festivities were concentrated in the downtown area, although other shopping districts throughout the city also planned their own events. Participants in a mass meeting of Buffalo retailers included the Broadway-Fillmore Business Men's Association, the North Main Citizens' Association, the North Park Association, the West Side Business Men's Association, and the North Jefferson Business Men's Association, among others.[1]

Merchants redoubled their efforts to woo western New Yorkers into Buffalo's retail districts, buying pages of newspaper space to publicize new shipments of goods and special savings. They decorated their stores in official Buffalo Day colors and declared 4 September the "One Great All-Buffalo Bargain Day." Local institutions went to great lengths in trying to mention the name of the city as much as possible in their advertising. R. B. Adam boasted that, as president of Adam, Meldrum and Anderson Company, a "Buffalo store, owned and supported by Buffalonians—the All-Buffalo Store that for more than half a century has led the way," he was confident that 1932 would be a year of prosperity "for Buffalo, for Buffalonians, for all who are interested enough to keep, mainstay and uphold Buffalo as the Queen City of the Lakes."[2] Bing and Nathan's furniture store featured a sketch of Buffalo City Hall in its advertising (see Plate 14).[3] Mayor Charles E. Roesch proclaimed 4 September a day "to uphold Buffalo's reputation as a great shopping center."[4] In addition to retailers, other local businesses and services pitched in to help with the success of the event. Bus fares within the city were lowered for the day, and designated parking lots also offered reduced rates. To encourage shoppers to "shop first" and then go to the movies, the Shea Theater chain advertised that it would feature afternoon matinee prices throughout the evening, not only downtown but also in all community movie houses. Hotels offered free rooms from 9:00 A.M. to 6:00 P.M. to "bona fide out-of-town shopping visitors" who needed a place to rest and regroup. Hotels and restaurants displaying the Buffalo Day seal offered reduced prices on special menus.[5]

The story of Buffalo Day helps revise our understanding of how local communities grappled with the Depression. Because of the dramatic developments of the New Deal, the story of the early 1930s is often told in light of what came afterward. The efforts of local communities, when they are recognized, are seen as laying the groundwork for the eventual development of the social welfare state. The arc of this narrative begins with the notion that in communities across the United States, people initially tried to solve the problems of the Depression privately, through voluntarism. Despite the valiant efforts of private charities, soup kitchens, and churches, however, these forms of private relief were not enough to mitigate the suffering of the vast ranks of the unemployed. Beginning in 1933, the federal government finally stepped in to pick up where these private initiatives left off. Among the most ambitious and lasting programs of the New Deal were relief programs such as the Unemployment Relief Act and the Social Security Act. For this reason, historians have tended to highlight those local initiatives in the 1930s that seemed to be pre-cursors to a federally sponsored social safety net.[6]

But as the story of Buffalo Day demonstrates, there was another dimension to local responses to the Depression. Even as local charities were grappling with diminishing relief resources, merchants and other business leaders in west-ern New York were seeking local solutions to the crisis. As it became appar-ent that western New York would not emerge unscathed from the Depression, area businesspeople brainstormed for possible solutions to the predicament they faced. The answers they came up with are notable for two reasons. First, many looked to private consumption as the answer to the economy's ills. Buffalo Day was not an attempt to increase the relief coffers of local welfare agencies, nor was it a charity drive. It—and many similar initiatives—broad-ened the conception of consumption, making it a civic act more than a self-interested activity. Consumption was redefined as a civic activity with benefits for the community as a whole. By consuming more, it was argued, citizens would grease the wheels of industry, creating jobs in the community and even-tually bringing the nation out of its slump. An increase in individual spending would give a needed boost to business, while avoiding the questionable moral-ity of providing "charity" to the unemployed.

Second, efforts to increase consumer spending had an emphatically local emphasis. Instead of simply encouraging the residents of Buffalo or Rochester to put more money into the economy generally, citizens were directed to spend these dollars *at home*, in order to create jobs and bring back good times within their own communities. It was only after initiatives to harness the power of local consumers came and went that western New Yorkers turned to more far-reaching solutions involving state and, later, federal intervention.

The stock market crash that closed the 1920s had brought new worries for merchants and consumers across the United States. In the nation's capital, political theorists, policymakers, and economists engaged in a battle over the very nature of the crisis. Did it originate at home, or were external factors to blame? Was the American economy generally healthy, or did it need a massive overhaul? How could one tell if the worst was over? For the administration of President Herbert Hoover, the Depression was initially believed to be a minor adjustment—a "natural" oscillation in the cycles of the capitalist econ-omy that would eventually correct itself. As a result, Hoover was reluctant to intervene in the economy, focusing instead on maintaining business confidence and renewing private investment. The president met with leaders in industry, agriculture, and finance, extracting promises that they would do their best to maintain employment levels and wage rates. Such, broadly stated, was the framework of discussion in Washington's corridors of power at the start of the 1930s. While later initiatives by Franklin Delano Roosevelt (FDR) would experiment with federally funded programs to create jobs, revive industry, and bail out agriculture, Hoover put more emphasis on encouraging countercyclical spending in the private sector. With the utmost faith in voluntarism, he urged both businesspeople and elected officials to maintain employment and wage levels and follow through on planned public works and expenditures. The crisis, he believed, could be solved without dramatic intervention by the national state.

Popular discussion of the economic crisis was even more prosaic. The debate over the economic situation in western New York lacked a sense of urgency in the early 1930s, in part because many remained hopeful that their cities would not be hard hit before the so-called slump was over. At least initially, Buffalo and Rochester were not as affected by the economic downturn as were other cities in the United States. Both enjoyed a level of industrial diversification, which provided a small (if, in the end, only temporary) level of protection from unemployment, and local business leaders remained optimistic that the economy would rebound.[7] As late as 1932, Buffalo's Chamber of Commerce continued to trumpet the resiliency of the city's diversified economy.[8] Steel production and flour milling were affected by the downturn, but other local businesses were thought likely to remain solvent and were good bets to survive the slump. Eastman Kodak, Rochester's largest single employer, was able to maintain its full workforce during the early years of the Depression. While cities such as Pittsburgh and Detroit that relied heavily on one industry faced immediate calamity, residents remained confident that Buffalo and Rochester were relatively well positioned to weather the storm.

Buffalo and Rochester boosters at first seemed to be in a state of denial about the seriousness of the situation. In the early months after the stock market crash of 1929, local pundits went to great lengths to stress the region's immunity to the economic downturn. The *Rochester Democrat and Chronicle* attempted to attract national advertisers by stressing the optimism of Rochesterians and the fact that the city was not suffering as much as the rest of the country. A full-page advertisement/editorial recounted the positive observations of recent visitors to the city. An economist making a survey of retail activity in the city was reported to have exclaimed, "The economic disease seems to leave no scars here." A financial man called his visit a "tonic," noting humorously that he had been in cities "where one is arrested if he smiles publicly."[9]

The paper also boasted that Rochester's 2,190 retail stores showed net sales in 1930 of almost $208 million. This evidence of Rochester's optimism holds a clue about the types of approaches with which western New York cities would experiment as the Depression lingered on. Retail sales were presented as an indication of the city's positive outlook. As long as Rochester's cash registers were ringing up sales, the ad copy suggested, conditions could not be that dire. And local citizens were sensible in their spending habits—economical but not *too* frugal. Residents were characterized as "thrifty in viewpoint, but generous in spending for self-betterment."[10] This emphasis on "good" spending would become the rallying cry for local initiatives to combat the Depression. Moreover, by differentiating Rochester from other cities, the paper reassured local readers that they, at least, were buffered from the chaos engulfing the rest of the nation.

The attractiveness of private consumption as an approach to ending the economic downturn of the early 1930s cannot be understood apart from the profound cultural change that preceded it. Consuming was an appealing course of action for a public that had come to equate spending with succeeding. As the previous chapters have explored, Americans during the early decades of the twentieth century had become more comfortable with material goods and self-indulgence as a part of daily life. Consuming, instead of producing, became the cornerstone of identity for most waged workers. This shift involved more than a quantitative increase in the amount of manufactured goods that were purchased by people in every income bracket. Guided by new institutions such as mass-market magazines and professional advertising, Americans increasingly found the purchase of consumer goods to be a means of self-expression and self-development, which overshadowed concern about religious salvation.[11] By the end of the 1920s, notions of self-control and restraint seemed old-fashioned and out of step with the times. In their place came a dominant ideology of consumption.

The proliferation of mass-produced goods, as well as the innovations in advertising and distribution that encouraged their purchase, was, indeed, a dramatic development. Yet the growth of a new "consumer culture" did not completely eclipse all that came before; not all Americans embraced this transformation. As Daniel Horowitz notes, even within the business community, whose members arguably had the most to gain from a public that consumed without restraint, "the acceptance of new values was far from complete."[12] Other, more detached observers also voiced reservations. While advertisers trumpeted the importance of consumption in maintaining an increased standard of living, social critics of the time such as Robert and Helen Lynd and Stuart Chase worried about the alienating and stultifying effects of excessive consumption.[13]

Moreover, older traditions of individualism and self-help did not vanish from the cultural landscape. Reverence for "Yankee thrift" and self-reliance was not completely eradicated. Indeed, the very strength of this new culture lay in its ability to incorporate older traditions. Just as local loyalties persisted in the face of national trends in advertising and selling, older notions of self-control and restraint were often reworked so that they reinforced ideas about the positive potential of consuming. On the one hand, advertisers and manufacturers encouraged Americans to give in to the hedonism of luxury goods and conspicuous consumption; on the other, a simultaneous emphasis on control and personal efficiency underscored their messages. A housewife who tried to be an efficient "domestic manager" through the proper selection of goods for her family did not exactly fit the stereotype of the hedonistic spender. She was a spender, to be sure, but was commended for taking the time to discriminate between products before selecting the right ones for her family. Men depicted in ads were most often ambitious office workers, not indulgent consumers of luxury items.[14] At the same time that ads encouraged people to buy, they often portrayed successful consumers as those who maximized their resources and made reasoned product choices.

Even new mechanisms of credit, which critics charged were creating a nation of impulse buyers, were not necessarily anathema to the idea of control. There was tremendous continuity in attitudes toward "responsible" spending. While the proliferation of consumer credit during the early decades of the nineteenth century has been characterized as a triumph of goods and luxury over self-control, installment credit imposed a form of discipline over consumer debtors, encouraging them to be industrious enough to make their monthly payments.[15] Even as people became more comfortable with spending, they still retained notions of the right way to make purchases, the responsible way to spend. Spending could be serious business, and during the Depression, the responsibility of the consumer was emphasized even more.

Furthermore, anxiety over the expansion of governmental powers ensured that private initiatives during the early 1930s would outpace any consideration of action by state or federal governments. As Michael Parrish has noted, Hoover took great pains to ensure that no effort to fight the Depression would "subvert the character of Americans by violating the fundamental principles of their social and political life: individualism, self-reliance, and voluntarism."[16]

The emphasis on the importance of local communities in solving the problems of their own citizens did not disappear even as the federal government began to experiment more broadly with the concept of a planned society after 1932. Despite his own growing commitment to increased federal intervention, even President Roosevelt himself maintained that traditional voluntarism would always have a place in American life. He commented, "We must never lose sight of the fact that no matter what contributions the Federal government makes, local communities will always have their peculiar duties to perform."[17] Roosevelt was careful not to insult the efforts of the local municipalities just as his administration was stepping in to take over some of the responsibilities that they had overseen.

What is striking about the campaigns to pull western New York out of the economic slump is the way that they fused these competing lines of rhetoric into one seamless justification for spending. If voluntarism was commended by both Hoover and Roosevelt at a national level, it is not surprising that it appealed to business leaders at the local level as well. Local efforts did not, however, focus solely on the expansion of traditional channels of relief such as churches or charity, although these institutions still remained active. Instead, local leaders set their sights on private consumption as the primary form of "voluntary" action. Merchants, manufacturers, and civic authorities in Buffalo and Rochester encouraged families to spend more money and to spend it at home. They played on notions of both frugality *and* self-gratification, of individualism *and* community service.

The idea that people from the region should try to keep dollars at home was not new in the 1930s. Just as they had during times of prosperity, business leaders used a language of localism to unite residents and marshal their available dollars. In the dark days of the 1930s, buying local was presented as an even more important answer to a variety of woes. Business leaders before the crash had tried a number of strategies to educate the public about the benefits of local spending. In 1928, the New Industries Bureau of the Rochester Chamber of Commerce sponsored a slogan contest to promote Rochester-made goods. The winner of the $25 prize came up with an instructive, if rather wordy, entry: "A Rochesterian purchasing a Rochester-made product is really investing in the industrial progress of the city, which pays dividends in the form of future prosperity."[18] After October 1929, the idea that "buying local" was beneficial to western New York gained new urgency. In the past, merchants had tried to use their local status to retain customers who might be straying to chain retailers or to Manhattan boutiques, but now, local business leaders felt that harnessing the power of area dollars was the only way out of the slump. Their campaigns encompassed both goods produced in the western New York area and all goods purchased there as well.

Consuming was an attractive solution to the economy's woes because it gave individuals the rationale to accumulate even more material possessions and also because it still was premised on a model of individualism and self-help. Those who had accumulated money should spend it, putting more funds into circulation and creating more demand for goods, which would *incidentally* create new jobs for the unemployed. This was a very different impulse from, say, the giving of a handout to an unemployed and possibly undeserving candidate. During the early days after the Wall Street Crash, commentators in Buffalo and Rochester carefully outlined plans that would improve local business conditions yet not undermine the moral character of the community by indiscriminately handing out charitable gifts. The *Buffalo Courier-Express* described shopping as the "best kind of philanthropy," for it "makes philanthropy unnecessary" by putting money into circulation, stimulating business, and creating jobs. This rhetoric married older notions of individualism and a reluctance to help others for fear of making them dependent with a new acceptance of spending and indulgence in material goods as both acceptable and positively virtuous. According to this scenario, all parties would win: shoppers could enjoy new goods, and employees could remain on the job.

Spending at the local level was particularly encouraged. A *Courier-Express* editorial qualified its advice by encouraging shoppers to direct their buying power into the local economy, not just spend money generally: "Such philanthropy," the writer argued, "begins at home—through the resumption of normal buying for normal needs on the part of everybody whose income remains steady." Early Christmas shopping would help to put many people back to work right away. The editorial closed with the rallying cry, "Come on Buffalo! Let's go!"[19] Significantly, this conception of the economy used a rather loose definition of local spending. Buying at home simply entailed shopping in local stores; no mention was made of selecting Buffalo-made products or even American-made ones. The site of consumption was what was important; a product's point of manufacture did not matter as long as it was bought locally.

The campaign also implied a certain understood level of "normal" buying that went beyond basic necessities. The use of the term *normal needs* implies a recognition of a division between necessities and frills. Yet in this instance, the purchase of gifts, arguably extras that marked special occasions, was consciously inserted within the parameters of so-called normal spending.

Christmas shopping was categorized as part of normal buying, which would presumably be conducted even during a time of economic crisis. This notion is especially striking given that the exchange of manufactured, as opposed to homemade, Christmas gifts itself was a relatively recent development. In his study of American gift giving, William Waits argues that this shift occurred between 1880 and 1920. Initially, manufactured gifts tended to be cheap, gaudy, and disposable gimcracks. The purchase of more expensive items, such as home appliances or luxury goods for family members and close friends, did not begin until the early twentieth century, most significantly after 1910. Christmas gifts had thus become normal purchases in a relatively short span of time.[20] That normal needs entailed more than subsistence purchases such as food and clothing went without saying; it was assumed that shoppers had reined in their spending and were only purchasing necessities. The free-spending days of the 1920s, when retail sales in Buffalo and Rochester had achieved record heights each year, were presented as the benchmark of normal buying, remembered fondly by retailers.

Buffalo newspaper writers and advertisers highlighted Christmas shopping as an opportunity for citizens to give to their own circle of family and friends while simultaneously making a civic contribution. A front-page story in the *Buffalo Courier-Express* in December 1930 excitedly described the beginning of the Christmas shopping season, encouraging gift buyers to congratulate themselves for their generosity on two levels. People who shopped early were "not only getting the choice of the entire display of Christmas goods" but also "making an appreciable contribution to unemployment relief." This unemployment relief was not in the form of charity but in job creation. It is also notable that the story focused on jobs in the service sector: shoppers could feel pleased that their actions were causing stores to hire "additional salesmen and saleswomen," beyond the regular ranks of store employees. The extra pay received by shop workers "means a lot to many families."[21]

Four days after this front-page editorial, a similar article urged shoppers to spend in Buffalo stores and "help others to help themselves." Additional crowds would require extra hands behind the shop counters of the city and result in "welcome pay envelopes" for jobless men and women in the community. The paper counseled, "Buyers make workers and prosperity is made by spending."[22] No mention was made of expanding the payrolls of local factories, perhaps indicating the belief that salespeople would be the first and most visible group to benefit from increased levels of retail sales. This emphasis on salespeople also reflected the increasing importance of the service sector in the Buffalo economy. Although manufacturing still remained central to the city's identity, an increasing percentage of Buffalo workers were employed in trade (most importantly in retail) by the end of the 1920s.[23]

The moral imperative of spending money locally to help reduce unemployment was highlighted in stories that underlined the deserving nature of those receiving jobs. In 1931, the *Courier-Express* featured an article about the "extras" who were hired as staff by Buffalo's stores. Interviews with a number of young women employed by retailers revealed the worthy goals toward which they were working. One of the clerks was trying to pay off debts from doctors' bills, another hoped to send a young sister to school, and others simply had to help feed their families. A typical story stressed the harsh home conditions faced by a young, hardworking shopgirl. "Behind Miss E.'s pre-holiday job in a local department store" lay the dream of giving her family "a real Christmas." Her father had been unemployed for four years, and her older brother also was unable to find a job. The family lived in a suburban cottage that was once their summer home and was not built for winter use.[24]

The emphasis on the meritorious nature of such workers was designed to alleviate any qualms shoppers might have that the legions of unemployed were down on their luck due to character flaws or personal failings. No one could dispute that contributing to "a real Christmas" was a worthwhile endeavor, particularly for a young woman who had been forced to assume the traditionally masculine mantle of provider for her family after her father and brother had failed. It is also striking that the paper celebrated the creation of jobs for women, given the prevailing belief that the nation's first priority was to get *men* back to work. Perhaps because department stores were traditionally places of female employment, there would be less weight to the argument that these shopgirls were taking jobs away from men.

Buffalo's newspaper pundits were not original in distinguishing between the "deserving" and "undeserving" poor. Yet the rejection of charity as a course of action, especially during the Christmas season, is revealing. Christmas charity for the poor was increasingly seen as old-fashioned by this time, as a host of Progressive era reformers had established the notion that assistance to the poor was best coordinated by large organizations, not left up to the individual, and spread throughout the entire year instead of concentrated in December.[25] Consuming was a less controversial solution to the problems of the 1930s than charity. By helping themselves, those who bought goods would also help others; they would not risk insulting the pride—or encouraging the laziness—of the less fortunate. This initiative would not entail a radical redistribution of wealth, for those with money were simply encouraged to spend it on themselves, with the happy by-product of helping others. The holiday season, a time traditionally associated with giving alms to the poor—or, more typically during the 1920s, with donating to the local Community Chest—was in this instance divorced from any hint of charity. One could buy gifts for friends and family members, indulging them while giving gainful employment, not handouts, to the poor.

In Buffalo's newspaper editorials, consuming was thus redefined as a civic act. Consuming had, of course, been imbued with political meaning before this time. During the American Revolution, for example, patriots identified themselves by their conspicuous nonconsumption of English goods. Yet what is striking about the western New York campaigns is that consumption involved little or no sacrifice. While patriots chafed in their homespun garments or housewives in a later era made the effort to look for the union label, western New Yorkers could congratulate themselves for *anything* they purchased that put more money into the economy.[26] All consuming, in this view, was good, civic-minded spending. Commentators in 1930 repeatedly pointed to private spending as the path out of the Depression. The underlying assumption of these messages was that once consumers understood their role in the system, they would make the rational decision to do their part and go out and spend. The *Buffalo Evening News* explained the workings of the economy in simple terms and highlighted the role of the consumer in an editorial in November 1930:

> The law of supply and demand is constant—consumer, retailer, manufacturer. It's logical and self-evident. Merchants supply the consumers' needs—your needs. Manufacturers supply the merchants— your merchants. . . . You are a necessary part of the business cycle, and upon your filling your place in this cycle depends the prosperity and welfare of the nation. If you stop buying, the merchants' shelves remain stocked, the sales force must be thinned, factories must shut down. Result . . . Unemployment.[27]

The solution was clear: individuals had to take the initiative to "buy out the Depression." This would not require abnormal or spendthrift behavior on the part of the public, only the resumption of normal buying. If the return to prosperity simply awaited the resumption of "normal buying for normal needs," the individual was warned, "stinting on your part means unemployment for others."[28] To hold back at such a time was not to be wisely frugal, in the mode of Ben Franklin in *Poor Richard's Almanack;* it was to be selfish and shortsighted.

These proposed early solutions to the Depression deployed a rhetoric of private initiative and market self-regulation, not state intervention, to encourage consumer spending. Consuming in this line of reasoning became not just a mode of self-expression but a marker of civic responsibility.

Retailers and editorialists picked up on the emphasis on "home buying" that had permeated advertising during the 1920s and in the battle against chain stores. It was foolish to spend the extra money to travel to New York seeking fashionable goods, for example, and beyond that, it was one's civic responsibility to spend those dollars at home and try to alleviate the crisis. The wealthy of the community, in particular, were thought to have a responsibility to the less fortunate. Those who made their fortunes in Buffalo were warned of the dire consequences that ensued when they chose to shop in New York City rather than at home. One editorial writer pointed out that women who shopped in New York were married to men who sold goods or services to the citizens of Buffalo. Given that these men had "worked hard for their salaries or their share of the profits of their companies," the writer asked, should they not be allowed to spend their money wherever they chose? Although the idea of limiting consumer choice seemed anathema to the whole culture of consumption, the answer was not so simple. The decision to shop away from home might be acceptable during ordinary times, but the Depression made every person's spending "a matter of public import. And just how shrewd, we ask, is it to trade out of town and then complain because your business does not pick up? In prosperous times, every one is buying. Today the wealthier citizens have a definite duty to perform. No one asks them to buy more than they should. But what they do buy should be purchased here in Buffalo. The profit to each individual is indirect. Today, however, we must have far-sightedness."[29] The same arguments that were marshaled to keep local dollars at home in good times gained a new urgency during the 1930s. If all else failed, appeals to self-interest were trotted out. It was simply good business to boost local merchants, for they, in turn, "bought from you" in the form of actual purchases of services or more abstractly in paying the wages of local people. Given that Buffalo products and Buffalo stores were of proven quality, there was simply no good reason to go away to shop. Anyone who disagreed was reminded that "money spent outside of Buffalo is poured into a bottomless well."[30]

In a time of economic crisis, consumers were not the only ones whose ethical behavior mattered. Local manufacturers and merchants took pains to assert that their business practices were above reproach and that they would not use hard times as an excuse to bilk the public. The Mitchell Knitting Mills of

Buffalo reported that a sale on their goods should not be viewed as a precursor to the firm's demise: "This is no bankrupt stock. Nor are these fine stylish and staple sweaters any tag-ends of stocks. They are all 1930 Fall and Winter goods. All made in Buffalo, by Buffalo workers. We are not thinking of loading up our Buffalo friends and then going out of Business. Quite the contrary. We have been in this sweater knitting business here for many years, and believe that Buffalo people in these times are entitled to these bargains."[31] As manufacturers and retailers encouraged people to spend locally, even banks tried to get into the action, implying that they, too, were local institutions that should be patronized. One Rochester newspaper ad proclaimed, "Your deposits Keep Workers on the Job. By depositing in a Rochester bank you help your community. Your savings are safe, available and earning interest."[32]

As the civic importance of consumption gained emphasis, sales appeals directed toward men increased. Shopping traditionally had been firmly categorized as a feminine activity, a notion underscored by commercial advertising directed at "Mrs. Consumer" throughout the early decades of the twentieth century.[33] Yet by the 1930s, when consumer spending was deemed a matter not of fashion or frills but of economic survival, it was increasingly presented as a serious subject, worthy of male attention. Appeals to economic reason most often appeared in ads directed at male shoppers as well as or even instead of women. Female customers had often been the main targets of department store newspaper advertising, but ads that used a "reason-why" approach, explaining the benefits of spending as a way out of the Depression, were as likely to speak to men as to women. When J. N. Adam's trumpeted the benefits of buying clothes in 1931 that were twice the value of those from 1930, its ad commended "thousands of Buffalo Women, Men and Children": "They're going to be better dressed than they were last year on the same money. They're going to put more money into circulation—and more money in circulation will help put more men back to work. They're going to get rid of the 'depression complex.'"[34] Ads regularly flattered readers by suggesting that they were intelligent enough to make the right choices, even when the rest of the nation foolishly panicked. One 1931 ad for J. N. Adam's pointed out that many of the great fortunes of America were created during "dull times" and that the wise families who had money to spend in an economic slump could take advantage of the opportunity. The ad argued, "Right now intelligent people are buying more and more—because quality is on the bargain table and because prices are so drastically low." Smart shoppers would maximize this opportunity to stock up on quality goods at low prices and simultaneously display their concern for their community.[35]

Yet even as men were congratulated for turning their attention to buying, women were acknowledged as experienced purchasers. Some of these appeals flattered women for not overreacting to the crisis: J. N. Adam's commended housewives for their ability to size up the economic situation and not be overcome with pessimism. They credited women with being able to recognize that conditions would soon be on the upswing, noting, "While all the keen-eyed 'Miracle Men' of America have been in serious conference—wondering where the bottom of the depression might be—the keen-minded housewives of America *have sensed that this is probably the bottom right now.* . . . So—J. N. Adam's takes a bow to the housewives of Buffalo—they know real values when they see them."[36] At least implicitly, the ad suggested that men were the ones who were holding back; if women were willing to spend, it was their husbands who needed to be educated with the hard facts of the economy. And despite some acknowledgment of women's superior economic sense, older stereotypes about women as innate, emotional spenders remained strong. Strikingly, ads that directly addressed women or referred to women shoppers separately from men were more likely to suggest that women *wanted* to buy. By simply maintaining their "natural" enthusiasm for spending, women could make a valuable contribution. This emphasis on the different perceptions of men and women on the economic situation was evident in a department store ad in Rochester. McCurdy and Company attempted to sympathize with women shoppers who felt fed up with talk of the Depression. Women were characterized as less concerned with financial conditions—while men actually enjoyed "moaning and groaning over juicy tales of bankrupts, busted prices and wobbly stocks," women missed the days when they spent freely. Men found in the Depression an inexhaustible topic of conversation, giving them a certain grim satisfaction as they suffered through hard times. "But we girls, that's different. We've been suffering from Repression. We can't go anywhere because we're practically *naked.* Home economy programs have ruined us."[37]

The ad played with notions of women as shoppers with no self-control. The stereotype of the middle-class woman who was easily seduced by department store displays became entrenched in the late nineteenth century. The extreme example of this figure was the woman who not only purchased on impulse or beyond her means but also stole items that tempted her. In her study of female shoplifting, Elaine Abelson argues that stores were reluctant to prosecute these newly diagnosed kleptomaniacs, who were often women of good social standing and regular customers. She notes that explanations for female shoplifting often rested on "woman's weak state of mind and frequent episodes of irresponsible behavior." A doctor testifying on behalf of a woman accused of shoplifting in 1893 excused her behavior by reinforcing the idea that "the female was often unstable, ruled by her nervous system and her emotions."[38] During the Depression, women expressed their supposedly natural desire for new fashions, no matter what the cost. While their husbands fretted over family finances, these deprived women longed for "gay evening things" that would help them forget their present troubles. McCurdy's took on the role of confidant, assuming the guise of the shopper who exclaimed, "We girls are just sick of it!" and speaking of the store workers in the third person. The dismissal of women as frivolous spenders more concerned about fashion than the harsh realities of the economic situation alternated with portrayals of women as budget-conscious domestic managers who maintained the family budget. The suggestion that women naturally craved luxurious items was not exactly complimentary; even as stores commended women for avoiding the "depression-mindset" of their husbands, the tone of ads directed at "we girls" suggested that women were interested in fashion for selfish reasons, not because they knew that spending would help the economy.

Merchants used newspaper ads to "educate" readers about the economic situation. The didactic quality of such appeals allowed merchants to claim that they were performing a public service by including whole paragraphs explaining the workings of the economy. Where a full-page newspaper ad during the 1920s might have been trumpeting the arrival of new stocks in the millinery department, for example, columns of text now painstakingly described the economy in layman's terms. A typical treatise appeared in a 1931 ad for J. N. Adam's:

If low prices will cause more people to buy more merchandise—more people buying more merchandise will necessitate greater production. Greater production will bring more workers back to their jobs. More people working and spending will put more dollars into circulation. And more money distributed through the channels of more buying, more wages, more production, more spending will help open wide the door to better times. J. N. Adam's dramatic presentation of today's low prices is made with the intention of showing Buffalo just how much sound, substantial value in good, dependable merchandise their dollars will buy today. The price of thousands of articles is lower than for years. Good merchandise has not sold so inexpensively for a decade. Right now is the time to stock up. . . . You can't afford to hold off any longer![39]

The altruism of stores encouraging home buying is open to question. On one level, merchants were probably genuinely committed to improving conditions in their cities. Many took their role as pillars of the community very seriously and were active in local politics and trade initiatives.[40] McCurdy and Company, for example, did its best to keep as many local citizens employed as possible—the store did not fire anyone during the entire Depression, though it curtailed employee hours week by week until economic conditions improved.[41] Another Rochester store staged a "community day" on which members of three women's organizations volunteered as shopkeepers for a day and a percentage of the day's sales receipts were turned over to the unemployment relief fund of the Rochester Community Chest.[42] At the same time, one should not take their protestations of acting for the public good entirely at face value. Merchants hoped to capitalize on local anxiety, turning around slumping sales by emphasizing the local responsibility of citizens to consume. Though these businesses often had long-standing local ties, their actions were motivated by concern for their own bottom lines as well as by the desire to improve the lot of western New Yorkers.

In 1931, local leaders in Buffalo and Rochester experimented with two organized campaigns to increase consumer spending in the area. Both of these initiatives assumed that a loosening of purse strings would help the community to rebound; in turn, these types of community efforts would have a ripple effect and eventually pull the entire nation out of its slump. This was not sophisticated countercyclical spending. It relied on a much more basic model of economic growth and the market. In retrospect, it is clear that it would take much more than an increase in private spending to turn the U.S. economy around. Yet the fact that these initiatives were boldly presented as the answer to such a crippling problem underscores how, at least early on in the 1930s, many believed that solutions were within the grasp of the local community. Once the proper course of action was outlined, consumers would step up to do their part to pump money into the local economy. Nowhere was this faith in the power of the individual consumer more evident than in the two campaigns organized by merchants and business leaders in Buffalo and Rochester in 1931: Buffalo Day and the Monroe County Pledge for Prosperity. Although each city had a different approach to encouraging local spending, both played up the responsibility of the local citizen and the importance of boosting local retail sales as a way to turn things around for the region and, in turn, the country.

Buffalo Day, as described earlier, was touted as the solution to the region's problems. Local pundits were optimistic about the potential for the Buffalo

Day campaign to improve economic conditions in the city. By holding a city-wide sale, merchants would give local citizens a reason to celebrate and indulge themselves, while helping to put their neighbors back to work in local stores and factories. The editorial cartoonist of the *Buffalo Evening News* depicted a female shopper in a car labeled "Business" who planned to spend the day taking advantage of bargains. In the distance, at the end of the road, lay her destination: "Normalcy" (see Plate 13). Weldon D. Smith, chairman of the Buffalo Day organizing committee, outlined the reasons for holding the event. As he saw it, the occasion was as much about overcoming a psychological condition as an economic one: "Believing that the so-called 'business depression' is now largely a mental condition, Buffalo Day was conceived by the merchants of this city to help restore confidence and encourage the public to resume buying. . . . Unless there is a return of buying consciousness, the wheels of industry will not revolve rapidly and any plan to bring back prosperity that does not include a restoration of the customary habits of spending a reasonable share of one's earnings wisely will necessarily fail."[43] That Smith could still refer to the Depression as "so-called" after nearly two years of unemployment and economic stagnation only underscores his belief that the crisis was one of perception, not reality. This emphasis on achieving a psychological breakthrough by means of symbolic activity echoed the language of earlier reformers who tried to jolt Buffalo's development by changing the name of Main Street. In a single day, planners of the event hoped to wipe away months of economic stagnation.

A mass meeting of all Buffalo retailers was held on 28 August in the prestigious Statler Hotel, and every store owner in Buffalo, "regardless of the store's size or location," was encouraged to participate.[44] The mayor addressed the store owners, and representatives from fourteen local merchants' and taxpayers' associations were in attendance. On an organizational level, their efforts were a success. To kick off the celebration, a parade of two hundred cars and floats wove through the city's West Side the night before Buffalo Day. Local radio stations featured short talks from notables including Mayor Roesch, outlining the purpose of the day and urging the public to participate. Large and small retailers, department stores, and specialty shops across the city opened their doors with special Buffalo Day bargains.[45] Independent merchants as well as chain stores with branches in the area participated. Sears, Roebuck boasted that it "Leads in Buffalo Day Bargains" and offered extra savings on everything from a Kenmore electric washer to a canary with cage and stand.[46]

Local leaders were unanimous in their support of the venture. Weldon Smith again emphasized that the local initiative would mean better days for Buffalonians and for all Americans. He stated, "This day was not planned just to bolster up sales, but is the merchants' contribution to the general plan to solve our national problem."[47] And sure enough, over two hundred thousand shoppers flooded the downtown core for the event, ringing up record cash register receipts. Downtown stores and Main Street were "literally jammed with shoppers," the *Evening News* reported on its front page.[48] Other cities imitated Buffalo in organizing shopping days—local papers crowed that Chicago was considering copying Buffalo's initiative.

Yet while the "shopping troops" were marshaled on Main Street, Buffalo Day did not achieve its larger goal of jolting the community—and the nation—out of the Depression. Department store sales in September 1931, though an improvement over the lull of the summer months, did not even match those of September 1930, never mind the high-water mark of the mid-1920s.[49] This failure did not end enthusiasm for home shopping as a solution to the economic situation, however. And Buffalonians were not alone in experimenting with initiatives to increase consumer spending, as the efforts of the residents of Rochester would demonstrate.

In November 1931, Rochester's Civic Committee on Unemployment also developed a strategy to inject more consumer dollars into the local economy. Like the Buffalo Day campaign, the plan was an ambitious one that would, it was hoped, turn the power of individual consumers to the benefit of the western New York region. Rochesterians were used to pulling together in the face of adversity. As city historian Blake McKelvey notes, local residents met the onset of the Depression with a sense of confidence that stemmed "from the triumphs they had won in the face of earlier cultural as well as civic and economic challenges."[50] Drives to build the university, to raise war bonds, and to support the city's museum and public library had been welcomed with enthusiasm. As the Depression wore on, however, unemployment soared, and work-relief projects initiated by the city seemed to accomplish little beyond increasing Rochester's debt. The Depression was not as bad in Rochester as it was in many other industrial cities, but, as Richard E. Holl observes, "It was bad enough."[51]

In February 1931, a group of Rochester employers led by Marion B. Folsom, assistant treasurer of Eastman Kodak, initiated a program of unemployment insurance for their workers. Employees laid off due to poor economic conditions who had been on the job for at least one year and earned less than $50 per week would be eligible for benefits of up to $18.75 per week. These benefits would last between six and thirteen weeks, depending on the individual's seniority.[52] Folsom conceived of the plan as a form of employment stabilization that would help some jobless workers but, more important, encourage management to retain workers through tough times.[53] One major drawback of the plan, however, was that it covered only a modest percentage of the city's workers. Smaller firms could not afford to participate in the plan, and only fourteen companies signed on in 1931.[54]

Another plan of action, one that could mobilize all Rochesterians, was needed. First conceived by the Civic Committee chair, Libanus Todd (and at times referred to as the Todd Plan in its early stages), the scheme targeted local people who were hoarding their savings. Todd and his brother were owners of a local manufacturing company that produced machines that protected checks against alteration. The outfit exported its goods to more than sixty-four countries around the globe.[55] As a local success story, Todd was viewed as an authority on the economic situation. In his opinion, unemployment was the result of the excessive frugality of those with money. Instead of spending, people were stockpiling. Left unchecked, this trend could have dire consequences, as a newspaper ad explaining the committee's strategy argued:

> Such penny-pinching is at present one of the major reasons for business stagnation. When people stop buying, mills stop manufacturing, men are laid off and their buying power is shut off. All this but leads to an endless cycle from one tragedy to another; more shut downs, more unemployment, again less spending, fewer dividends, less income, more charity, greater taxes for relief. Finally, if these things continue, all buying would cease, all production would be dammed up and the suffering of every industry, every community and every individual would be beyond imagination. This is not a pretty picture.[56]

The committee hoped an organized effort to encourage spending would ameliorate the situation. By December, the *Democrat and Chronicle* first featured an ad for the Pledge for Prosperity campaign, which was designed to have local citizens promise to spend a certain amount of money "in an intelligent effort to bring back normal times."[57] Readers were advised to include in their total pledges any direct hiring of labor (for example, hiring a contractor for home renovations), as well as "the indirect employment of labor in the consumption of products already made or produced."[58] A list of over 150 suggestions for home improvements included cosmetic changes such as "replace tub, lavatory, and water closet with modern types" or "provide improved toilet seat," as well as more ambitious domestic projects such as replacing pipes and wiring, building a sleeping porch, or installing a telephone.[59] The committee enlisted the help of other sponsors who stood to gain from the project, including the Rochester Retail Merchants Association, the Industrial Management Council, and the Builders and Contractors' Association.

For ten days, fifteen hundred workers canvassed Rochester and Monroe County, asking local residents, "Have you signed the Pledge for Prosperity?" Anyone missed in the door-to-door campaign could mail in a pledge form to be included in the total. The *Democrat and Chronicle* kept a running tally of the total pledges made on the front page of every issue. The written statement formed a sort of pledge of allegiance for local consumers, asking the individual to promise to hold up his or her end of the economic relationship for the benefit of the community. Instead of national honor, the campaign required a commitment to local spending. Subscribers endorsed the following statement:

> Believing that a dollar invested in employing labor does more good than a dollar given as charity, and desiring to help to increase employment, I hereby pledge that I will, during the next three months, (or before _____ 1932), expend at least $_____ in improving my home, factory, store, buildings or grounds by purchasing desirable equipment or by making needed additions, repairs or alterations; or by making personal purchases for myself, family or friends, which otherwise might be deferred.[60]

The campaign offered Rochesterians the opportunity to give a special Christmas gift to their families, neighbors, and community. Monroe County was taking the bit in its teeth, setting an example for the rest of the nation in "how to dynamite the dam of accumulated dollars and turn loose the reservoir of wealth to flood the dried up fields of prosperity."[61]

The language of the pledge was a bundle of contradictions. Monroe County residents were exhorted to help others by abandoning "Perverted Thrift." Self-denial, in this context, was characterized as stingy and shortsighted. Those who had money "salted away" yet persisted in living below their means were "pettily denying themselves and their families the comforts and luxuries they really would like and really can afford."[62] Instead, good local citizens were "generously selfish," indulging themselves not only for personal pleasure but also to help others. The very idea that selfishness or self-sacrifice was necessary for the success of the plan was challenged by pledge organizers, who emphasized that their campaign was "not a plea exhorting you to unselfishness." On the contrary, citizens were instructed, "it is a plea urging you to be selfish for *the sake of Self-Preservation*—preservation of yourself, your family, your home, your business, your city and your nation."[63]

The Victorian triumvirate of frugality, thrift, and financial planning was transformed during the 1930s, so that saving became selfish hoarding and spending was presented as a form of civic activism. During the nineteenth century, thrift and self-denial were considered indicative of one's character and commitment to the community. Lendol Calder notes that Victorians viewed personal savings as key to capital formation and thus necessary for national wealth. Those who saved were "lauded as public benefactors."[64] Daniel Horowitz has argued that the emergence of a new culture centered around buying divorced Americans from meaningful personal and political expression. In his view, consumption "became a substitution for compelling moral commitments, engaged political activity, or genuine selfhood."[65] In this instance, however, Rochesterians did not have to choose between consuming and fulfilling a civic responsibility; they were encouraged to view spending money as a positive political act. Like Buffalo Day, Rochester's Pledge for Prosperity campaign took the relaxation of Victorian restraints on spending one step further: in addition to being morally acceptable to consume, it was actually one's civic duty. By denying themselves the luxuries they could afford, local families were hurting their neighbors and their city.[66] A resurgence of local spending would reverse this trend.

In 1920, along with seven hundred other cities throughout the United States, Rochester had celebrated Thrift Week, a commemoration of the 214th anniversary of the birth of Ben Franklin, the "father of thrift." Each day had a different theme and motto. For example, Bank Day emphasized the importance of bank accounts and was backed up with the theme "A bank account guards money from burglar and fire and the worst thief of all—foolish spending."[67] Other days promoted prompt payment of bills and household budgeting. Now, just over a decade later, Rochesterians were being assured that all spending was good spending and that hanging on to excess savings was foolish and shortsighted.

Thrift, in this instance, was more than old-fashioned; it was actually detrimental. While the "idle dollar benefits no one," as one pledge ad noted, money that is put into circulation "keeps on working for the benefit of the entire community."[68] How much actual engaged political activism was engendered by the pledge campaign is unclear. Unlike a consumer boycott or wartime conservation effort, the campaign did not require tangible sacrifice on the part of citizens or even much modification of activity beyond a return to purportedly normal spending. Indeed, area residents were encouraged to give in, to buy all items they secretly coveted yet had been holding back from purchasing. Yet the language of the drive merged consumption and civic activity, equating consumption with community commitment.

Military metaphors underscored the urgency of the cause. The hundreds of volunteers canvassing local homes and businesses in the pledge drive were "shock troops in seven divisions." In bringing millions of dollars into circulation, Rochesterians would "rout completely this stupid and devitalizing depression," engaging in a "counter-attack" against hunger, sickness, misery, and distress. Cooperation would combat the "evils of today." The rhetoric of wartime bond drives was picked up in exhortations: "The county can afford *no* slackers."[69] During World War I, Rochesterians had been active participants in Liberty Loan drives and thus would have been familiar with the idea of setting aside money for a cause. Spurred on by the leadership of George Eastman, who personally donated $2.5 million to the Liberty Loan campaign, the city frequently outstripped goals for Liberty Loan and Red Cross campaigns in 1918.[70] Bond drives had commonly emphasized the necessity of frugality and self-discipline in a time of crisis. For example, a Liberty Loan ad distributed by the U.S. Government Committee on Public Information noted, "You are called upon to economize in every way. It is sometimes harder to live nobly than to die nobly. The supreme sacrifice of life may come easier than the petty sacrifices of comforts and luxuries. You are called to exercise stern self-discipline. Upon this the Allied Success depends."[71] There was an acknowledgment of self-restraint and the idea that Americans had to give "'til it hurt" during the war, but Rochester's Pledge for Prosperity only asked people to "spend *'til it helps,* because there will be no real prosperity for any until there is prosperity for all."[72]

In addition to recalling bond drives from wartime, the promotions for the Prosperity Pledge drew freely from the vernacular of commercial advertising, often echoing the language and sloganeering of magazine ads. One full-page pledge ad in the *Democrat and Chronicle* urged readers to take a critical look at their homes, making an inventory of what was needed and "noting down what a guest *could* tell" about the occupants. The suggestion that a "guest-eye inventory" would provide a much more critical evaluation of one's home played on a theme much utilized in commercial advertising during this time period.

Roland Marchand finds numerous examples of magazine ads in the 1920s and 1930s that cultivated consumer anxiety by suggesting that unwise purchases could give the wrong impression to others. He notes that in the tableaux created by advertisers, "friends, casual acquaintances, and strangers peered under people's rugs or inspected their handwriting for such signs of deficient character as might be revealed by a leaky pen. They retreated with disgust from bathrooms in which the 'otherwise perfect appearance' had been spoiled by a 'mussed towel' or a 'slow-draining, gurgling lavatory.'"[73] Homes, in this view, were much more than shelter; they were a reflection of their owners' character, and as such, they had to be continually maintained to ensure that they projected the correct impression about their occupants. Rochester's Civic Committee on Unemployment similarly reminded local citizens that they were not always objective in viewing their own surroundings, warning them, "The place you live in—the things you love. How different they look when stripped of the film of romance with which you and yours have lovingly entwined them!"[74]

Just as ads cautioned consumers to avoid making the wrong impression by overlooking a single detail in their homes, the pledge campaign counseled Rochesterians to be vigilant in evaluating their environs. Only by taking a critical view, in the way a stranger or guest to the home would, could the individual be assured of projecting the correct image. An ad for the campaign featured a checklist of over eighty "Needs" to be surveyed within the home, ranging from repairs such as new paint jobs to purchases such as new furnaces, towel racks, and modern lighting systems. Fostering this type of self-doubt would serve to encourage people to buy—not specific, branded goods but any additional goods or services that would contribute to "Monroe County's Magic Circle of Prosperity."

The campaign fused commercial advertising's messages about fulfillment through consumption with rhetoric about private spending as a civic responsibility. Everyone would win by the acquisition of new products. Families that had been misguidedly denying themselves would get a lot of pleasure from these expenditures and at the same time help to relieve unemployment. Any guilt over "unnecessary" purchases was summarily dismissed. A different promotion for the campaign outlined not only home improvements but also a range of personal purchases:

> Concretely this means that . . . the individual who usually purchases two suits should not now provide himself with merely one, and that the purchase of all other apparelling should be considered in the same

way; that if new furnishings or equipment for home are contemplated, they should be purchased immediately rather than deferred; . . . that if you want a new radio, buy it now; that if a new automobile is being considered, contact a dealer at once; that so-called luxuries should not be considered as non-essentials, that the Christmas list should be extended rather than curtailed.[75]

Local Community Chest clerks were given the task of coordinating the campaign. Canvassers were instructed to distinguish between everyday spending and emergency spending, moneys that would not have been spent except for the campaign. The plan was to stimulate extra spending, above and beyond the necessities of daily life. Even Christmas gifts came under scrutiny. When asked by those solicited if they could include their Christmas gifts in the amount they pledged to spend, canvassers were instructed to reply, "'No' unless the giver agreed to spend $10 for a gift where it was originally planned to spend $5."[76] Just as the Buffalo newspaper categorized gifts as part of normal spending, Rochester's campaign classified presents as either "necessary" or "additional." A certain level of spending would be expected at holiday time; only *additional* generosity would qualify for credit under the campaign. To prevent harassment of the pledgers by those seeking work, the names of those who had committed to spend in the campaign or hire contractors to do repairs were not released to the public.

Local leaders were confident that Rochester could serve as an example to the rest of the nation. The Chicago Tribune News Service reported that the Rochester plan of "emergency employment and business stimulation" was under discussion in Chicago, although Edward L. Ryerson of that city's Joint Emergency Relief Fund expressed doubt that private expenditures could solve the problem of immediately needed relief.[77] Such criticism did not dampen enthusiasm in western New York. Rochester's civic leaders, perhaps under less pressure to supply immediate relief to the unemployed than their Chicago counterparts, remained confident that local spending in the community could provide a sufficient jolt to conditions, thereby helping the area and eventually showing "the rest of the country the way out." Libanus Todd expressed confidence that Rochester would be able to take a leading role in publicizing this type of strategy. He argued that Monroe County was "one of the best places— perhaps the best place" to try such a cooperative effort, for "here we are accustomed to pulling together—we know how to do team work—and in this particular effort, we have outdone ourselves."[78] He predicted that as the plan spread across the nation, it might "as a byproduct" become associated with the city itself: "It might be termed the Rochester depression remover, or the new Monroe Doctrine."[79] Todd filled a scrapbook with clippings from around the country. San Francisco, Minneapolis, Hartford, and Utica were among the cities that expressed interest in trying the "Rochester method." President Herbert Hoover himself wrote a brief note to Rochester resident Col. Oscar Solbert (who had written the White House about the plan), stating that he was "greatly interested in the plan and in the success of the movement so ably directed in Rochester.[80]

The *Democrat and Chronicle* on 15 December trumpeted a figure of $6,026,351 that had been pledged by a total of 10,771 residents.[81] The headline boasted, "Canvass succeeds beyond best hope of its sponsors," with the article beneath it noting that the original figure projected for the campaign was $2 million. In addition to the volunteer force of 1,550 canvassers, members of the Rochester Community Chest did the clerical work. Local leaders were ecstatic. "There has never been a campaign waged in Rochester since the war, with more determination, or with more individual concentrated interest," said Henry H. Stebbins, chairman of the Civic Committee on Unemployment. "It has been a most unusual campaign, in that we helped ourselves in helping others. So we may say it was a mutual campaign; a wonderful thing for the community."[82] The newspaper reported the number of pledges and total amounts in each city ward. No ward in Rochester lacked participants, and the average amount pledged ranged from a few hundred dollars to a few thousand.

The breakdown of pledges reported in the *Democrat and Chronicle* on 15 December 1931 provides a sense of the distribution of pledges. Ward 7, one of the wealthier areas of town, reported only 14 pledgers, but the average pledge was over $5,000. Even working-class neighborhoods, such as Ward 24, still reported pledgers—in this case, 447, although the average pledge was a more modest $185. This amount was still a considerable sum in an era when a new Ford Roadster could be purchased for just over $400. Perhaps the fact that the pledge was designed to indicate spending over the following three months encouraged people to enter a rather generous amount. Since there was no real way to enforce the pledges, some expressed doubts that all of them would be fulfilled.[83]

Like Buffalo Day, the pledge campaign promised the best of both worlds: if city residents helped themselves to the consumer goods that they had been foolishly avoiding, things would get better. The plan did more than simply alleviate guilt over personal indulgences and purchases; it turned spending into a virtue, a way to help the community itself. Rochester's pledge campaigners shared the inflated rhetoric and unstinting optimism of the Buffalo Day organizers. Both initiatives redefined consumption as a civic act, making *all* spending a positive contribution to the local situation. They also underscored the role of men in making spending decisions. The suggestions in Rochester's Pledge for Prosperity emphasized major expenditures, on items for which the decision to purchase would probably rest with the male head of the household. Although renovations or new appliances would improve the "feminine" realm of the home, it is likely that final say over such expenditures rested with men and that even the signing of the pledge would often be up to the male authority figure. Although convention made it more likely that ad copywriters would refer to the individual as "he," often shoppers were categorized as "she" or "Madam." It is therefore interesting to note that the Pledge for Prosperity campaign described how canvassers were trying to "show each individual how *he* can help by signing the pledge printed above."[84]

The rhetoric of these campaigns was essentially democratic. Just as advertising during the 1920s had emphasized how specific products could improve the lives of the rich and poor alike, all citizens were instructed to do their best and take part in the pledge.[85] Rochester's *Democrat and Chronicle* ran editorials emphasizing that each and every person living in the city, no matter his or her financial or social rank, could help out by spending more: "It doesn't require a lot of money to help—every dollar swells the total, every hundred dollars is multiplied over and over as it passes from hand to hand, the thousands of dollars grow to hundreds of thousands and there will be millions for work, for happiness, for prosperity—if everyone helps."[86]

Libanus Todd, evaluating the success of Rochester's Pledge for Prosperity, excitedly informed a visiting journalist that citizens of ample as well as modest means were taking part in the program. George Eastman, the city's wealthiest citizen, "was sold on [the] idea from the beginning." In fact, after looking over his stately mansion for needed improvements, he could not find anything that required fixing so he instead decided to build a private sewage disposal plant for his home.[87] At the same time, Todd warmly praised a citizen of much more limited resources who did her own small part to improve Rochester's situation. A woman who had little money but a big desire to help the cause "looked about her small home for a spot she could afford to spend a few dollars in fixing up" and decided to have an old sofa recovered. Todd argued that the two cases were typical of the responses received by his committee.[88] The inclusiveness of these campaigns is significant, for it emphasized that all citizens, not solely the wealthy, had a responsibility to act. The hard times of the

Depression put everyone in the same boat, from the millionaire capitalist to the humble but respectable worker.

On another level, however, the extent to which these campaigns *avoided* dividing participants according to class is quite remarkable. The two figures in the preceding example did provide a contrast in means: the woman's small home and old sofa were no match for Eastman's new sewage facility in terms of the amount of money put into the local economy. Yet the campaign praised both for doing their part. What was missing from this discussion was the possibility that some people could not afford even modest expenditures. Campaigns that emphasized the power of "hoarded" dollars to grease the wheels of the economy suggested that most people were not actually impoverished by the Depression but simply were holding on to their money until conditions stabilized. The unemployed and those who had exhausted their savings or lost their homes were overlooked in campaigns that emphasized the importance of having everyone participate. The discussion of perverted thrift as a psychological barrier to be overcome did not acknowledge the rising numbers of jobless in Rochester. This emphasis on focusing the resources at hand to benefit local people was not unique to Rochester, however.

On 6 February 1932, Herbert Hoover appeared at a Washington rally for civic leaders from across the nation. Audience members included representatives of forty national associations, including the American Legion, American Federation of Labor, American Bankers' Association, and the General Federation of Women's Clubs. Hoover urged the creation of a national antihoarding association to combat individual currency withdrawals from banks across the nation and hoped to unite 20 million citizens in an "antihoarding war." Charles G. Dawes, president of the Reconstruction Finance Corporation, suggested that a return to the drive methods of World War I would stop what he called "a mass movement toward currency deflation." Ogden L. Mills, Undersecretary of the Treasury, linked the antihoarding drive with efforts to expand spending. Consumers should not withdraw their bank deposits and keep the money hoarded at home: they should instead spend and "put hoarded dollars to work." The development of a national campaign, with "branches in every community," was to be headed by Col. Frank Knox, publisher of the *Chicago Daily News*. A White House statement issued after the meeting noted that most of the audience agreed with the president that "a large portion of the hoarding was due to misunderstanding of the national effect of such acts, that it arose out of unnecessary fears and apprehension and that nothing could contribute more to the resumption of employment, to the stability of agriculture and other commodity prices, than to restore this money to work to turn the tide of depression on the way to prosperity."[89] Although most attendees of the meeting promised to put the support of their respective organizations behind the antihoarding drive, at least one representative expressed doubts. J. E. Spingarn, a representative of the National Association for the Advancement of Colored People and the sole black delegate to the meeting, argued that it was "merely ironical" to invite black Americans to join in such a movement "when they have no money to hoard."[90]

Local initiatives to encourage spending complemented later, national campaigns to encourage consumer spending, including those that emphasized purchasing American-made products. By the fall of 1932, renewed interest in "Buying American" was noted in newspapers and retail trade periodicals, in part encouraged by William Randolph Hearst. Hearst used the twenty-seven newspapers in his empire as a pulpit from which to preach the Buy American concept. Dana Frank argues that Hearst's pronouncements "landed in a fertile field," making it easy for him to enlist the resources of upper-class club women and others alarmed at America's economic situation.[91] One could argue, however, that the situation Hearst found in America in 1933 was something more than a reflection of Americans' desire to "turn inward" from engagement with Europe, as Frank contends. It was also an outgrowth of all the efforts local communities had made to harness consumer dollars, thereby laying the groundwork for a national campaign. Organizers in Buffalo and Rochester were articulating a "buy local" argument and running ambitious campaigns based on this notion at least a full year before Hearst began his Buy American editorials. In 1933, the Hearst papers featured Buy American pledge forms that were designed to function like the Monroe County Pledge for Prosperity, except on a national scale. Frank asserts that the movement was quickly spun off into local calls to "buy state" or "buy city," and she refers to campaigns in California and by New York canneries in 1933. While she acknowledges that many campaigns "antedated the Depression," she emphasizes that the national Buy American campaign brought a new swell of support to the idea of state and city economic "nationalism."[92] The story of Buffalo Day and Monroe County's Pledge for Prosperity suggests that at least some of the impulse behind economic nationalism came from the local level and then gained national momentum.

Trade journals, as well as the national mass media, picked up on the Buy American rhetoric. An article in the *Merchandise Manager* noted that some store executives were reporting a slump in imported goods, including Irish linens and French perfumes. Although these items usually accounted for only a small percentage of sales, their symbolic value was much more important. The article reported how purchasing decisions could often be the cause of domestic strife, noting that a recent incident in a Buffalo department store illustrated the "psychology of the movement." A businessman reportedly rebelled at paying his wife's monthly department store bill because it covered primarily French-made articles. "Why," he asked indignantly, "should I, who am contributing liberally to the support of the unemployed in my own country, exert my family purchasing power in directions which give employment to French workers instead of our own?"[93] Finally, he paid the bill, after it had been tactfully pointed out that the problem he raised was "one of domestic relations," not international trade. In this vignette, it is the man who knew the workings of the economy and the true value of his wages in turning America's economy around. His wife, preoccupied with fashion, had no grasp of the impact of her actions. Yet even as Hearst and others tried to whip up economic nationalism, regional loyalty remained a touchstone of proposed solutions to the Depression. An editorial in the Buffalo magazine *Town Tidings* in 1933 exhorted, "*Buy American* if you want to, but BUY BUFFALO first."[94]

Hindsight permits us to evaluate these campaigns more critically than observers at the time did. Buffalo Day, though a successful one-day sale for retailers, by no means solved unemployment in the city. The predicted psychological breakthrough for local shoppers did not materialize, and one can argue that even if it had, the combined spending power of western New Yorkers would not have reversed economic conditions in the region, never mind in the entire nation. In Rochester, despite the sincerity of the thousands of individuals who solemnly swore to do their best to spend their way out of the Depression, the Pledge for Prosperity did not have the desired effect of jump-starting the city on the path to normalcy. Given the eventual limitations of these plans, how do we account for these two communities embracing such initiatives?

In one sense, this marshaling of local spenders can be seen as a way for people to feel that they were doing their part to end the Depression. By emphasizing the responsibility of every individual to contribute in some fashion to ending the economic downturn, these shopping and spending campaigns asserted that the individual *could* make a difference. To relegate all action to Washington or the state government was to acknowledge the powerlessness of individuals over the course of the nation's progress. These proposals appealed to individuals who wanted to do something—anything—to try to improve economic conditions.

The popularity of this strategy also had much to do with the common understanding of the workings of the economy. It made sense for residents of the area to think of all individuals as participating in a large "circle of distribution," for they had been hearing this message for some time in local editorials and advertising. During the 1920s, local merchants had encouraged people to spend at home as a way to further boost their region's prosperity; now this became a matter of survival. Similarly, merchants borrowed the rhetoric of civic campaigns such as the Pledge for Prosperity to emphasize the role of the individual in the local economy. Retailers turned around the popular language of fiscal responsibility to encourage people to go back to the stores. Spending was not about giving in to desire, in this view; rather, it was the outcome of a rational decision.

As time wore on, it became clear that local initiatives such as Buffalo Day or the Rochester Pledge for Prosperity were not effective in ending America's slump. In Buffalo, relief expenditures in December 1933 reached a high of $611,677, and over 21,000 families relied on public assistance. In contrast, a decade earlier, expenditures in December 1923 had been under $12,000, and 453 families were on assistance.[95] By 1934, some expressed doubt that the private consumer had the power to make a difference in the economy. As one newspaper article noted, the slogan "Buy Now and Aid Recovery" was "a good one, but of limited effectiveness for the excellent reason that ole John Consumer is, at the moment, a trifle short of spending money."[96]

In the end, Rochester suffered from a serious loss of morale, and many fled the city. In order to screen the overwhelming numbers of applicants for public assistance, officials used work projects, including a rock pile, to distinguish "the worthy from the shiftless male vagabonds."[97] Even Rochester's Community Chest, which had received generous bequests from city patron George Eastman, was unable to meet the needs of the unemployed. After Eastman's death by suicide in 1932, residents fell into a torpor and abandoned many local initiatives.[98]

By the mid-1930s, solutions that called on the federal government for funding became more attractive, and FDR's willingness to spend money on New Deal programs prompted some local residents to entertain creative new notions of government intervention. Beginning in 1935, Buffalo received federal relief money, primarily for public works. Between 1935 and 1937, the city received over $45 million for projects, including the building of a downtown auditorium, new police headquarters, public housing, modernization of the zoo, and countless other renovation efforts.[99] Buffalo's George C. Andrews, a prominent city engineer and former Water Department official, developed a plan to help "Uncle Sam put some money in the consumer's wallet."[100] Andrews presented his "Federal Handout Scheme" in speeches before various luncheon clubs and in a pamphlet entitled "Why Postpone Prosperity?" He argued that the government should provide "taxable money" that would have to be put into circulation immediately or would lose its value over time. To prevent anyone acquiring this special currency from simply saving it, the plan would require the attachment of a stamp to each unspent dollar bill every fifteen days, which would reduce its value by 2 percent. According to Andrews, the government would redeem the bill in ordinary currency two years after the date of issue, provided fifty stamps were attached.

The Andrews plan had parallels to the Old Age Pension Plan advocated by Francis Townshend, which also relied on the government to provide handouts of cash to consumers. Townshend, a California doctor, rose to national prominence as the spokesperson for Old Age Revolving Pensions, Ltd. He advocated a monthly pension for seniors, with the stipulation that they retire from work and spend the whole amount within thirty days.[101] By 1935, a network of Townshend Clubs had stretched through California and into the Midwest and Northeast.[102] It is not clear whether Andrews was familiar with Townshend's plan. Alan Brinkley points out that Townshend himself was not the first to suggest such a scheme, as others (including adman Bruce Barton and Seattle dentist Stuart McCord) had proposed similar plans.[103] Late in 1934, Louisiana senator Huey Long devised his own form of wealth redistribution, the Share Our Wealth Plan. Long's plan would heavily tax the wealthy—for example, any income an individual made above $1 million would simply be confiscated, and strict limits would be set on inheritances. The money gained by the government would be distributed to every needy family in the country.[104]

In contrast to Townshend and Long, Andrews targeted home owners as the main beneficiaries of his plan. Stating that it was impossible for the government to give employment on public works to all of the jobless, he proposed that home owners be used to create employment. Each home owner would receive an amount of this "taxable currency" equal to 5 percent of the assessed valuation of his or her property, with the stipulation that the money be expended to repair or improve the home. The plan would provide employment for "all carpenters, plumbers, painters, et cetera" as well as those in other industries such as construction supplies or furniture. The workers hired to improve homes "would be allowed to spend the money paid them by the home owner in any way they desired," but naturally, every recipient would spend it immediately so as to avoid the necessity of attaching stamps. Andrews believed that "with hoarding penalized in this way," the money would turn over at least twenty-five times in a year, or about three times faster than did currency with no such penalty. His plan would have entitled Buffalo residents to about $200 million for home rehabilitation.

In one sense, Andrews's plan can be seen as a compromise between wholly private spending initiatives and state employment and public works ventures. While the citizens who went shopping on Buffalo Day or pledged money in the Monroe County campaign were trying to make a difference by putting their own savings into circulation, Andrews recognized that not everyone had sufficient funds to contribute. His plan relied on government money, but it put that money in the hands of individual consumers. The desired result would be very similar to goals announced by the promoters of the Rochester Pledge for Prosperity: home owners would hire extra labor or make additional purchases that, in turn, would fuel the economy. Andrews did not go so far as to advocate that the state simply hand out this money directly to the most needy. Nor was he willing to entertain a radical redistribution of wealth, as Long proposed. Where Long wanted to take money from the wealthy and give it directly to "the people," Andrews would reward home owners (presumably including the most wealthy citizens of the country) with money to spend, and they would then hire workers and put these additional funds into the economy.

Despite the fanfare surrounding its announcement, Andrews's plan was never adopted. By 1935, federally funded public works had become the main strategy to alleviate unemployment in western New York. People in the area grew more resigned to the idea that individuals had little power when it came to changing the direction of the economy. Robert Riegel, a professor of statistics in the School of Business Administration at the University of Buffalo, mused on this change in the *Buffalo Times.* Riegel drew a distinction between "old-fashioned" businessmen who followed common sense and scorned statistics and economic theory and those who recognized their dependence on much larger market forces. The former group had been rendered "extinct as a dodo bird" by the Depression. "Besides its extraordinary length and the vast unemployment situation it has created, there is one thing that distinguishes this depression from all that have gone before it," Riegel declared. "That distinguishing characteristic is the absolute dependence of the individual on general economic conditions, certainly nation-wide and in many respects world-wide. The businessman, the industrialist, the workingman, the professional man and the investor have all come to realize that only a general

recovery on a large scale can change their individual lot for the better."[105]
Riegel argued that in former times, this was not the case, as conditions in one
community were not so closely linked to those in another—"one could be
prosperous and flourishing and the other depressed at the very same time."

The growing belief in the powerlessness of the individual to have an impact
on the Depression is not surprising. By the mid-1930s, neither Rochester nor
Buffalo could claim immunity from the economic slump. Local unemployment soared, as those businesses that did manage to stay afloat sharply curtailed their payrolls. Local leaders increasingly appealed to the state and federal
governments for aid. And although stores would still experiment with "buy
local" efforts in advertising, few entertained grand proposals along the lines
of Buffalo Day or the Pledge for Prosperity as the solution to the continuing
crisis.

These initiatives, which aimed to harness the purchasing power of the individual for the good of all, reveal the continued power of local identities.
Faced with the downturn of business conditions, the people of western New
York first looked for solutions at home, hoping that by coming together in
their communities, they could help themselves and perhaps even the rest of the
nation. They also focused on consuming as the most effective means by which
every individual could make a difference. Consuming was seen as a win-win solution, allowing citizens to indulge themselves and simultaneously give a boost
to the economy. Finally, in proposing plans that encouraged consumer spending, western New Yorkers attempted to redefine older notions of thrift and
fiscal responsibility. By the early 1930s, spending eclipsed saving as the ideal for
the civic-minded residents, as merchants and local leaders promoted buying as
the way out. These local spending initiatives show the resourcefulness of Buffalo and Rochester merchants and citizens. As it turned out, however, the resources they had at hand were not enough to turn the tide.

Plate 1. The Rochester Chamber of Commerce adopted the slogan "Rochester Made Means Quality" in 1908 and continued to use it throughout the 1920s and 1930s. *From the Rochester City Hall Photo Lab vintage collection. Reprinted courtesy of the City of Rochester.*

Plate 2. This photograph appeared in the *Rochester Herald* on 13 December 1920. The caption says that the girl is watching her baby brother while her mother "interviews Santa Claus." She is standing outside Duffy-Powers department store, and a sign on the door proudly boasts of "Men's Rochester Made Suits." *From the Albert R. Stone Negative Collection, Rochester Museum and Science Center, Rochester, NY.*

Plate 3. Adults and children gather in front of a department store toy display, circa 1919. *From the Albert R. Stone Negative Collection, Rochester Museum and Science Center, Rochester, NY.*

Plate 4. Children admiring store window, Rochester, circa 1919. *From the Albert R. Stone Negative Collection, Rochester Museum and Science Center, Rochester, NY.*

Plate 5. Cartoon showing the "circle of business" in Buffalo, as money changes hands between a local manufacturer, workman, housewife, and retailer. The cartoon appeared in *Buffalo Saturday Night* magazine on 10 December 1921. *Collection of the Buffalo and Erie County Public Library.*

Plate 6. This photograph of the Sibley, Lindsay and Curr Company float appeared in the *Rochester Herald* on 6 September 1923. The store often participated in community events like the Floral Carnival Parade. *From the Albert R. Stone Negative Collection, Rochester Museum and Science Center, Rochester, NY.*

Plate 7. A crowd of shoppers in the 1920s crosses the street at the corner of Main Street and Clinton Avenue in Rochester. On the far corner the awnings and first floor of the Sibley, Lindsay and Curr Company are visible. *From the Albert R. Stone Negative Collection, Rochester Museum and Science Center, Rochester, NY.*

Plate 8. A man (possibly Elmer N. Baxter himself) stands behind the counter in the E. N. Baxter grocery store, circa 1930. The store was located in Brighton, New York, near Rochester. Note the array of branded goods on the shelves along the wall, including Maxwell House Coffee, Grape-Nuts Flakes, Lux soap, Argo cornstarch, and Salada tea. *Reprinted with permission of the Town of Brighton.*

Plate 9. This photograph of Main Street East in Rochester during 1930 or 1931 shows that pedestrians and cars still gathered in the downtown despite the economic crisis. Some of the businesses pictured, including The Father and Son Shoe Store, J. R. White jewelry store, and Rowe Underwear Stores, would not survive the Depression. *From the Albert R. Stone Negative Collection, Rochester Museum and Science Center, Rochester, NY.*

Plate 10. Looking west along Main Street East in Rochester during the late 1930s or early 1940s. A billboard for Coca-Cola looms over the crowds and streetcars. *Courtesy of the Rochester Municipal Archives.*

Plate 11. Map of the "Niagara area," produced by the Buffalo Chamber of Commerce to visually suggest the region's role as the hub of a large trading area. It appeared in the magazine *Niagara Area* in January 1932. *Reprinted with permission of the Buffalo Niagara Partnership.*

Plate 12. Cartoon from the *Buffalo Evening News*, 3 August 1931. The cartoonist shows some skepticism about the effectiveness of buying campaigns and price cuts to rejuvenate the public's spending habits. *Reprinted with permission of the* Buffalo News.

Plate 13. Cartoon from the *Buffalo Evening News*, 2 September 1931. The image suggests that the Buffalo Day campaign might put gas in the tank of business and speed the return to normalcy. *Reprinted with permission of the* Buffalo News.

Plate 14. Advertisement from Bing and Nathan demonstrating the store's participation in Buffalo Day. The ad features a drawing of Buffalo City Hall, an instantly recognizable landmark to people from the region. It appeared in the *Buffalo Evening News* on 3 September 1931.

ĦARD TIMES AND GOOD TIMES AT ĦOME

LOCAL IDENTITIES BOTH ENDURED and were transformed during the late 1930s. This chapter will explore the continued significance of the community appeal as a selling tool after 1931 and the persistence of local stores as sites not only of consumption but also of entertainment, education, and celebration. Further, it will suggest that other groups, including national advertisers, tried to tap into local loyalties with varying amounts of success. In this sense, it challenges the narrative of national homogenization that frames much of the literature on American popular culture during the interwar period. Scholars have emphasized how Americans from coast to coast were becoming more and more alike and were increasingly prone to see themselves as part of a national culture. The spread of consumer culture is assumed to have had a homogenizing and unifying effect on all areas of the United States. Urban historians suggest that the nation was becoming integrated in broad networks of communication and distribution and less tied to the "island communities" of the nineteenth century, to use Robert Wiebe's famous phrase.[1]

The development of a mass market, in this view, encouraged a sense of participation in a world beyond one's hometown. Advertising campaigns further contributed to the development of a national vernacular, whereby people across the country could identify the slogan of Wrigley's gum or Lucky Strike cigarettes.[2] Magazines, movies, and radio programs served as common experiences for consumers in all regions of the country, encouraging individuals to feel they were sharing something that spoke to the nation as a whole.[3]

On one level, this emphasis on a growing national consciousness rings true. As the previous chapters have demonstrated, an examination of Rochester and Buffalo during the 1920s reveals that residents did feel better connected to others in the rest of the country. By the 1930s, certain well-established mechanisms enabled the residents of these cities to keep well abreast of developments across the nation. As we have seen, improvements in roads and railways made it easier for people to venture beyond their immediate surroundings. At the same time, improvements in distribution and transportation brought brand-name goods to western New York, and businesses based in other parts of the country, in particular chain stores, had a growing presence in the region.

Yet on another level, what has been described as the new "national" culture in the early 1920s could more accurately be considered a "big-city" culture. More specifically, the entertainments, fashions, habits, and lifestyles of those living in centers such as New York, Los Angeles, Philadelphia, and Chicago became increasingly familiar to all Americans. As movies came out of Hollywood and as Madison Avenue ad agencies cranked out national campaigns, Americans in all regions became better acquainted with the goings-on in these places. The artistic and cultural output of the metropolises seemed to make these places matter in a way that smaller cities such as Buffalo and Rochester did not. Scholars interested in America's emergence as a nation of consumers have invariably emphasized how profound changes in a few key cities had resonance throughout the country.

What is missing from this equation is the persistence of local identities in the formation of American consumer culture. Even in the late 1930s—by which time the various apparatuses of the mass market (including national advertising, magazines, and media) were firmly in place—local particularities still shaped the experiences of consumers in western New York. The emphasis on local identities and local roots cultivated by retailers endured through the 1920s and well into the Depression and beyond.

In the 1930s, merchants in smaller cities served as mediators between the mass market and local interests. Department stores boasted of carrying wide ranges of branded goods, allowing the citizens of Buffalo and Rochester full access to the wonders of American mass production. At the same time, they asserted their own place in the continued evolution and success of their communities. Throughout the 1930s, retailers in western New York used local sentiment as a tool for selling, whether by linking sales events to significant dates in the history of the city or by using appeals to community solidarity in newspaper advertising. In 1934, for example, the B. Forman Company tied in its own twenty-fifth anniversary with the Rochester Centennial, affixing a twenty-five-foot replica of an early map of the Rochester area to the front of the store. The canvas map covered almost the entire face of the building, noted the *Dry Goods Merchants Trade Journal*, extending from close to the top down to the second-floor windows. Treated to withstand the elements, it was lashed to the building with decorative ropes. The *DGMTJ* noted approvingly the high level of local interest in the map: "At night the map is lighted from below and causes much comment. In fact, it has aroused so much interest that its picture has appeared in local newspapers, with resultant free publicity to the firm."[4] Crowds reportedly gathered to examine the map and marvel at how the city had developed since its founding.

Even after the failure of "local spending" initiatives such as Buffalo Day and the Rochester Pledge for Prosperity in 1931, retailers continued to emphasize the importance of patronizing area retailers. During the Christmas season of 1936, the *Rochester Democrat and Chronicle* editorialized that businesses were "human" and reacted best when under the "stimulus of local encouragement and support." Readers were encouraged to begin their gift shopping to demonstrate their commitment to Rochester. The paper admonished readers that citizenship carried "a definite responsibility to the community."[5] Shopping was portrayed as a painless way to encourage local businesses and foster employment for fellow citizens.

As a guest, be loyal to your host. As an employe [*sic*], be loyal to your business. As a citizen, be loyal to your community. If you live in Rochester, patronize Rochester's stores. Give your business to the merchants who give employment to your fellow citizens. . . . Rochester merchants are of, by, and for the community in which they are doing business. They hire Rochesterians for clerical and executive staffs. Payrolls are made up from money you spend over the counters and in various departments. As the stores prosper, the community prospers. Yes, shop in Rochester, and shop early. But when you think of the many fine business institutions in this city, and when you realize that every dollar spent in Rochester aids the people and prosperity of Rochester, you cannot help resolving to spend even a higher percentage of

your money here. . . . Be a booster and share in the pride of building
a greater Rochester.[6]

Such entreaties emphasized the money spent by local retailers in wages,
while disregarding the fact that most of the products available in the stores actually were not locally manufactured but were shipped in from all over the
country and the world. No mention was even made of trying to buy American-
made goods. The more immediate transfer of funds from the shopper to the
retailer and then to the salesclerk seemed the most crucial aspect. This logic
persisted, and the retail trade press continued to report "buy-at-home" drives
in communities across the nation throughout the late 1930s.[7] Local consumption was the main focus of such drives, although recognition of area manufacturers might occasionally accompany promotions for local retailers.

During the dark days of the Depression, residents of western New York
continued to visit area stores, even if their actual purchases were limited. The
economic downturn hit department stores hard. Figures for Sibley, Lindsay
and Curr in Rochester suggest a steady decline in net sales from 1929 to 1933,
with a slow recovery for the rest of the decade.[8] Buffalo department stores similarly hit bottom in 1933 and only gradually made their way back up to sales levels seen in the 1920s.[9] Yet even though unemployment and relief numbers grew
throughout the 1930s, people still strolled down Main Street and still visited
stores, at least to look. Indeed, some of the people walking by show windows
in the downtown were undoubtedly among the newly unemployed who were
out pounding the pavement in search of work, and they might have had ambivalent reactions to seeing goods that were beyond their means. At the same
time, perusal of wares in department or discount stores remained a popular
pastime for many people, including the unemployed. The distractions of the
store and the fantasy world that merchants had so carefully cultivated in prosperous times had a particular allure in hard times. Visitors to the store could
revel in the luxurious surroundings, perhaps forgetting the privations they endured at home. Further, the transformative power of goods appealed to people
in desperate times. Throughout the 1920s, advertisers and retailers had stressed
the importance of choosing the right products in order to ensure personal success. During the Depression, the notion, however fanciful, that one might be
able to reverse bad fortune simply by selecting the proper new necktie for a job
interview had a potent appeal.[10]

Some impressionistic evidence supports the view that the central business
district remained a place of activity, if not actual purchases, throughout the

later 1930s. Buffalo's Main Street Association performed periodic counts of pedestrians at various points in the downtown. According to one count on Wednesday, 1 November 1933, almost 3,000 people passed in front of Adam, Meldrum and Anderson during two half-hour blocks from 11:00 to 11:30 A.M. and 2:30 to 3:00 P.M. A similar count outside Lerner's discount store on the west side of Main Street indicated there were 4,446 passersby and another 2,047 outside J. N. Adam's across the street. These figures suggest that the downtown area did not become a ghost town even during 1933, the year that Buffalo's department stores reported their lowest sales during the Depression. Throughout the 1930s, literally thousands of people walked through the retail district every business day. During subsequent counts in June and November 1934, 1935, 1936, 1937, and 1938, no fewer than 2,000 people were counted outside J. N. Adam's during two thirty-minute segments, with the average reaching over 3,000.[11]

In particular, special events staged by the department stores drew crowds regularly. The unveiling of store improvements was an event attended by local leaders and residents alike. The installation of the first store escalators in Rochester (explained as "electric stairways" to those unfamiliar with the term) became an occasion to celebrate the city's advancement and the wonderful possibilities of modern technology. Sibley's management boasted that the new feature could move shoppers from the main floor to the fifth floor of the store in ninety seconds.[12] These new conveyors were greeted with a high level of excitement. Men, women, and children flocked to the stores to ride the escalators, some for the first time in their lives. In certain ways, both the public excitement over escalators and the leading roles taken by department stores in adopting this new technology echoed similar developments surrounding the adoption of electric lighting in the late nineteenth century. During the 1880s, clothing and department stores had been among the first locations to be wired for electricity. In Buffalo, merchants had spearheaded the drive for electric lighting in the downtown area. Now, crowds gathered to see the escalators set in motion.

In 1936, a group of over three thousand Rochesterians jammed the main floor aisles of Sibley, Lindsay and Curr to witness Mayor Charles Stanton press a button that started the escalators between five floors of the store. The new feature cost the store over a quarter of a million dollars.[13] Before the unveiling, the store's board of directors and officials hosted a breakfast for 350 local officials, Chamber of Commerce executives, presidents of civic clubs, and other Rochester citizens. The store proclaimed that the installation was the largest in New York State outside Manhattan. After the assembled crowd was brought to attention by the sound of bugles, Rochester's mayor praised the store for its leadership in the community. Stanton noted that Sibley's was "keeping up to the minute, as always. . . . Sibley's has become an institution in Rochester. It is a landmark for thousands who go shopping. This new equipment will add to their convenience."[14] The crowd roared its approval as the mayor set the escalators in motion. The fact that this event could draw such a large crowd at 9:30 on a Wednesday morning perhaps also indicates that the local business leaders present at the occasion were joined by at least some of the ranks of Rochester's unemployed.

In Buffalo the following year, the opening of the escalators at J. N. Adam and Company similarly became a civic event, with people lining up on Main Street to await the initial run of the "moving steps." Samuel W. Reyburn, chairman of the board of the Associated Dry Goods Corporation, was on hand to speak, but the highlight of the evening was the chance for Buffalonians to ride the stairs for the first time. The *Buffalo Courier* reported on the revelry associated with the starting of the escalators. A line of citizens formed on the sidewalk outside the store at 7 P.M. An audience watched attentively as the current was turned on to start the moving steps. "Maybe it was the 'kid' in them," the newspaper reported, "but lots of folks joined in riding both up and down the five flights of 'stairs,' and then up and down again." As store executives had planned, the debut became an open house party, with crowds of shoppers roaming into every department of the store, asking questions of salesgirls.[15] Store management viewed the opening of the escalators as a selling occasion, to be sure, but it also was a chance for local residents to experience the new technology, free of charge, and celebrate the advancement of their city. Buffalo's health commissioner noted approvingly that the new escalators would eliminate the nausea or fainting spells associated with "old-fashioned" elevators.

The opening of new or expanded stores drew similar attention. The 1930s witnessed considerable reinvestment in downtown stores. Despite the constraints of the Depression, many stores either extended or renovated their buildings. Buffalo saw quite a few new developments. Just prior to the installation of the escalators in 1937, J. N. Adam's completed a $500,000 renovation, building a new six-story structure at the corner of Main and Eagle Streets and modernizing the existing structure. At the ceremony to lay the cornerstone of the new building, Reyburn, from Associated Dry Goods, explicitly equated the retailers' investment in the city with the larger efforts by the American private sector to lead the way out of the Depression. Taking the opportunity to criticize Roosevelt's New Deal, Reyburn rejected the notion that the state should become more involved in regulating the economy. He compared the role of government to that of officials at a football game, who should "enforce the rules but leave the actual playing to the players."[16] Only by giving business a chance to "fight its way out" would both state and federal officials help the return to normalcy.

Walter Brunmark, president of J. N. Adam, explained that the decision to embark on a huge expansion program indicated the company's faith in the future of downtown Main Street and in Buffalo as a whole. He argued,

> This new building and expansion program, involving so substantial a capital investment . . . has come about after several years of careful study of all the important facts that determine a logical, successful location for a large, modern department store business. . . . It is also very gratifying that we find it necessary and logical to embark on this important development at this time because it will provide employment for hundreds of Buffalo's skilled craftsmen engaged in the building trades and allied industries in our immediate trading area. It is also a sincere expression of our faith and belief in Buffalo as a community and expresses our confidence in the future of this splendid city.[17]

Research into traffic patterns, transportation, and parking facilities reinforced the company's decision to expand. The location was also close to large office buildings, banks, and other stores, leading the store's management to conclude that the site would be "most desirable, not only for this generation, but for those that will follow." The J. N. Adam's construction contract was awarded to the same Buffalo firm that constructed the $7 million City Hall, an art deco downtown landmark.. All materials were from the Buffalo area, and all labor employed was local. The only exception to this rule was the selection of the architectural firm Starrett and Van Vleck of New York City. The firm had earned a reputation for department store design since overseeing the redesign of Lord and Taylor's Fifth Avenue store in Manhattan twenty-three years previously.[18]

The modern styling of the new building, featuring horizontal lines, was commended in the local press.[19] After the completion of the project in 1936, the Main Street Association awarded a prize to the store for the finest major building construction in the city. Accepting the award, Brunmark stated confidently that "Main Street never would degenerate into a Coney Island boardwalk" if businesses continued to invest in maintaining and modernizing their buildings. He noted that the satisfaction of store executives and employees, combined with the public's positive response to the project, had provided ample compensation for the company's investment.[20]

In Buffalo, Hengerer's spent $1 million modernizing its Main Street store in 1937 and 1938. New fixtures, fire-resistant enclosed stairways, new departments, and a 36,000-square-foot addition were designed to make Hengerer's "the most modern store in New York State."[21] Five Westinghouse elevators with blue-green leather doors and bronze trim were installed. Attention went into every facet of the store's design. The interior featured alternating pilasters and a glass-and-brick penthouse for the store's office workers. The exterior of the building was refaced in white granite and trimmed in bronze, with an off-white terra-cotta facade running from the second floor to the penthouse. Sweeping display windows encouraged shoppers to linger in front, while bronze revolving doors ushered them inside. The tearoom was "redone in the modern style," with bleached straw walls, maple woodwork, and "strong accents of turquoise."[22] Despite Hengerer's long-standing image as a "store of specialty shops," catering to Buffalo's elite, the new building featured budget dresses, coats, and millinery, as well as a new dress thrift shop, perhaps indicating that even Hengerer's had to make concessions to the Depression. The Store for Men had a contrasting interior, with walnut and simulated pigskin walls. To further encourage the sense that male shoppers were distinct from their feminine counterparts, the men's shop was arranged as a "store within a store" and had a facade of its own and a separate entrance.

In 1938, E. W. Edwards and Son of Buffalo opened a new store with what were described by the *Courier-Express* as "impressive ceremonies," attended by civic and company officials and 150 merchandisers' and buyers' representatives. Some 500 salespeople were on hand to welcome customers. The store had planned to give each visitor a rose, but the supply of an estimated 15,000 to 20,000 blossoms was exhausted by three o'clock in the afternoon; the total number of visitors reached between 30,000 and 40,000.[23] Attendants at the nearby Statler Garage reported that 1,000 shoppers took advantage of the free parking spaces arranged for the occasion. The store's design was the culmination of an extensive study of department stores in New York and other cities. The structure was guaranteed to be fireproof, and the interior had a state-of-the-art ventilation system. Twenty-seven show windows brought natural light into the store and were supplemented by a lighting system installed jointly by

General Electric and Niagara Hudson. The feeling of light and openness was echoed in the pale peach blossom hue chosen for the interiors and the cream ceilings. The layout of store departments was also revised according to new research. The men's department was designed with separate street entrances, which, according to the store's promotions director Adam Eby, allowed "men, who usually despise shopping, [to] duck in one door, make their purchases, and duck out the other door."[24] Kleinhans of Buffalo also modernized, hiring the local architectural firm Bley and Lyman and awarding the construction job to another city business. The store hoped its new facade of pink granite and enhanced display windows would complement the other improved buildings in the downtown area.[25]

Even as the independent merchants of Buffalo and Rochester rejuvenated their stores, chain stores were increasing their profile in the central business districts of the two cities. Department stores were, of course, long-standing fixtures in the downtown. Now, a range of discount stores and chains (both regional and national) invested in new, modern facilities. Buffalo, in particular, saw a mix of chain stores popping up in its downtown area. Some of these stores were new to the area; others were expanded versions of existing chain branches.

Neisner's five-cents-to-a-dollar stores opened a new branch in Buffalo at 450 Main Street. The Rochester-based chain already had two Buffalo branches, one that had opened in 1923 in the Broadway shopping district (traditionally home to more discount retailers and five-and-dime chains than the Main Street area) and another on Bailey Avenue, which had been in business since 1935. By the time this new "flagship store" was being built in Buffalo, the Neisner chain had 103 stores in sixty-three cities, spread out over sixteen states.[26] According to the *Buffalo Times,* the new store featured the "longest lunch counter in the world," seating eighty diners, who faced a wall of green and white tiled glass, inset with diamond-shaped lights and soft multi-colored effects."[27] Green leather swivel chairs featured convenient built-in footrests, and a special rack under the counter allowed shoppers to relax while eating lunch with their purchases safely stowed away. Food preparation was done using stainless steel equipment and methods "parallel [to] those of the best modern hospitals in sanitation."[28] The trained staff of three hundred on hand for the grand opening were "all Buffalonians," the manager was careful to point out.[29]

Some merchants joined forces to capitalize on the publicity surrounding new store openings. When Woolworth's held a special reopening ceremony to unveil improvements to its downtown Buffalo store, its neighbors on the block bounded by Main, Clinton, Washington, and Eagle Streets held their own programs. Kleinhans held fashion shows in the shop for men and featured orchestra music in its own newly refurbished lobby, while J. N. Adam held women's fashion shows. The joint "good neighbor celebration" was designed to call the public's attention to the central location of the stores, served by twenty-one bus and streetcar lines.[30] Woolworth's unveiled a new selling floor with a two-hundred-foot lunch counter (extending from Main Street to Washington Street), new fixtures, lighting, and air-conditioning.

Chain stores, including W. T. Grant and Sears, Roebuck, reinvested in Buffalo's downtown during the 1930s. Buffalo welcomed yet another chain flagship: W. T. Grant's new store at Main and Huron was the largest of the Grant chain of 497 units. The *Courier-Express* reported that over 3,500 applicants were given interviews for 750 jobs in the store, and all saleswomen were "either high school graduates or college girls, and every one [was] a Buffalonian."[31] The Grant organization, founded in Lynn, Massachusetts, as a twenty-five-cent store, adopted a "1 cent to 1 dollar" merchandising strategy after World War I and maintained a centralized staff of buyers in New York City. The new Buffalo branch had a modern, streamlined design with a blue terra-cotta exterior on the first floor and long rows of tapestry glass above. The *Courier-Express* described the new design features in detail. A large mezzanine lounge at the back of the store allowed customers a bird's-eye view of all the merchandise on the street floor and proved especially convenient on "the many occasions on which Mrs. Buffalo wants to arrange for a meeting with a friend who is doing some shopping down town."[32]

Paul Gleason, manager of the Grant store, explained that the company had "faith in the future growth and prosperity of Buffalo" and thus felt that the $500,000 spent on the store was a good investment. Ninety percent of the appliances in the store were purchased from local concerns, and all the steel used in construction came from the nearby Bethlehem Steel Company. Sears, Roebuck joined the ranks of stores that were expanding in downtown Buffalo. The company enlarged its store at 1905 Main Street in 1939. The *Buffalo Evening News* excitedly reported that a $300,000 addition was planned, increasing the size of the store by 40 percent and enlarging practically every department.[33]

The considerable reinvestment in the downtown core by department stores and chain stores alike during the late 1930s underscores two points that are often overlooked in hindsight. First, while suburban development in the Buffalo area was under way during the two decades prior to World War II, few business leaders felt that the downtown area was in decline as a retail district.[34] Indeed, companies such as Neisner's and W. T. Grant were constructing new stores on Main Street in the 1930s. The fact that suburban development (and the growth of suburban malls) would outpace and eventually replace reinvestment in the central business district in the postwar period would seem to suggest that Main Street was in decline. From the perspective of store owners during the 1930s, however, Buffalo's Main Street was still the primary retail area of the city, and companies (both locally owned ones and those based elsewhere) viewed expenditures for the fixtures, display areas, building facades, and restaurants of the downtown stores as wise investments.

This observation leads to a second important point about the 1930s. Even though unemployment had reached unprecedented levels in Buffalo and despite the low volume of retail sales that persisted throughout the decade, many still believed that private initiatives and the power of consumer spending would be able to bring America out of its economic slump. Historians now know, of course, that it would take more than private spending and even more than the New Deal to turn the U.S. economy around. Yet the underlying optimism of businesses that invested millions of dollars in renovating facilities or constructing new stores even as the Depression continued is striking. The president of the Associated Dry Goods Corporation (which owned J. N. Adam's and Hengerer's by the 1930s) explained to stockholders why it was necessary for retailers to put money back into the communities in which they were located:

> During the early years of the depression prices declined, volume of business shrank, and work on the maintenance of physical properties was held to a minimum. . . . Revival of business required larger investments in merchandise inventories and accounts receivable, and justified expenditures for improvement of plants, fixtures and equipment. . . . Distribution is a barometer of all industry and of general welfare. It can only prosper with prosperity, and it cannot protect itself against loss in a period of recession. To attempt to do so would cause such a curtailment in the selection of goods offered for sale and lowering of standards of service, that the loss of goodwill and position in the community would far outweigh any possible temporary decrease in losses.[35]

It was worth it, in Oswald W. Knauth's view, to continue to spend on both inventory and fixtures in order to retain community goodwill. The new and revamped stores were tangible evidence that retailers believed conditions in

Buffalo would get better and their investments would be recouped as consumers loosened their purse strings and spent as freely as they had done in the 1920s.

Even as hard times persisted, the stores continued to act as cultural brokers within their communities. At a time when many families had little cash to spare for anything beyond the bare necessities, local stores offered entertainments that attracted huge crowds. Retailers naturally hoped that these promotions would help business, but many people who attended fashion shows, parades, and other ceremonies could do so without having to make a purchase. Throughout the Depression, merchants continued to devote considerable resources to sponsor public entertainments. Celebrities were a huge draw for major department stores in Rochester and Buffalo. Booking special appearances by entertainers, musicians, sports heroes, or other famous figures was not a new practice in the 1930s, although the hard economic times made such free shows especially popular. Some famous individuals combined autograph sessions at department stores with other local appearances. For example, in 1938, Guy Lombardo and his orchestra played at the Rochester Main Street Armory, but the bandleader also autographed records in Sibley's radio department.[36] Yet others would probably not have visited western New York without the promotional efforts of the department store. Baseball player Walter Johnson autographed baseballs and sold copies of his new board game in Hengerer's Toyland in Buffalo.[37] Yvonne Leroux, nurse of the famed Dionne quintuplets of Canada, gave talks twice a day in Sibley's as part of a thirty-city tour in 1937. She promoted baby goods while relating stories of the "fun and headaches" associated with caring for the five babies.[38]

Guest appearances often occurred in the store departments that carried related merchandise. Other promotions required much more elaborate staging. Sibley's regularly held fashion shows in the store auditorium, hiring models and arranging seating for preferred customers. As noted in chapter 2, the store often boasted that it was bringing the best of New York and Paris to Rochester.

> So smartly clad they seemed to step from fashion portraits, and stamped with the style and cut of the world's most famous designers, twelve models paraded today along a flower-bordered runway in two showings of the annual fashion revue of the SL&C Co Store. . . . Eight professional models from New York were among those who wore the latest creations of Aliz, Lanvin, Mainboucher and Hattie Carnegie and the copies of Paris and New York designed apparel which will be on sale in the Sibley store.[39]

The emphasis on cosmopolitan design did not, however, preclude local tie-ins. At times, stores used local women as models. One type of show that was particularly well received relied on the talents of local high school girls to walk the runways. An audience of friends and family ensured the success of these types of shows.[40]

Some attractions were decidedly more exotic. Department stores occasionally sponsored attractions similar to exhibits seen at world's fairs. From the late nineteenth century onward, "anthropological" exhibits of native peoples from North America, Africa, and the South Pacific were expected features of international and trade fairs. By showing "primitive" civilizations in their "natural" habitats, these exhibits purported to allow a new understanding of human development.[41] Buffalo's Pan-American Exposition in 1901 had showcased an exhibit of native "savages." The popularity of such attractions persisted into the 1930s, and department stores staged them for a nominal fee or, more frequently, free of charge.

Buffalo and Rochester merchants experimented with these types of attractions. In 1932, B. Forman's of Rochester presented a display of Hopi Indians, along with their "curios and craftsmanship." Response to the exhibit was so positive that an extra opportunity for schoolchildren to meet "these picturesque native Americans" was scheduled.[42] The Believe It or Not Odditorium, famous as a big draw at the World's Fair in Chicago, opened in the annex of the E. W. Edwards and Son store in Buffalo in 1933. Performances sponsored by the American Legion ran from noon until midnight. Buffalo residents could see a range of "living wonders," including "Jon T. Bowers, who speaks without vocal chords; Freda Pushni, the armless and legless half girl; Edna Price, swallower of swords and electric bulbs; Singalee, Hindu fire worshipper, whose body apparently is immune to fire; Betty Williams, a Georgia baby with four legs and three arms; Juan and Martina de la Cruz, 'world's smallest people;' Roy Bard, the ossified man; Medusa, with the body of an infant and the head of an adult, and Marden J. Laurello, 'the man with a revolving head.'"[43]

That department stores were willing to house such exhibits, even those considered less educational and more seedy "midway" fare, is not surprising. Even though the odditorium was not linked to the sale of goods per se, it attracted huge crowds that would pass through the store, and at least some audience members would make purchases. These attractions reinforced the role of the store as a cultural center, providing inexpensive or free entertainment to the Buffalo public. Department stores had used these types of attractions from the turn of the century as part of a strategy to dazzle consumers and create the impression of a fantasy world where wishes seemed easily fulfilled. In hard

times, these exhibits remained popular even if the number of sales they produced for the stores dropped. Visits to stores to witness a new exhibit or the
unveiling of a new technology may well have become even more attractive when
the average family's entertainment budget was constrained. Movie attendance
in Buffalo dropped (particularly at first-run theaters, where the price of admission was higher) from 1932 to 1935, with a slight recovery in 1936.[44] Free exhibits such as the odditorium would have been especially appealing to those
who had curtailed other types of entertainment.

Stores were also responsible for hosting entertainments in other venues in
the city. McCurdy's of Rochester rented the Columbus Civic Center in order to
stage a benefit for the store's employee welfare fund. At this benefit, a group
with the unfortunate designation McCurdy's Kotton Klub Komics produced an
old-fashioned minstrel show for a large paying audience; the production included the stereotypical characters Sambo, Rambo, Hambo, and Siambo. Appearing against a "vivid backdrop of the river wharf of a Mississippi-River
plantation," the cast presented stories and songs of the South. White actors
wore blackface. Other stock figures, including the plantation owner's wife, were
trotted out to the delight of patrons. It is unfortunate but perhaps not surprising that the group would openly adopt a name with a KKK acronym and
stage a show based on a nostalgic view of the plantation South, complete with
white performers in blackface. Western New York had been home to active Ku
Klux Klan chapters during the early 1920s; there may have been little stigma to
the name Kotton Klub Komics. Although it had reached its zenith in the mid-
nineteenth century, minstrelsy continued as a popular form of entertainment,
and many of its traditions were incorporated in vaudeville acts and in Harlem
clubs in New York City into the 1930s. The Rochester show appears to have
been a more traditional minstrel show, but it was not an anomaly at the time.[45]

Educational exhibits drawing on local history or the achievements of area
businesses were mainstays in department stores in both Rochester and Buffalo.
Adam, Meldrum and Anderson, in conjunction with the Electrical League of
the Niagara Frontier, held a commemorative show of electrical lights, recognizing the fifty-year anniversary of the opening of the Westinghouse Electric
Company and the building of Buffalo's first commercial generating station.
The store had been the "pioneer user" of electricity in the downtown area, installing the first electric lighting system in Buffalo in 1886.[46] Newspaper coverage of the event pointed out how, in hosting the exhibit, the store was carrying
on a long tradition: "Fifty years ago crowds of local folk jostled each other in
broad aisles, standing entranced to watch 'light that can be turned on and off

like gas, but with no odor, no heat, no matches, and no danger." Yesterday a younger generation stood and chortled at a historical lamp display and the lamps that lighted the Columbian exposition in Chicago in 1893 where millions saw for the first time 'flameless' lighting."[47] Robert B. Adam, president of the store, recalled being present the first time the store was lit. The drama of the event remained a vivid memory for him: electricity—"the flash between the thunder clouds, the omnipotent, indescribable force in the universe, harnessed and tamed and made subservient to the will of man, who refuses to bow before creation"—took the place of the dim yellow gas jets and dangling gas chandeliers in the store. By staging the educational display, the store reminded Buffalonians of its past contributions to the development of the city.

Sibley, Lindsay and Curr hosted a display in 1938 that conflated civic aspirations with local sales. Its "Made in Rochester" exposition featured nearly one hundred local businesses. All of the store's display areas, including its forty-five show windows and areas on every selling floor, were taken over by demonstrations of the manufacture of Rochester products. From Tuesday to Saturday, 10 to 14 May, crowds thronged the exhibits. The range of displays was astounding, covering technical instruments, luxury items, industrial products, and more. Counters were heaped with everything from radios to fishing tackle, playing cards, perfume, and even spaghetti and spices. A report in the paper promised that visitors could see how a necktie was made; learn to hand-dip candy, make eyelash curlers, cut shoes from the original hides, make women's hats, upholster chairs, and play solitaire bridge; or get lessons in modern ironing, sweeping, and coffeemaking. Everything "from potato chips to upholstered chairs, including brooms, mattresses and telephone switch boards," would be made in front of the public, and a large display of the latest cameras, lenses, and instruments would be of further interest. Most of the manufacturers that were granted exhibit space in Sibley's sold their wares in the store throughout the rest of the year. Others were included as well, as the store hoped to "make Rochesterians realize the national and international importance of local companies."[48]

The slogan "What Rochester makes—makes Rochester," adopted previously by the Chamber of Commerce, was emblazoned on signs in the display windows and throughout the store. Classes of schoolchildren visited the store with their teachers to benefit from the educational presentations, and the chance to witness the actual production of goods drew men into the store "in great numbers to see displays of household products bought usually by women."[49] The store's transformation into a place of industrial demonstration and civic expression, rather than simply feminine indulgence, made it a more comfortable destination for Rochester men. A total of one hundred thousand visitors were estimated to have seen the exhibits in the store, not including the many who lined up outside the Main Street windows for a glimpse of live demonstrations. Sibley's presented the exhibit as a chance for the store to express its pride in the community and to encourage others to share this civic spirit. The exhibit proved so popular that it was sponsored in following years. In 1939, Sibley's boasted that it showcased home industries at the city's own "World's Fair."[50]

Sibley's continued to promote local pride and local history in another window exhibit, this one designed in conjunction with the Rochester Museum of Arts and Sciences starting in 1939. Museum staff member Norman Akely created a miniature-scale model of part of downtown Rochester as it had appeared a hundred years previously. Using sketches of the city's oldest buildings (including the First Presbyterian Church, St. Luke's Church, and the Court House) as well as interviews with older residents, Akely hoped to be historically accurate in his portrayal of Rochester in 1839. After completing a few scale buildings, he was going to stop the project when Sibley's approached the museum with the idea of reproducing the whole city at the time. To supplement the museum's sketches, engravings, and watercolors from the nineteenth century (which gave a general sense of the appearance of many buildings), the city engineer's maps of the period were consulted to gauge the location and actual size of the sites that the buildings occupied.

Raymond Shantz began construction of the entire village in Sibley's own workshops, on the eighteenth floor of the store. He was aided in historical research by three museum employees. Ultimately, Shantz made more than fifty buildings and homes. Each model had a framework of balsa wood, with walls created from cardboard cut to shape. Windows were made from transparent acetate, with threads for partitions. Three store display artists painted the buildings, using colors in "as close an approximation of the hues used in early Rochester as could be deduced from the data available."[51] The entire village was assembled using a scale of three-eighths of an inch to one foot. It was then moved down to the store's largest show window. On the Main Street side, the display stretched for twenty-four feet. Completion of the project took four months of work. The finishing touch was the placement of lampposts along the streets of the model—it was thought that dim lighting would best re-create the sense of life in the community during the 1830s. The educational display attracted passersby on Main Street and eventually was donated to the

Museum of Arts and Science, where it became part of the permanent collection (and was still available for viewing in 2003). The creation of the diorama
was the result of the investment of personnel, work space, and resources by
Sibley's, and the painstaking attention to detail by all involved indicated a re-
spect for Rochester's history.

It was not such a stretch for department stores to take on these types of
projects. With their glass display cases and rows of carefully arrayed objects,
these stores in many ways resembled museums.[52] Given that their definition of
service to the community was more flexible than the museum's, however, retailers hosted both the educational exhibits usually associated with trade fairs
or museums and more "lowbrow" attractions such as the odditorium. While
museums took seriously their role in shaping the intellectual life of America,
department stores were not limited to providing strictly edifying fare. Displays
explaining the history of the city or the achievements of local industry were, indeed, promoted as educational, yet even these appeared in the same space
where customers were encouraged to touch and try out different types of merchandise. And while retailers emphasized the public service they provided in
staging such shows, their main goal was simply to draw as many people as possible to the attractions (and, by extension, their stores). They had no com-
punction about switching from an educational exhibit to a display that offered
only entertainment. Thus, the store could act as both industrial fair and midway, museum and sideshow.

Not all events sponsored by retailers took place within the confines of the
stores themselves. Among the most popular of the attractions organized by
area stores were the Christmas parades. During the 1920s, the tradition of a
Thanksgiving Day parade had been famously adopted by Macy's in New York
City.[53] The practice was embraced with enthusiasm by western New York merchants and continued throughout the Depression. In 1936, Sibley, Lindsay and
Curr staged a procession of giant balloons, floats, and clowns in Rochester
that passed down East Avenue and Culver Road and continued to Main Street.
According to the *Democrat and Chronicle,* parents and children gathered early and
jostled for the best vantage points to view the parade. The crowd reached
record proportions, causing congestion in the downtown core. The paper estimated the crowd at eighty thousand. Every artery in the downtown was
choked with cars, streetcars, and pedestrians, despite the efforts of police to
keep traffic moving. Streetcars ran behind schedule for the entire day.[54] Rochester police made a statement that the crowd reached one hundred thousand,
and the *DGMTJ* noted that from atop Sibley's roof, "not a foot of sidewalk

could be seen." Police worked hard to keep the throngs of children and parents from entering the road. Thirty-nine giant balloons made by Goodyear Rubber, including an eighty-foot dragon and the "world's biggest edition of Mickey Mouse," entranced the viewers.[55] After making his way along the parade route, Santa Claus stepped down from his float to enter Sibley's and assume his post in Toyland. At this point, a crowd of children surged into the store, sweeping aside photographers who had been positioned inside to capture the event. Sibley's was able to cope with the crowds, although the counters who stood at the foot of the escalators were unable to keep up with patrons crowded "four and five to a step." The store asserted that nearly ten thousand visitors were counted proceeding to Toyland, with "an unestimated number missed."[56] The fourth floor of the store was roped off into aisles that led to and from a Toyland display with the theme "Twenty-Thousand Leagues under the Sea." The following year, Toyland featured a preview with music of Walt Disney's motion picture *Snow White and the Seven Dwarfs.*[57]

The continued ability of department stores to attract crowds and their new investments in store upgrades and openings should not be taken as an indication that they did not suffer during the Depression. Retail sales slumped as unemployment soared. Buffalo's department store sales in 1933 were only 56 percent of what they had been in the boom years 1925, 1926, and 1927. In fact, sales would not recover to even 80 percent of what they once were until the 1940s.[58] New York merchants felt particularly put-upon because of the tax strategy adopted by the state. In 1933, New York proposed a 1 percent retail sales tax in a desperate attempt to raise revenue to cover growing relief roles and mounting debt. In April of the same year, W. H. Bramley, director of Sibley, Lindsay and Curr, spoke out against the proposed tax. Invoking the ideal of public service, he compared the role of retailers in the community to the role of the state: "Upon retailers, as well as upon government, rests a mandate for the preservation of service to the public. And upon retailers rests also the dire economic necessity of rendering that service within limits of the available funds."[59] In this instance, the rhetoric of service went beyond simply providing assistance in the store. In Bramley's view, retailers played a key role in the functioning of the economy and thus of the nation. Any restrictions that interfered with the ability of merchants to serve the public were counterproductive and would run contrary to the spirit of government efforts to end the economic crisis.

The New York State Council of Retail Merchants quickly passed a resolution against the sales tax measure, and retailers from Buffalo and Rochester formulated arguments against it. Gilbert J. C. McCurdy, president of Mc-Curdy and Company in Rochester, wrote an eloquent essay in the pages of the *Bulletin of the National Retail Dry Goods Association* indicating the special role that merchants could play in solving the economic slump.

> It is a matter of common knowledge that the problems of the depression under which the entire world has labored during these last three years, are problems of distribution. The application of science to industry has long since made possible the production of the necessities of life, and indeed of the complete range of luxuries, in quantities vastly larger than would suffice for our entire population. Yet we behold today the incomprehensible spectacle of want in a land of plenty, of unsatisfied desires in the midst of agencies eager to fulfill those desires, of poverty in a nation of untold wealth, and in the mightiest State of that great Nation.[60]

Retailers, he noted, were precisely the agencies that might fulfill the "unsatisfied desires" of the public, but the proposed legislation would handicap them in their efforts to provide both the necessities and the luxuries that had come to be associated with the American way of life. McCurdy and his fellow members of the New York State Council of Retail Merchants stepped forward to comment not as government experts but as representatives of the retailers in their state, "whose lives have been devoted, in good times and in bad, to the business of distribution, to the sale of goods, to the exchange of the products of labor for the wherewithal to employ more labor." In other words, McCurdy argued, these were people who had spent their careers studying the exact problem facing the country.[61] But how were merchants supposed to help the country and aid recovery, they asked, when a new tax would sap their strength? Bearing the "responsibility for providing the vital impulse for the recovery of employment," merchants were now being asked to provide revenues out of the very capital required to do the job of distribution.

Despite the concerns of merchants, New York passed the 1 percent tax as an emergency bill, which was set to expire on 30 June 1934. Mobilized to respond, civic and commercial groups representing communities in every county and section of the state flocked to a meeting on 15 January 1934 at the ballroom of the Hotel Pennsylvania in New York City. They passed a unanimous motion opposing the present tax, condemning any extension of it beyond the emergency period, and petitioning the governor of the state and all state officials to wipe out the existing tax.[62] Meanwhile, for months after the measure was enacted, the National Retail Dry Goods Association published statements condemning the tax. One Albany department store president suggested that a state retail sales tax was "absolutely opposed to the principles of the National Recovery Act," for it slowed the buying power of the public, which, in turn, slowed the business of the merchant, and that meant only a reduction in factory production and employment.[63]

Buffalo and Rochester merchants continued to be among the tax's most vocal opponents. Weldon Smith, general manager of Adam, Meldrum and Anderson, president of the Retail Merchants Association of Buffalo and director of the New York State Council of Retail Merchants, decried the "psychological effect" of a sales tax, which would only "create buying resistance and diminish spending."[64] Smith argued that merchants in Buffalo and across the state were doing their best to keep the wheels of the economy rolling by encouraging people to buy instead of hoard and to help increase employment. He felt a tax that hit consumers would only delay recovery and impede the efforts of merchants to return to normalcy. The Rochester Retail Merchants' Council added its name to the list of critics of the measure. Gilbert McCurdy presented a brief at a Rochester hearing of the Commission for the Revisions of the Tax Laws of the State of New York, in which he condemned the sales tax not only on behalf of retailers but also "in the interest of our customers, the citizens of Rochester."[65] Ultimately, the combined efforts of retailers across the state proved successful: the sales tax measure was not extended past the June 1934 deadline.

Department stores and other merchants in Buffalo and Rochester continued to cultivate community loyalty and maintain an image of civic leadership in their cities during the Great Depression. Another measure of the persistence of local identities during this period is the way in which those outside the area attempted to capitalize on local sentiment. Department stores and area retailers were not the only ones to recognize the importance of local selling during the 1930s. A number of national manufacturers used local references when selling to area consumers, a phenomenon overlooked by many historians of advertising. In part, this oversight stems from the fact that scholars have not devoted much attention to local or regional advertising. The extensive literature on national advertising and mass-market magazines persuasively demonstrates the emergence of a new style of selling and new techniques to capture the attention of the reader. National advertisers were the originators of the most sophisticated strategies of modern advertising, so it is not surprising that they have attracted so much attention. But at the same time that Americans were poring over the pages of magazine advertising described by scholars including Roland Marchand, Jackson Lears, and Jennifer Scanlon, they were also faced with newspaper ads from businesses in their own communities that often combined new selling techniques with appeals to area pride and loyalty.

Manufacturers with local roots would be expected to use their community connections to foster local pride and thus local sales. Just as retailers pointed to their long-standing history in Buffalo or Rochester or their employment of local people, manufacturers hoped that by suggesting they were from the same place as their patrons, they would encourage brand loyalty. A typical campaign for a local business was one created for Arpeako sausage. It featured a Rochester couple who went away to vacation in the Adirondacks with less than enough sausage meat but were pleasantly surprised to find they could purchase more of their favorite brand from a dealer near their campsite.[66] In this case, patrons of Arpeako were informed of the growing distribution of a local product to a wider circle of stores.

One of the more significant twists on this theme of community promotion involved national ad campaigns that were tailored to the local market. This phenomenon was especially prevalent in campaigns using testimonials. The use of consumer endorsements was nothing new in the 1930s, for the approach dated back well into the nineteenth century. Patent medicines, for example, had long used statements from satisfied customers. To be sure, the use of testimonials had declined by the turn of the twentieth century, in no small part due to the increasing disfavor with which these drug- and alcohol-laced remedies were received. The technique did not fade completely, however, and agencies experimented with ways to increase the reader's confidence in the words of "satisfied customers."[67] Advertisers believed that the most effective ads presented praise for a product coming from an "apparently disinterested party," rather than from the manufacturer or sales representative.[68] Recognizing the negative publicity associated with some testimonial ads, the Advertising Federation of America circulated a statement in 1929 asserting that most advertising was honest but abuse of testimonials needed to be curbed because of its "disproportionate impression upon the public mind."[69] While not wanting to go so far as to suggest coercive measures for advertisers who persisted in using "insincere" testimonials, the federation condemned those who used unscrupulous methods to elicit testimonials.

Endorsements from celebrities and society figures during the 1920s and 1930s were viewed as one way to distance the testimonial from the taint of patent medicines while conveying impressions of high class and good taste. A

very successful campaign for Pond's cold cream, launched in the mid-1920s, re-
vived the use of the testimonial for mainstream products.[70] Celebrity endorsements were effective in selling cosmetics or other luxury items, but not all
products were suited for this strategy. When selling a brand of soap flakes, for
example, testimonials from "average" wives and mothers appeared more be-
lievable than an endorsement from a Hollywood star. Roland Marchand thus
has argued that advertisers in the late 1920s and early 1930s emphasized a new
realism, where stereotypical character types (the businessman, the doctor, the
housewife) were replaced by "real people."[71]

It is here that we see how advertisers combined national campaigns with appeals to the local market. Newspaper ads, though in some ways similar in
layout and copy to magazine ads, offered the additional opportunity for advertisers to feature typical consumers from the actual community in which the
ad would appear. In other words, readers of the *Buffalo Evening News* or the *Rochester Democrat and Chronicle* saw testimonials from real people with similar occupations and concerns who were also western New Yorkers. To give an added
air of authenticity to these statements, advertisers included the full home address as well as the name (and often the job) of the "person on the street."

Ads in western New York papers throughout the 1920s and 1930s included
statements from area residents such as Mrs. Sara Dubawsky, of 10 Winslow
Avenue in Buffalo, who exclaimed, "I'll never go back to those slow-sudsing,
lazy soaps. Not as long as I can get Rinso, the hard-water soap!"[72] Lux soap
featured a letter from "local woman" Mrs. Margaret Furey, of 24 DeWitt
Street in Buffalo, claiming that it was "LIKE THROWING AWAY MONEY TO WASH
COLORED SILKS THE OLD WAY" and demonstrating her new resolve to switch
from other cake soaps, chips, and powders to Lux.[73] Some campaigns would
combine two of the most popular styles of selling in the same ad. In the 1930s,
ad agencies became increasingly enamored of using comic strips to sell. An ad
for Rinso combined the company's typical comic strip with local testimonials.
The strip told the story of two housewives who were comparing their laundry,
while in a separate statement, Mrs. W. MacDermot, of 29 Huetter Avenue in
Tonawanda, New York, exclaimed, "Never saw such suds! I'll never forget the
first time I used Rinso in my washer."[74] She commented that the water was very
hard in Buffalo, and so Rinso was necessary. Another ad that echoed the layout of a news story referred directly to the women of western New York: "You
washed CLOTHES. . . . You washed DISHES. . . . You VOTED 'new improved Chipso
is best'—in Rochester—Albany—Syracuse—Buffalo—Women tried the new
improved Chipso. For two weeks they tested Chipso—for laundry—for

dishes—for cleaning. And the way those speedy Chipso suds got the dirt, opened their eyes."[75] The sense that the ad was speaking directly to the reader (a technique known as appellation) was intensified because Chipso was endorsed by women in the specific area where the reader lived. Chipso based its campaign on the notion of a consumer democracy, where housewives "voted" for their product choices. Another ad featured the testimonials of six women from Albany, Rochester, Buffalo, and Syracuse who were "TYPICAL OF HUNDREDS IN 4 NEW YORK CITIES WHO VOTED 'NEW IMPROVED' CHIPSO BEST PACKAGED SOAP BY FAR."[76] Accounts from women such as Mrs. John Ryan, of 317 Helen Street in Syracuse, were enhanced by personal details: Mrs. Ryan had eight children to wash for and so was qualified as a skilled judge of washing soap.

Given their long associations with testimonial advertising, it is not surprising that the manufacturers of patent medicines would continue to employ this technique. Here, too, the extent to which advertisers included testimonials from area people is notable. Doan's Kidney Pills used the slogan "Ask your neighbor!" to accompany lists of "Rochester cases" who had been cured of aches and pains by the medicine.[77] Some ads included the address of the person endorsing the product as well as the place where he or she purchased it. "Read How These Rochester Folks Found Relief," proclaimed an ad that explained how Elmer E. Laning, stationary fireman, used "two boxes of Doan's Pills from Jones' Drug Store" and was rid of his back pains and how Geo. Wilcox, heating contractor, purchased his pills from Reynolds' Drug Store.[78] In Buffalo, visits from company representatives created an opportunity to solicit testimonials. The words of Mrs. Emma Turner, of 213 Sycamore Street, Buffalo, to a Konjola sales representative at her usual drugstore were reprinted in newspaper ads. She attested, "Konjola proved to be exactly what I needed, and I found this wonderful medicine just when I was about to give up in despair."[79] Readers were encouraged to "Meet the Konjola Man" at the Harvey and Karey Drug Store and hear the praise from a "Grateful Buffalo Lady" for the special medicine.[80]

Even more respectable products, with many national campaigns behind them, experimented with local pitches. An ad for Lifebuoy soap alerted readers that "THIS HAPPENED IN BUFFALO" as a Delaware Avenue woman told of her neighbor's embarrassing body odor experience. Although this woman had many wonderful qualities, she eventually lost her place in Buffalo society because of her hygiene problem. "When we first met her, we all thought her charming. Her clothes were so smart and becoming—her manner so friendly and pleasant. But what a sad disappointment when she spent an evening with us. It was tragic that such apparent charm should be completely ruined by 'B.O.'"[81] The woman went on to explain that while she "wouldn't dream of mentioning" the name of her former friend, she wished that she had the courage to tell her about Lifebuoy. The ad presented a high-class, respected confidant who clearly outlined the worst fear of the socially ambitious: the notion that one improper product choice could jeopardize even the most carefully cultivated image. Readers were encouraged to reflect on their own grooming habits and to wonder whether their own friends would make a similar confession. Yet readers in Buffalo could take their association with the ad one step further; not only was the friendless "B.O." sufferer a real person, she was also identified as someone from their own city. The woman who confessed that "we finally stopped inviting her . . . *all because of 'B.O.'"* was not just any society matron but a resident of one of the Delaware Avenue mansions and as such instantly identified with the upper echelons of Buffalo society.

This ad was different, however, from other testimonials that used local people. The ad's claims to realism rested on the testimony of an unnamed local woman. Given the premise of the ad, the notion that the speaker wanted to preserve both her own anonymity and that of her former friend when speaking of such a delicate subject presumably precluded the listing of her name and address. The ad copy assured the reader that "the above experience was related to us by a woman in this city. It is by no means unusual. It happens far oftener than we realize." Yet it is unlikely that this ad was based on actual testimony or had anything to do with Buffalo in particular. The Lifebuoy ads were created by the New York ad agency of Ruthrauff and Ryann, part of a national campaign linking use of the soap with elimination of body odor.[82] The agency staffers had clearly done some research, enabling them to suggest Delaware Avenue by name as the place where fashionable people were likely to live in Buffalo.

On another level, the Lifebuoy ad had very little to do with the city. It evoked "localness" without the participation of an actual Buffalo resident. The lip service paid to locality was another way for advertisers to personalize their messages and give the impression of relating to the concerns of residents in a particular community. Other examples of this tactic were frequent in newspaper advertising. Climalene water softener asserted that local women had come to realize that "this city's water is too hard for the best washing results." Despite repeated references to "local housewives," "this hard water," and "this city," the ad did not specifically name Buffalo and thus could have been repro-

duced in any city's newspaper with equal success.[83] A Lux soap ad similarly featured an endorsement from an ostensibly local woman who had been dis-
satisfied with her soap until "a buyer in our best department store advised me
always to use Lux."[84] The department store was not named.

Advertisers recognized that different regions had different shopping habits.
In 1938, Scripps-Howard Newspapers commissioned a study of the buying
habits and brand preferences of consumers in sixteen cities, including Buffalo.
Nationwide, over fifty-three thousand housewives completed the survey. Over
four thousand randomly selected Buffalo housewives filled out questionnaires,
providing an inventory of household products and describing their choice of
stores.[85] In Buffalo, women were encouraged to fill out the forms by Marie
Daigler, president of the Buffalo Council of Parents and Teachers (the PTA).
Since PTA groups did not exist in all areas to be included in the survey, the
ladies' auxiliaries or other clubs from twenty different churches were used to
help distribute and return the cards.[86] Scripps-Howard paid all these organizations for their participation. The reports represented 3 percent of Buffalo's
population. Punch cards were then used by IBM to tabulate the results of the
questionnaires. The completed study allowed a comparison of the sixteen cities
with the national average and each other.

The respondents to the survey were in some ways self-selecting, for only
those who could read and write in English and were involved in community or
church organizations were able to fill out the questionnaires. For this reason,
the survey likely provided a more accurate picture of the shopping habits of
middle-class, native-stock Buffalo as opposed to the practices of the residents
of working-class or ethnic neighborhoods. As mentioned, the ladies' auxiliaries
of churches scattered across the city were involved in collecting the survey, but
it should be noted that Scripps-Howard did not focus on Buffalo's white,
Anglo-Saxon, Protestant elite in its selection of churches: Catholic, Protestant,
and Jewish groups were all represented. Members from two Polish churches,
one missionary society, and one Seventh-Day Adventist Church were participants. Respondents were also most likely married women and, more specifically, mothers (given that the PTA was a major force in collecting the surveys).
This fact would also skew the sample toward established households in which
wives had sufficient time to respond to the survey. Newly married couples, single people, the unemployed, the poor, the illiterate, non–English speakers, and
single parents would be less likely to participate in the survey.

Nevertheless, Scripps-Howard endeavored to gain a cross-section of the city.
The map of Buffalo was divided so that each census tract was put into one of

three groups. The median rental cost for each tract was used to determine whether residents in a particular district fit into the top 17 percent, the middle 58 percent, or the bottom 25 percent of probable income levels. The company's representatives gathered reports from a proportionate number of families in each group, and within the groups, a proportionate number of respondents from each tract were culled for the sample. The representativeness of the sample was tested in each city against findings that included the numbers of renters and owners of homes in each area, types of homes, and number of persons per family.[87] Because the sample included families from every tract throughout the city and because Scripps-Howard consciously included proportionate numbers from areas representing a range of income levels, we can take the findings of the survey as representative of larger consuming patterns in the city. Although certain groups were excluded by the methodology of the inventory, the Scripps-Howard Home Inventory, as it was titled, provides a useful snapshot of the shopping habits of Buffalonians for the purposes of this volume.

The Scripps-Howard survey suggests that by 1938, nationally branded goods dominated the shelves in Buffalo homes (as well as homes in other cities in the survey). When asked about their brand preferences for over twenty products, the Buffalo housewives overwhelmingly chose national brands. From Pond's Cold Cream to Coca-Cola, respondents displayed a familiarity with and a preference for nationally established products. When asked to name their favorite mayonnaise, for example, 55.8 percent said Kraft and another 15.6 percent named Hellmann's.[88] The only "regional" brand to make the list was Red and White (the house brand of the Red and White grocery chain), which was mentioned by only 2.1 percent of respondents. Buffalonians overwhelmingly chose brand names when selecting grocery items such as canned soups. Thus, 82.3 percent of Buffalo households named Campbell's tomato soup as their favorite brand. Such was the case for all three class groups in the survey: respondents from the top income group (ranked according to the real estate value of the census tracts in which they lived) were slightly less likely to choose Campbell's than respondents in the other two groups.[89] Some brands that were nationally available but had local ties did comparatively better in Buffalo than in the other cities surveyed. Nabisco's Shredded Wheat, which was produced at a factory in nearby Niagara Falls, New York, was preferred by 19.0 percent of Buffalo households surveyed, compared with the average in all sixteen cities of 11.7 percent.[90]

The Scripps-Howard Home Inventory did reveal regional differences in product choices. Yet in most categories, the competition for market share was between two or more national contenders. In other words, while more people preferred Kraft packaged cheese in Cleveland, Columbus, and Washington than in Buffalo, it was still the overwhelming favorite in all four cities, and the next choice for housewives in Buffalo, Cleveland, and Columbus was Borden's, not a locally produced brand.[91]

More distinctive than the brand choices were the shopping habits of residents in different cities. Scripps-Howard was able to conclude that Saturday was the heavy food marketing day in all cities, where an average of 41.2 percent of the week's food budget was spent (42.7 percent in Buffalo).[92] Less consistent was the day of the week when people shopped in the downtown area. Although Saturday was the most popular day to shop overall, different cities had distinct patterns in weekday shopping. Buffalo reported Thursday as the busiest weekday, while for Washington, D.C., Thursday was the least busy day of the week. Residents of Akron, Ohio, shopped on Wednesday, whereas those in Cleveland shopped on Tuesday.[93]

The study revealed that whereas certain items were likely to be purchased at a chain store, others were much more the domain of the independent merchant. Thus, although over a quarter (25.7 percent) of Buffalo housewives surveyed reported that they shopped most frequently at the A&P, when asked where they last purchased fresh meat, only 5.2 percent said that they had done so at the national chain. In contrast, 55.3 percent reported buying meat from an independent grocer, and another 11.5 percent patronized a butcher or meat market. Similarly, while only 18.9 percent said that they patronized independent grocers most frequently, 54.5 percent reported that they had last purchased fresh vegetables from an independent grocer.[94] In contrast, a packaged item such as canned milk or cold cereal was much more likely to have been purchased at a chain grocer.[95] This wide discrepancy in the preferred point of purchase for groceries, meats, and vegetables indicates that many households went to independent stores for certain items, even if they considered themselves chain store shoppers.

The impression of Buffalo housewives as chain store shoppers becomes even more complicated when the existence of regional chains is taken into account. A&P was, indeed, identified as the most popular grocery store in the city. Yet closer study reveals that local stores still accounted for more business than national chains. If those who shopped at various *regional* chains (including Danahy-Faxon, Loblaw, Red and White, and Mohican Markets) were grouped together, they would make up a larger percentage than the A&P shoppers. Regional chains, as discussed in chapter 4, hoped to combine the purchasing power of a large organization with appeals to local loyalty and thus enjoy the best of both worlds. From the statistics developed by the Scripps-Howard survey, they appeared to be successful in doing so.

Moving away from the grocery trade, when asked about cosmetic items or household goods, Buffalo housewives indicated that they bought nationally advertised goods but from independent merchants. The 4,191 Buffalo housewives in the sample were asked at which one department store they shopped most frequently. Women in all three income groups overwhelmingly selected independent department stores as their first choice: J. N. Adam's was named as the favorite by 27.3 percent of Buffalo housewives, followed by Adam, Meldrum and Anderson at 21.9 percent, Sattler's at 11.9 percent, and Hengerer's at 11.9 percent. Sears, Roebuck was chosen by only 4 percent of those surveyed.[96] Again, however, if we imagine a typical shopper's range of purchases, we can see that Buffalo housewives shopped at department stores for some items and chain or discount stores for others. Prestige items such as face cream, dry rouge, or lipstick were more likely to be purchased at department stores.[97] Department stores faced much stiffer competition from five-cents-to-a-dollar stores for smaller items such as nail polish, safety razors, or toothbrushes.[98]

The findings of the Scripps-Howard study reinforce the value of using local and regional perspectives when considering the history of consuming. Moreover, a focus on the history of a specific type of retail institution can reveal certain things but mask others. For example, in considering the rise of chain stores, one might posit a point in time when most consumers switched from patronizing old-fashioned independent stores to embrace the modernity of the chain store. The household inventory suggests that often the same shopper might go to a locally owned department store for clothing, purchase cosmetics at the five-and-dime, buy canned goods at a chain store, and shop for meat at an independent grocer. Only by considering the range of options available to residents in particular regions or communities can we get a full sense of how consumers interacted with the marketplace. This study has tried to suggest that the interaction of both retailers and consumers in western New York with the American mass market was a complex process of negotiation. The same Buffalo woman who shopped at Woolworth's one day went to J. N. Adam's the next; similarly, the same family that read national magazines and saw ads for nationally branded goods read the Rochester newspaper and its ads for local businesses.

This chapter has suggested that even in the hard times of the late 1930s, appeals to local loyalty and identity remained a significant component of the selling strategy of area merchants and were even picked up by national advertisers. Even (or perhaps especially) during hard times, the retailers of western New York were still deeply connected to the very psyche of the communities in which they were located. During the Depression, merchants continued in their roles as cultural brokers, bringing diverse entertainments to their cities and staging celebrations of local achievements and potential.

Department stores and other downtown retailers assumed a mantle of economic as well as cultural leadership during hard times; many felt that as experts in distribution, they had a special part to play in ensuring America's economic recovery. The high level of reinvestment in downtown stores in Buffalo reflected not only this sense of authority but also a feeling of underlying optimism in the future of western New York. That things did not turn out as the retailers and other area leaders predicted perhaps indicates a certain naïveté and a tendency toward boosterism that, in retrospect, seems misguided; retailers did not solve the problems of the Depression, and in the postwar period, suburban development would outstrip the growth of the downtown. This observation should not be taken to indicate, however, that the connection between community identity and retailers did not have a certain resonance or that local citizens did not respond to such appeals. Retailers in Rochester and Buffalo assumed many different roles. Their fostering of local pride was, in many ways, inseparable from their other economic and social functions.

Epilogue

In August 1957, the board of directors of Sibley, Lindsay and Curr in Rochester voted unanimously to recommend acceptance of an offer from Associated Dry Goods to buy all of Sibley's common stock. At the time, the vast majority of the store's shares were held by descendants of the company's founders or early investors.[1] The board of directors assured staff and customers that even if Sibley's was bought by Associated Dry Goods, the store's traditions and policies would remain the same. All twelve hundred Rochester employees of the store would retain their jobs. Local patrons as well were reassured that they would not see major changes at their beloved store. Although Associated Dry Goods was a national company, it allowed its stores a high level of independence in their operations. John R. Sibley, son of the store's founder, explained to the *Rochester Times-Union* why he had given his personal seal of approval to the deal: "One of the many things I like about Associated is the strict home-management aspect of its operation. The corporation calls it 'autonomy.' I prefer to look on it as home-management. Associated is a huge organization which, with the Sibley business, will do about 250 million dollars worth of business a year, yet in its headquarters on Madison Avenue, New York, it employs a staff of only 15 people. That's an indication of how thoroughly autonomous its various store operations are."[2] Sibley stated that he had long observed Associated Dry Goods operations in other cities and noted that although he had received many offers for the store over the years, he settled on that company because he "wanted to live to see that all that my father and his partners built should come into the best possible hands."[3]

Robert J. McKim, president of Associated Dry Goods, stressed that Sibley's would not become a chain store because of the sale. Describing his organization as "a group of stores, rather than a chain," he emphasized that "our stores have strong individual personalities reflecting their many years of operation in their own communities."[4] Although the company's overall management was centralized, many aspects of store operations remained under local control. Buying was not done through a central office but by the stores themselves.

Further, the company encouraged stores to assert their individuality in terms of display and merchandising. The main function of the head office in Manhattan was to analyze and disseminate information on sales, costs, finance, and administrative techniques. Sibley's board of directors underscored that in joining Associated Dry Goods, the store would operate as an autonomous division, while enjoying the competitive benefits of being part of a much larger organization. Above all, the store would retain its local character. A statement released to the public asserted, "It will be a store managed and operated by Rochesterians, who know Rochester and its people."[5]

As this study has demonstrated, the assertion that the store was maintaining its proud local traditions even as it joined a new type of business organization was nothing new. Sibley's was not even the first western New York store to join Associated Dry Goods, as J. N. Adam's and Hengerer's of Buffalo had long been part of the organization. Other area stores had participated in buying groups, which combined the power to bargain for low prices from suppliers with the ability to assert independent status. What is clear from the statements by both store officials and Associated Dry Goods spokespeople is that it remained very important to Sibley's public image to be perceived as a local institution, with a proper appreciation for Rochester's particular history and tastes. The sense that the store served Rochesterians in a way that other interlopers could not survived well into the postwar period.

During the 1920s and 1930s, retailers in Rochester and Buffalo affirmed their position in the communities they served. They were active in civic life, providing a range of services and entertainments that went beyond the simple sale of goods. In some ways, though, the interwar period witnessed significant changes in the business of selling. As Buffalo and Rochester stores became more integrated into national networks, they risked losing what had made them distinct. The sale of stores to Associated Dry Goods, the joining of group-buying associations by other independent stores, and even the very success of Buffalo and Rochester merchants in bringing the world to western New York were all developments that had both positive and negative implications. Retailers who changed how they did business, even in the interest of bringing more selection or better prices to local markets, risked diluting whatever local identity there was left in these institutions.

A close examination of retailing and marketing in western New York during the 1920s and 1930s reveals, however, that the local remained important in the way consumers experienced the market. Residents of Buffalo and Rochester took pride in knowing about the latest fashions or being able to purchase the same mass-produced item advertised in national magazines. Yet they also responded to retailers' appeals to local loyalty. Consumers flocked to exhibits of city-made goods and celebrated the opening of new stores or improved facilities as symbolic of the growth of their communities. During hard times, they attended special promotions that promised to help area businesses or they pledged to spend more money locally.

For their part, retailers were happy to cultivate the notion that they had played a prominent role in the evolution of Buffalo and Rochester. Merchants were visible business leaders, active in local chambers of commerce, and tireless in their boosting. In their advertising, they trumpeted the advances of their cities as well as their stores. In the 1920s, they navigated new forms of competition by asserting their local roots while simultaneously keeping an eye on developments in the rest of the nation and the world. Retailers in western New York used new innovations in communication to keep abreast of trends around the globe. They assured patrons that they could purchase the best of Parisian fashion or the same items advertised in the *Ladies' Home Journal* without going to New York City. When chain stores appeared to threaten their position, Buffalo and Rochester retailers adopted strategies such as group buying yet never conceded the moral superiority of their independent status. Chain stores as well learned to cultivate local goodwill by emphasizing how they recruited area personnel and stocked locally produced goods.

As economic conditions worsened, retailers used the same emphasis on home buying to encourage patrons to spend money in their own cities. They devoted columns of their advertising space to explanations of the chain of distribution and the need for increased consumer spending. They blamed hoarding and "selfish thrift" for creating unemployment, and they formulated different strategies to engage the public. Merchants in Buffalo organized a special day of sales that was intended to restore consumer confidence and provide a boost to the local economy. Rochester's Pledge for Prosperity campaign was premised on a similar understanding of private spending as the key to ending the Depression. Even after the failure of such initiatives, retailers remained active in their communities and devoted considerable resources to store improvements throughout the late 1930s. We must always keep in mind, of course, that the retailers who made local appeals were not purely altruistic. By evoking local sentiment, they often hoped to gain a competitive edge over newly arrived chain store branches or stores in nearby cities. Yet at the same time, merchants took their role in civic affairs seriously. They were active in promoting local causes, helping charities, and finding solutions to area problems.

In his study of Buffalo's automobile clubs, Ernest Grogan Brown argues that trends in mass leisure cannot be understood without paying close attention to local particularities. He notes, "Despite fears of local institutions being unable to resist the hegemonic pressures of mass society, many have flourished, giving a local character to mass phenomena, and acted as mediators or agents between mass society and the individual."[6] Brown's observations about car culture can be broadened to include larger developments in leisure and consumption. Buffalo and Rochester consumers experienced the mass market through the filter of local institutions. Retailers in western New York often assumed the role of cultural mediators, bringing not only specific types of goods but also celebrities, entertainments, and exhibits to Rochester and Buffalo for the edification and amusement of local patrons.

I have argued in this work that the study of medium-sized cities is important to an effort to fully comprehend the history of American consumerism. While many scholars interested in examining trends in retailing, advertising, and consuming have looked to developments in larger cities such as New York or Chicago as emblematic of national cultural changes, I have worked from the premise that New York City was not America and that there is much to be learned from examining the experiences of retailers and consumers who lived outside the metropolis.

And while cities such as Buffalo and Rochester are crucial to a full understanding of the American mass market and the development of a consumer culture, retailers are key to a nuanced view of the life of these centers. Examining the consumption patterns of the city can provide many insights into civic life in the 1920s and 1930s. Stores, particularly the major retailers clustered on the Main Streets of Buffalo and Rochester, were central to the cultural lives of these cities. Taking a closer look at retailing in western New York allows us to better understand how Americans in different regions and communities of different sizes interacted with the mass market and found their own ways to "consume locally." As we enter an age when not merely national but also global trends seem to have more and more impact on our daily lives, it is worth remembering the ways in which the local continued (and continues) to matter.

Appendix

Consumption Patterns in Upstate New York, 1920 to 1940

Table 1: Urban Territories in the United States, 1920

Size	Number	Population	% Urban Population	% Total Population
All urban areas	2,787	54,304,603	100.0	51.4
1,000,000 or more	3	10,145,532	18.7	9.6
500,000 to 1,000,000	9	6,223,769	11.5	5.9
250,000 to 500,000	13	4,540,838	8.4	4.3
100,000 to 250,000	43	6,519,187	12.0	6.2
50,000 to 100,000	76	5,265,747	9.7	5.0
25,000 to 50,000	143	5,075,041	9.2	4.8
10,000 to 25,000	459	6,942,742	12.8	6.6
5,000 to 10,000	721	4,997,794	9.2	4.7
2,500 to 5,000	1,320	4,593,953	8.5	4.3

Source: U.S. Department of Commerce, *Abstract of the Fourteenth Census of the United States*, table 14, page 74.

Table 2: Major Downtown Retailers in Buffalo, 1920–1940

Name	Location
J. N. Adam and Company	383–393 Main Street
Adam, Meldrum and Anderson Company	396–408 Main Street
E. W. Edwards	460–470 Main Street
Davis Brothers	West Ferry and Grant
Flint and Kent	554–562 Main Street
Wm. Hengerer Company	457–471 Main Street
Hens and Kelly Company	478–488 Main Street
W. T. Grant Company	546–552 Main Street
Jahraus-Braun Company	977–979 Broadway
Oppenheim, Collins and Company	Main and Huron
Sears, Roebuck and Company	1095 Main (at Jefferson)

Table 3: Major Downtown Retailers in Rochester, 1920–1940

Duffy-Powers	Main Street at Fitzhugh
E. W. Edwards	110 and 144–158 Main Street East
B. Forman	46 Clinton Avenue South
McCurdy and Company	219–274 Main Street East (at Elm)
National Clothing Company	159 Main Street East
Neisner Brothers	200 Main Street East (main branch)
Sibley, Lindsay and Curr Company	228–280 Main Street East (at Clinton)
W. T. Grant Company	293 Main Street East

Table 4: Net Sales, Gross Earnings, and Net Earnings of Sibley, Lindsay and Curr, 1920–1940

Year	Net Sales	Gross Earnings	Income Tax	Net Earnings
1920	10,680,726	970,260	345,256	625,004
1921	11,094,573	1,438,940	136,974	1,301,966
1922	11,522.685	1,557,505	408,180	1,149,325
1923	12,684,411	2,009,616	187,950	1,821,666
1924	12,668,293	1,416,831	213,280	1,203,551
1925	12,623,774	1,323,711	161,385	1,162,326
1926	13,504,706	1,024,489	148,024	876,456
1927	13,107,305	1,346,591	123,358	1,223,233
1928	12,816,108	1,055,961	127,766	928,195
1929	12,606,898	936,199	115,157	821,042
1930	11,504,721	584,865	143,126	441,739
1931	10,248,562	302,319	30,000	272,319
1932	7,994,247	19,986	5,000	14,986
1933	7,710,850	98,802	11,000	87,802
1934	8,052,629	188,838	25,000	163,838
1935	8,382,970	221,004	26,000	105,004
13 months ending 31 January 1937	9,923,347	306,578	49,500	257,078
Fiscal year ending 31 January 1938	9,911,941	51,912	18,000	33,912
1939	9,248,762	152,435	24,000	128,435
1940	9,693,219	418,074	52,000	366,074

Source: Carton "Annual Reports, Homer Hoyt, Market Survey and Appraisal," table 18, Sibley Collection, Strong Museum.

Table 5: Buffalo Business Indexes, 1928–1936 (1933 = 100%)

	Motion Picture Receipts	Bank Debits	Department Store Sales	Factory Payrolls
1928	N/A	235	171	247
1929	N/A	284	170	263
1930	N/A	214	157	210
1931	N/A	159	138	153
1932	130	110	107	98
1933	100	100	100	100
1934	98	109	108	130
1935	91	119	115	150
1936	96	136	130	186

Source: SS, May 1937, 3.

Table 6: Index of Sales of Buffalo Department Stores, 1925–1935, by Month
(Not adjusted for seasonal variation or number of days in month)
1925–1926–1927 = 100%

	1925	1926	1927	1928	1929	1930	1931	1932	1933	1934	1935
January	82.2	83.1	75.2	74.5	79.6	70.6	65.6	54.7	39.3	44.0	47.7
February	80.1	77.9	74.4	74.9	73.7	66.4	60.4	54.3	37.7	44.2	45.6
March	91.3	82.0	81.6	84.3	89.4	81.6	75.6	59.3	42.4	63.6	57.6
April	113.8	101.1	109.9	96.8	95.4	100.8	98.1	71.8	63.4	63.0	67.0
May	107.7	104.8	103.6	102.2	107.2	97.4	76.4	55.7	59.9	62.3	61.2
June	102.8	96.6	95.4	91.4	92.9	84.7	80.8	58.7	54.9	59.1	61.7
July	75.9	72.1	70.3	68.3	70.3	63.3	56.2	38.8	41.2	39.2	44.3
August	73.9	76.8	82.3	70.1	72.8	64.5	60.8	45.0	54.0	51.7	54.7
September	98.3	97.8	96.7	101.9	99.1	100.2	79.6	65.0	58.6	59.9	68.6
October	134.1	114.5	120.0	119.2	115.3	95.4	82.6	62.9	65.6	71.1	71.0
November	102.4	104.3	101.4	100.4	97.8	86.5	71.7	59.0	56.2	62.9	77.2
December	173.6	169.8	172.0	171.8	158.1	149.1	126.4	96.8	103.3	112.5	123.0

Source: BBSR, Data for Statistical Surveys, Box 2 "Sales," Folder "Department Store Sales," UBA.

Table 7: Pledges for the Rochester Pledge for Prosperity Campaign, by Ward

Ward	Total Pledges	Amount	Average Pledge
1	77	$ 69,045	$ 896.69
2	39	105,275	2,699.36
3	88	84,865	964.38
4	143	318,600	2,227.97
5	137	91,807	670.12
6	271	201,927	745.12
7	14	70,650	5,046.43
8	197	129,118	655.42
9	75	29,655	395.40
10	1,391	438,230	315.05
11	100	47,690	476.90
12	716	456,806.69	638.00
13	176	37,188.50	211.30
14	611	256,879.75	420.43
15	107	155,321.50	1,451.60
16	116	31,027	267.47
17	368	106,547.50	289.53
18	514	144,802.50	281.72
19	1,919	829,491.25	423.25
20	227	543,421.28	2,393.93
21	228	205,934.50	903.22
22	447	82,812.10	185.26
23	232	83,724	360.88
24	537	668,315.11	1,244.53
Totals	8730	$ 5,189,133.00	$ 594.40

(Totals are for city wards; pledges in the rest of the county are not included)

Source: *RD&C*, 15 December 1931, 14.

Table 8: *Index of Sales of Buffalo Department Stores, 1928–1937, by Year*
(Not adjusted for seasonal variation or number of days in month)
1925–1926–1927 = 100%

Year	Monthly Average
1928	96.3
1929	96.0
1930	88.4
1931	77.9
1932	60.2
1933	56.4
1934	61.1
1935	65.0
1936	73.7
1937	78.2

Source: "Buffalo Business Indices," BBSR, Box 2 "Sales," Folder "Department Stores," UBA.

Table 9: *Department Stores Most Frequently Patronized by Buffalo Housewives, 1938*

J. N. Adam	27.3%
Adam, Meldrum and Anderson	21.9
Sattler's	12.8
Hengerer's	11.9
Hens and Kelly	6.2
Edwards	5.4
Sears, Roebuck	4.0
Baker's	3.8
Flint and Kent	1.5
Others	5.2

Source: Scripps-Howard Newspapers, *Market Records*, 247.

Table 10: Grocery Stores Most Frequently Patronized by Buffalo Housewives, 1938

A&P	25.7%
Danahy-Faxon	16.6
Loblaws	16.2
Red and White	4.4
IGA	4.3
Bishop Stores	4.3
Sattler's Grocery Dept.	3.9
Mohican Markets	3.8
BWG Stores	1.9
Others	18.9

Source: Scripps-Howard Newspapers, *Market Records*, 247.

Notes

Abbreviations Used in the Notes

NEWSPAPERS AND PERIODICALS

BCE	*Buffalo Courier-Express*
BEN	*Buffalo Evening News*
CSA	*Chain Store Age*
CSM	*Chain Store Manager*
DGMTJ	*Dry Goods Merchants Trade Journal*
DSB	*Department Store Buyer*
MM	*Merchandise Manager*
NATMA	*National Association of Teachers of Marketing and Advertising Bulletin*
NRDGA	*Bulletin of the National Retail Dry Goods Association*
RD&C	*Rochester Democrat and Chronicle*
RTU	*Rochester Times-Union*
SS	*Statistical Survey*
TT	*Town Tidings*

ARCHIVES AND COLLECTIONS

BBR	Bureau of Business Research, Harvard Business School
BBSR	Bureau of Business and Social Research, University of Buffalo
BECHS	Buffalo and Erie County Historical Society
BECPL	Special Collections and Local History Room, Central Branch, Buffalo and Erie County Public Library
BLHU	Special Collections, Baker Library, Harvard University
RHS	Rochester Historical Society
Strong	Special Collections, Margaret Woodbury Strong Museum, Rochester, New York
UBA	University Archives, State University of New York at Buffalo

Introduction

1. David Potter, *People of Plenty: Economic Abundance and the American Character,* and Daniel Boorstin, *The Americans: The Democratic Experience.* Even some critics of consumer culture have emphasized the homogenizing (if alienating) tendencies of these developments. See, for example, Warren I. Susman, *Culture as History: The Transformation of American Society in the Twentieth Century.* The literature on American consumer culture is sizable. One good starting point is the bibliographic essay by Lawrence B. Glickman in his edited collection *Consumer Society in American History: A Reader,* 399–414. See also Tom Pendergast, "Consuming Questions: Scholarship on Consumerism in America to 1940."

2. William Leach, *Land of Desire: Merchants, Power, and the Rise of a New American Culture,* 15. A number of scholars have tried to push back the date of a "consumer revolution" into the early nineteenth and even the eighteenth centuries. See T. H. Breen, "'Baubles of Britain': The American and Consumer Revolution of the Eighteenth Century," *Past and Present* 119 (1988): 73–104; this article, as well as others by James Axtell and Joyce Appleby on the "Roots of American Consumer Society," appear in Glickman, ed., *Consumer Society,* 84–144. In English historiography, see Neil McKendrick, Colin Brewer, and J. H. Plumb, eds., *The Birth of a Consumer Society: The Commercialization of Eighteenth-Century England.* For a review of this debate, see Peter N. Stearns, "Stages of Consumerism: Recent Work on the Issues of Periodization," 110–17. There appears to be some consensus, however, that any discussion of *mass* consumption properly begins in the years after the American Civil War and that the early twentieth century witnessed a new phase in the maturation of retailing, advertising, and marketing techniques in the country.

3. See Leach, *Land of Desire;* Susan Porter Benson, *Counter Cultures: Saleswomen, Managers, and Customers in American Department Stores, 1890–1940;* and Elaine Abelson, *When Ladies Go A-Thieving: Middle-Class Shoplifters in the Victorian Department Store.*

4. Roland Marchand, *Advertising the American Dream: Making Way for Modernity, 1920–1940.* For other works that focus primarily on national advertising, see T. J. Jackson Lears, *Fables of Abundance: A Cultural History of Advertising in America;* James D. Norris, *Advertising and the Transformation of American Society, 1865–1920;* Daniel Pope, *The Making of Modern Advertising;* and Michael Schudson, *Advertising, the Uneasy Persuasion: Its Dubious Impact on American Society.* On marketing, see Susan Strasser, *Satisfaction Guaranteed: The Making of the American Mass Market;* Richard S. Tedlow, *New and Improved: The Story of Mass Marketing in America;* and Pamela Walker Laird, *Advertising Progress: American Business and the Rise of Consumer Marketing.*

5. Matthew Schneirov, *The Dream of a New Social Order: Popular Magazines in America, 1893–1914;* Helen Damon-Moore, *Magazines for the Millions: Gender and Commerce in the* Ladies' Home Journal *and the* Saturday Evening Post, *1880–1910;* and Jennifer Scanlon, *Inarticulate Longings: The* Ladies' Home Journal, *Gender, and the Promises of Consumer Culture.*

6. Richard Ohmann, *Selling Culture: Magazines, Markets, and Class at the Turn of the Century.*

7. Roy Rosenzweig, *Eight Hours for What We Will: Workers and Leisure in an Industrial City, 1870–1920*; Francis G. Couvares, *The Remaking of Pittsburgh: Class and Culture in an Industrializing City, 1877–1919*; Kathy Peiss, *Cheap Amusements: Working Women and Leisure in Turn-of-the-Century New York*; Lizabeth Cohen, *Making a New Deal: Industrial Workers in Chicago, 1919–1939*; Andrew Heinze, *Adapting to Abundance: Jewish Immigrants, Mass Consumption, and the Search for American Identity*; and George Sanchez, *Becoming Mexican American: Ethnicity, Culture, and Identity in Chicano Los Angeles, 1900–1945.*

8. On the South, see Ted Ownby, *American Dreams in Mississippi: Consumers, Poverty and Culture, 1830–1998.* For rural consumers, see David Blanke, *Sowing the American Dream: How Consumer Culture Took Root in the Rural Midwest*; Ronald R. Kline, *Consumers in the Country: Technology and Social Change in Rural America*; and the chapter on rural consumers in Susan J. Matt, *Keeping Up with the Joneses: Envy in American Consumer Society, 1890–1930.*

9. Douglas makes a good case for New York's significance, although she expands her scope to include figures who lived far from Manhattan, claiming Ernest Hemingway, T. S. Eliot, Sigmund Freud, Gertrude Stein, and Henry James as intellectual and spiritual New Yorkers. The city's indisputable artistic and cultural output should not, however, be simply taken as wholly representative of a new national culture. Ann Douglas, *Terrible Honesty: Mongrel Manhattan in the 1920s*, 3–28.

10. Gary Cross, *An All-Consuming Century: Why Commercialism Won in Modern America.*

11. See, for example, William Leach, *Country of Exiles: The Destruction of Place in American Life.*

12. U.S. Department of Commerce, Bureau of the Census, *Abstract of the Fourteenth Census of the United States: 1920*, table 14, page 74.

13. Bertha M. Nienburg, *The Woman Home-Maker in the City: A Study of Statistics Relating to Married Women in the City of Rochestester, N.Y. at the Census of 1920*, 8.

Chapter 1

1. David A. Gerber, *The Making of an American Pluralism: Buffalo, New York, 1825–1860*, 5.

2. See Carol Sheriff, *The Artificial River: The Erie Canal and the Paradox of Progress, 1817–1862.*

3. John F. Barry and Robert W. Elmes, *Buffalo's Text Book*, 13.

4. Gerber, *American Pluralism*, 5.

5. Quoted in ibid., 7.

6. Paul E. Johnson's *A Shopkeeper's Millennium: Society and Revivals in Rochester* remains the definitive study of religious revivals in the area.

7. Federal Writers' Project, Works Progress Administration, State of New York, *Rochester and Monroe County: A History and Guide*, 73.

8. Barry and Elmes, *Buffalo's Text Book*, 13.

9. Mark Goldman, *High Hopes: The Rise and Decline of Buffalo, New York*, 129.

10. Blake McKelvey, *Rochester on the Genesee: The Growth of a City*, 63.

11. Ibid., 34.

12. "Great Industry Outgrowth of New Idea in Merchandising," *Buffalo Live Wire*, May 1925, 4.

13. McKelvey, *Rochester on the Genesee*, 64, 108.

14. Joseph W. Barnes, "The City's Golden Age," 6.

15. Ibid., 7.

16. Federal Writers' Project, *Rochester and Monroe County*, 74–77.

17. *The Industries of Buffalo: A Resume of the Mercantile and Manufacturing Progress of the Queen City of the Lakes, Together with a Condensed Summary of Her Material Development and History and a Series of Comprehensive Sketches of Her Representative Business Houses*, 73–74.

18. *Buffalo Evening News* (hereafter *BEN*), 14 November 1929, 6.

19. *Industries of Buffalo*, 245.

20. Charles S. Illingworth, "This I Remember—VIII: Down Town," 89–90.

21. *The Pan-American Exposition, May 1 to November 1, 1901: Its Purpose and Plan*.

22. Historian and retired surgeon Jack C. Fisher has argued that McKinley's doctors were unfairly blamed for his death, for their treatment was entirely appropriate given the state of medical knowledge at the time. Fisher contends that no physician in 1901 would have been able to save the president, although similar wounds would be treatable today. See Jack C. Fisher, *Stolen Glory: The McKinley Assassination*.

23. Blake McKelvey, "Historic Predecessors of the Central Business District," *Rochester History*, 2. Buffalo Street would eventually be renamed Main Street East (perhaps as a slight to a nearby rival city), so by the 1920s, the term *Four Corners* would refer to the intersection of Main, State, and Exchange.

24. Advertisement for McCurdy and Company, *Rochester Democrat and Chronicle* (hereafter *RD&C*), 1 January 1926, 3.

25. Blake McKelvey, *Rochester, the Flower City—1855–1890*, 23.

26. McKelvey, "Historic Predecessors," 7.

27. Ibid.

28. Ibid., 10, 22.

29. "A Glorious Past," *News and Notes from the Rochester Historical Society*.

30. Untitled document dated 1947, Carton "History 1868–1926," Folder "Reports," Sibley Collection, Strong Museum, 1. The store continued to act as a wholesaler until 1929, when many of the dry goods merchants in smaller towns that had relied on Sibley's were pushed out of business by branches of stores such as Sears, Roebuck; Montgomery Ward; and J. C. Penney.

31. McKelvey, "Historic Predecessors," 15.

32. Goldman, *High Hopes*, 187.

33. Charles S. Illingworth, "Buffalo Theatres—1898–1908," 42–43.

34. Goldman, *High Hopes*, 187. Ad for the Deco Restaurant, featuring the "Queen City" sandwich—"20¢ Hamburg with bacon, cheese and cole slaw"—*Buffalo Courier-Express* (hereafter *BCE*), 9 December 1933, 7.

35. *Buffalo Live Wire*, May 1923, 11.

36. "Golden Jubilee of Electric Lighting," 29 February to 7 March 1936, pamphlet celebrating golden jubilee of Westinghouse Electric, commemorated by an electrical exhibit on Adam, Meldrum and Anderson's fourth floor, Vertical Files, Retailers A, Buffalo and Erie County Historical Society (hereafter BECHS).

37. "Modern J. N. Adam & Co. Store Far Different from First One," *BEN*, 14 November 1929, 6.

38. Goldman, *High Hopes*, 153.

39. Edmund D. McGarry, "The Structure and Stability of Retail Trade in Buffalo, 1929, 1933 and 1935—Grocery Stores," *Statistical Survey* (hereafter *SS*) *Supplement* 14, no. 7A (March 1939): chart 4.

40. "Sibley's Grocery and Bakery" [mimeographed page], Carton "History 1868–1926," Folder "Histories," Sibley Collection, Strong Museum.

41. "The History of Sibley's, 1868–1955" [notebook], Carton "Sibley's Misc. Store History," Sibley, Lindsay and Curr Company Collection, Rochester Historical Society (hereafter RHS), 18.

42. "Something about This New Store Here in Rochester" [pamphlet], Fall and Winter 1901–1902, private collection of Lynda McCurdy Hotra.

43. Ad for B. Forman, *RD&C*, 1 January 1926, 21.

44. Blake McKelvey, *Rochester, the Quest for Quality*, 255.

45. McKelvey, "Historic Predecessors," 17.

46. Barry and Elmes, *Buffalo's Text Book*, 19.

47. "America's Leading Markets: Buffalo," *J. Walter Thompson Company Newsletter*, 17 July 1924, 6. Box 2, J. Walter Thompson Company Archives, Special Collections, Duke University.

48. Many Buffalo employers claimed to prefer Polish workers over Italians. See Goldman, *High Hopes*, 178; Virginia Yans-McLaughlin, *Family and Community: Italian Immigrants in Buffalo, 1880–1930*, 42–43.

49. Yans-McLaughlin, *Family and Community*, 27–54.

50. Niles Carpenter, *Nationality, Color, and Economic Opportunity in the City of Buffalo*, University of Buffalo, 115–18, 155–67.

51. Edmund D. McGarry, "Retail Trade Areas in Buffalo," *SS Supplement* 6, no. 8A (April 1933); Carpenter, *Nationality*, 96–99.

52. Federal Writers' Project, *Rochester and Monroe County*, 47.

53. McKelvey, *Rochester, the Quest for Quality*, 3.

54. Federal Writers' Project, *Rochester and Monroe County*, 45.

55. U.S. Department of Commerce, *Abstract of the Fourteenth Census*, 378–81; McKelvey, *Rochester, the Flower City*, 379.

56. U.S. Department of Commerce, *Abstract of the Fourteenth Census*, 108.

57. Barry and Elmes, *Buffalo's Text Book*, 11.

58. U.S. Department of Commerce, *Abstract of the Fourteenth Census*, 50–52, 55.

59. Barry and Elmes, *Buffalo's Text Book*, 98.

60. J. Walter Thompson Company, *Retail Shopping Areas: A Suggested Grouping of Counties about 683 Principal Shopping Centers, with 642 Sub-centers Indicated*, 21.

61. "America's Leading Markets: Buffalo," *J. Walter Thompson Company Newsletter*, 17 July 1924.

62. J. Walter Thompson Company, *Retail Shopping Areas*, 22.

63. "Merchants Aid Extension of Rochester Trade Area," *RD&C*, 16 October 1924, 1.

64. Ibid.

65. "America's Leading Markets: Buffalo," 6.

Chapter 2

1. "Befriending the Fat Man—With a Good Word for the Bridegroom, Too," *Dry Goods Merchants Trade Journal* (hereafter *DGMTJ*), December 1922, 86.

2. "Modernism Ties Up with Popular Prices," *DGMTJ*, September 1929, 148. The article features a photo of a Sibley's window display, which highlighted sportswear by using three panels of geometric prints.

3. "New Interiors at Sibley, Lindsay & Curr's," *DGMTJ*, February 1927, 50.

4. "McCurdy's Forced to Enlarge Store Owing to Growth of Trade," clipping as part of McCurdy time line, n.d [1923], private collection of Lynda McCurdy Hotra.

5. Untitled typed sheet with times and descriptions of shoppers, 30 October 1915, Folder "From Internal Memos Scrapbook, 1909–1917," Sibley Collection, Strong Museum.

6. "Public Benefactors!" *Town Tidings* (hereafter *TT*), June 1933, 10.

7. For a discussion of the department store as an "Adamless Eden," designed for women, see Benson, *Counter Cultures*, 75–123. See also Leach, *Land of Desire.*

8. "We Make It Easy for Out of Town Patrons to Meet Their City Friends," *RD&C*, 18 October 1920, 17.

9. "Program of Music," Rochester Ladies' Trio [program from Tea Room concert, 3 April 1909]; "A New Cafe for Men," n.d. [1909], John White Johnson, Advertising Department, Scrapbook 1909–1912, Sibley Collection, Strong Museum.

10. "The New Beauty Salon Takes a Formal Bow Tomorrow," Advertisement for J. N. Adam's, *BCE*, 28 December 1930, 3.

11. August 15, 1938, Binder "Operating Committee," Sibley Collection, RHS.

12. Advertisement for B. Forman Co., *RD&C* 15 December 1927, 25.

13. "Delivery Route Leads to Lush Pastures for Veteran Horse—Ira Perkins to Drive Cy over Path for Last Time," *RD&C* 25 April 1938, Scrapbook "Clippings, Local Press 1936–1941," Sibley Collection, Strong Museum.

14. "Interesting Facts" [two typed sheets, undated but probably 1940], Carton "Sibley's Misc. Store History," Sibley Collection, Strong Museum.

15. Advertisement for Larkin Company, *TT*, October 1931, 31.

16. Benson, *Counter Cultures,* 128–53. See also Abelson, *When Ladies Go A-Thieving.*

17. "From Internal Memos Scrapbook 1909–1917," 25 May 1917, Sibley Collection, Strong Museum.

18. "Employee Hand Book" [pamphlet], 1 June 1927, Sibley Collection, Strong Museum, 6–7.

19. "Operating Committee" [binder], 25 January 1937, Sibley Collection, RHS, 103.

20. "Hens and Kelly Adapt Sales Talk to Each Customer," *DGMTJ,* July 1928. Emphasis in original.

21. Advertisement for Sibley, Lindsay and Curr, *RD&C,* 19 December 1927, 5.

22. Jessie Cary Grange, "Fruit Cakes as Christmas Presents," *Rochester Gas and Electric News* 16, no. 5 (November 1928): 174.

23. *A Year Book and Rochester Gas and Electric News* [special edition of *Rochester Gas and Electric News*], January 1930, 303, collection of Rochester Gas and Electric Corporation.

24. *RD&C,* 19 December 1927, 5; *BEN,* 11 November 1930, 12; *RD&C,* 7 October 1930, 2.

25. *Juvenile Magazine* (hereafter *JM*), April 1927, back cover, publication of Sibley, Lindsay and Curr Company, Folder "Juvenile Magazine, 1923–1931," Sibley Collection, Strong Museum.

26. *JM,* May 1924, 3.

27. *JM,* August 1924, 3.

28. Ibid.

29. *JM,* December 1925, 11.

30. *JM,* March 1925, 11.

31. *JM,* December 1925, 3.

32. *JM,* November 1926, 12.

33. *JM,* January 1925, 12.

34. *JM,* December 1925, 8.

35. "Toyland Open," *RD&C,* 30 October 1920, 15.

36. "The Christmas Store Bountiful," *BEN,* 2 December 1921, 7.

37. "Buffalo's Main Street Is Going to Be the Place—The Big White Way of All the World," *BCE,* 20 December 1930, 3.

38. "Buy it in Buffalo," *Buffalo Saturday Night* 1, no. 39 (10 December 1921): 3.

39. Advertisement for Sibley, Lindsay and Curr, *RD&C*, 19 December, 1927.

40. Leach, *Land of Desire*, 115.

41. Advertisement for B. Forman Company, *RD&C*, 1 January 1928, 3.

42. Advertisement for B. Forman Company, *RD&C*, 6 November 1927, 3.

43. Advertisement for Wm. Hengerer, *BEN*, 19 November 1927, 5.

44. "All Buffalo Stands Silent with Heads Bowed at Noon," *BEN*, Financial Edition, 11 November 1921, front page.

45. "Voters, Be Fair! A Communication from William A. Morgan," *BEN*, 7 November 1921, 21.

46. "Rochester Opinions on Daylight Saving," Advertisement for Rochester Citizens' Daylight Savings Committee, *RD&C*, 6 November 1927, Section 2, 28.

47. *Rochester Gas and Electric News* 15, no. 3 (September 1927): 112.

48. Advertisement for Sibley, Lindsay and Curr, *RD&C*, 18 October 1927, 26.

49. *Official Program and Guide of Buffalo Centennial*, Vertical Files, Celebrations, BECHS, 33.

50. Advertisement for B. Forman Company, *RD&C*, 3 December 1931, 2.

51. Advertisement for Jahraus-Braun, *BEN*, 31 October 1929, 4.

52. Adam, Meldrum and Anderson Papers, Box 1, Folder 9, BECHS, n.d. [1917].

53. Advertisement for Danahy-Faxon Stores, *BCE*, 15 December 1933, 17.

54. Advertisement for Bing and Nathan, *BEN*, 22 November 1920, 7.

55. Advertisement for the Reliable Furniture Company, *RD&C*, 20 November 1927.

56. "Our Inferiority Complex," *TT*, October 1928, 13.

57. Ibid., 14.

58. Ibid., 15.

59. "The Superiority of Feeling Inferior," *TT*, November 1928, 13–14.

60. Ibid., 14.

61. Ibid., 15.

62. Ibid.

63. Ibid.

64. Sinclair Lewis, *Main Street* (New York: Harcourt Brace Jovanovich, 1920; New York: Signet Classics, 1980), 38–41.

65. "Our Inferiority Complex," *TT*, October 1928, 16.

66. "Main Street the Un-Magnificent," *TT*, December 1928, 26.

67. "The Superiority of Feeling Inferior," *TT*, November 1928, 19.

68. "The Main Street Label," *TT*, February 1929, 24.

69. Ibid.

70. *TT*, July 1930, 8.

71. "Concerning 'Main Street'—A Symposium," *TT*, October 1929, 44.

72. "Concerning 'Main Street,'" *TT*, June 1929, 80.

73. "Concerning 'Main Street'—A Symposium," *TT*, October 1929, 44.

74. "VALUE OF THE NAME 'MAIN STREET' APPRECIATED," *Main Street* 2 (February 1927): 3, official publication of the Main Street Association, Inc., Vertical Files, Retailers, BECHS.

75. The manager of the *Buffalo Evening News* expressed this idea. "Concerning 'Main Street'—A Symposium," *TT*, October 1929, 46.

76. Ibid., 44.

Chapter 3

1. "416 Retail Stores Swap Ideas," *DGMTJ*, January 1924, 179.

2. "All Sections Represented," *DGMTJ*, August 1928, 188.

3. "Under 10,000," *Dry Goods Journal*, June 1936, 30.

4. "Befriending the Fat Man—With a Good Word for the Bridegroom, Too," *DGMTJ*, December 1922, 86.

5. "How Sibley's Makes Corsets of Storewide Importance," *DGMTJ*, March 1933, 57–58.

6. "'Budget Control Pays in Smaller Stores,' Says Beir's," *DGMTJ*, April 1928, 39.

7. Untitled Report from 1947, Carton "History 1868–1926," Folder "Reports," Sibley Collection, Strong Museum.

8. Untitled mimeographed sheet, n.d. Flint and Kent Department Store Papers, Box A70–100, Folder 1 "History," BECHS. The same piece appears in the Bureau of Business Research (hereafter BBR) Office Files, Folder "Amusing Letters," 1931, Special Collections, Baker Library, Harvard University (hereafter BLHU).

9. Don Herold, "The Macy Complex," *The Merchandise Manager* (hereafter *MM*) 3, no. 1 (July 1932): 34.

10. "New York Is Not America," *Department Store Buyer* (hereafter *DSB*), February 1940, 23.

11. Thomas Robb, Elmhurst, Long Island, two letters to Adam, Meldrum and Anderson, Buffalo, 4 April 1934 and 8 May 1934, Adam, Meldrum and Anderson Papers, B95–2, Box 1, Folder 1, BECHS.

12. M. E. Osgood, "The Bureau of Business Research," *The Alumni Bulletin*, November 1929, BBR Office Files, BLHU.

13. *New England Grocer and Tradesman*, 2 January, 1925, "The Grocery Clipping Book," in Notebooks on Retail Trade, BBR Office Files, BLHU.

14. Entry for 1 May 1940, Binder "Operating Committee," Sibley Collection, RHS.

15. *SS* 1, no. 1 (April 1926): 1.

16. Seldon O. Martin, "Applications of the Experience of the Bureau of Business Research of Harvard University to the Retail Jewelry Business," Address before the Ohio Retail Jewelers' Association, Columbus, Ohio, 24 April 1914, BBR Correspondence Files, Division of Research, Folder 5, BLHU.

17. Letter dated 1 July 1923, BBR Correspondence Files, Folder "Letters to the Dean of HBS, 1923–1926," BLHU.

18. David Monod, *Store Wars: Shopkeepers and the Culture of Mass Marketing, 1890–1939,* 170.

19. Letter dated July 1, 1923, BBR Correspondence Files, BLHU.

20. *New York Times,* 9 July 1930, financial section, clipping in BBR Office Files, File "Publicity—Department Store," BLHU.

21. H. L. Post, "The Independent Does Not Need to Surrender," first of a series, *DGMTJ,* January 1934, 22.

22. "Smaller Stores Have Better Opportunity Now Than Ever," *DGMTJ,* July 1924, 26.

23. "Sales Possibilities in Group Merchandising," *DGMTJ,* January 1929, 33.

24. "Under 10,000," *Dry Goods Journal,* June 1936, 30.

25. "Selling Best Sellers," *DGMTJ,* December 1934, 76.

26. *DGMTJ,* February 1920, 108.

27. "Fabric Promotion Weeks Increase Demand for Piece Goods in Rochester Store," *DGMTJ,* October 1929, 66.

28. "How Fraser's Ties in Nationwide Publicity," *DGMTJ,* May 1929, 47.

29. Ibid.

30. Advertisement for Cannon, *DGMTJ,* November 1924, 35.

31. Advertisement for Kleinert's Rubber Company, *DGMTJ,* January 1926, 132–33.

32. Advertisement for American Viscose Coporation, *Dry Goods Journal,* February 1940, 35.

33. "Contact," *MM,* December 1933, 28.

34. "Contact," *MM,* September 1933, 32.

35. "Contact," *MM,* December 1933, 29.

36. Leonard S. Marcus, *The American Store Window,* 41–42.

37. Ohmann, *Selling Culture,* 231.

38. "Fashion Bureau," *RD&C,* 7 October 1930, 8.

39. *Rochester Gas and Electric News* 15, no. 10 (April 1928): 385.

40. "NRDGA Convention Notes," *Dry Goods Journal,* February 1936, 86.

41. Edmund D. McGarry, "Consumers' Buying Habits in Satellite Cities," *SS Supplement* 8, no. 3A (November 1932): 5.

42. Ibid., 6.

43. Advertisement for Sibley, Lindsay and Curr, *RD&C,* 28 November 1927, 19.

44. *RD&C,* 20 December 1936.

45. Ibid.

46. Advertisement for B. Forman Company, *RD&C*, 20 July 1926, 18; *RD&C*, 1 January 1928, 3.

47. "Importations: The Wm. Hengerer Co." [pamphlet], n.d., Vertical Files, Retailers H, BECHS.

48. Advertisement for L. L. Berger, *TT*, March 1929, 51.

49. Harry Serwer, "Is Paris Losing Her Fashion Crown?" *MM*, September 1932, 33–34, 53.

50. Ibid., 33.

51. "The Gentle Shopper," *TT*, June 1928, 59.

52. "Money in Your Pocket," *TT*, April 1932, 6. The article was reprinted June 1936, 34.

53. *RD&C*, 9 December 1936, 10.

54. "Money in Your Pocket," *TT*, April 1932, 6.

55. Advertisement for B. Forman, *RD&C*, 2 December 1934, 24.

56. "Fabric and Piece Goods: Fabric Promotion Weeks Increase Demand for Piece Goods in Rochester Store," *DGMTJ*, October 1929, 63–64.

57. Ad for McCall Printed Patterns, *DGMTJ*, May 1929, 81.

58. *BCE*, 14 November 1935, 8; *BEN*, 6 November 1930, 3; *BEN*, 18 November 1930, 3; *BEN*, 9 December 1930, 20; *BEN*, 22 November, 1935, 5; *BEN*, 10 November, 1920, 5; *RD&C*, 12 October 1920, 145.

59. *BEN*, 10 October 1920, 5.

60. *DSB*, February 1940, 24.

61. Advertisement for McFarlin's Clothiers, *RD&C*, 9 October 1932, 3.

62. See Blake McKelvey, "Men's Clothing Industry in Rochester's History," 22–31.

63. Advertisement for The National Clothing Company, *RD&C*, 3 January 1926, 27.

64. Advertisement for Eastwood Shoes, *RD&C*, 18 November 1923, 37.

65. *DSB*, February 1940, 34.

66. "In the Marts of Trade," *DSB*, June 1939, 22.

67. "In the Marts of Trade," *DSB*, January 1939, 68.

68. "In the Marts of Trade," *DSB*, March 1940, 25–26.

69. "In the Marts of Trade," *DSB*, September 1940, 23.

70. "In the Marts of Trade," *DSB*, January 1939, 68–70.

71. "In the Marts of Trade," *DSB*, November 1938, 63.

72. "In the Marts of Trade," *DSB*, September 1939, 22.

73. Ibid., 23.

74. "In the Marts of Trade," *DSB*, August 1939, 25.

75. "In the Marts of Trade," *DSB*, February 1939, 43.

76. "The Hunting Season," *DSB*, September 1939, 13.

Chapter 4

1. Homer Hoyt & Associates, "Market Survey & Appraisal," March 1953, table 18, Carton "Annual Reports," Sibley Collection, Strong Museum.

2. "Why These Independents Do Not Fear Chain Stores," *DGMTJ*, January 1929, 40.

3. "Common Elements of Success," *DGMTJ*, January 1929, 48.

4. Quoted in "Meeting Chain Store Competition," *DGMTJ*, January 1929, 43.

5. "Is This the Chain Store," *Chain Store Manager* (hereafter *CSM*), March 1926, 28.

6. Ibid., 23.

7. Monod, *Store Wars*, 171.

8. "Group Buying—How Stores Are Using It Profitably," *DGMTJ*, January 1929, 42.

9. "Pelletier's Meet Chains with Powerful Pep," *DGMTJ*, June 1929, 36.

10. "Meeting Chain Store Competition," *DGMTJ*, January 1929, 43.

11. Ibid.

12. Clarence P. Foster, "A Brief History of the Wm. Hengerer Co. Store," 1936, Vertical Files, Retailers, BECHS.

13. "The History of Sibley's, 1868–1955," n.d. [1955], Carton "History 1868–1926," Folder "Histories," Sibley Collection, Strong Museum, 21.

14. "Group Buying—How Stores Are Using it Profitably."

15. Advertisement for E. W. Edwards and Son, *BEN*, 18 November 1929, 13.

16. W. Bruce Philip, "The Position of the Independent Retailer," *Commonwealth*, Part Two: Official Journal of the Commonwealth Club of California, San Francisco, 7, no. 28 (14 July 1931): 224, McGarry Papers, Box 2, Folder "Chain Stores—Correspondence and Clippings," University Archives, State University of New York at Buffalo (hereafter UBA).

17. Philip, "The Position of the Independent Retailer," 229.

18. *Business Week*, 16 July 1930, n.p.; BBR Office Files, Carton "Publicity: Dept. Stores," BLHU.

19. "Why Chains Strive for What Independents Have," *DGMTJ*, September 1928, 37.

20. Theodore N. Beckman and Herman C. Nolen, *The Chain Store Problem: A Critical Analysis*, 70.

21. Lew V. Day, "Fitting the New Store into its Community," *Chain Store Age* (hereafter *CSA*), April 1932, 221.

22. E. K. Moore, "Building up the Neighborhood Drug Chain on Personality," *CSA*, April 1928, 29.

23. "Some Plain Facts for Independent and Chain Stores," *DGMTJ*, January 1929, 48.

24. Advertisement for J. C. Penney, *DGMTJ*, November 1929, 168.

25. Advertisement for J. C. Penney, *DGMTJ,* September 1929, 208.

26. Ibid; *DGMTJ,* November 1929, 168.

27. Beckman and Nolen, *Chain Store Problem,* 64.

28. McGarry, "Retail Trade Areas," 11.

29. Cohen, *Making a New Deal,* 100–20.

30. Ibid., 120.

31. McGarry, "Structure and Stability," 24.

32. Ibid.

33. Ibid.

34. Paul D. Converse, "Prices and Services of Chain and Independent Stores in Champaign-Urbana, Illinois, *National Association of Teachers of Marketing and Advertising Bulletin* (hereafter *NATMA Bulletin*), 1931 Series, no. 4: 25.

35. Editor of the *Michigan Tradesman,* comments in *Modern Merchant and Grocery World,* April 13, 1929, quoted by James L. Palmer, assistant professor of marketing, University of Chicago, in "Economic and Social Aspects of Chain Stores," an address given before the Iowa Association of Economists and Sociologists, 10 May 1929, McGarry Papers, Box 2 "Chain Stores: Correspondence and Clippings, 1928–1929," UBA, 5

36. Advertisement for Butterick Company, *RD&C,* 3 November 1920, 3.

37. Strasser, *Satisfaction Guaranteed,* 249–51.

38. Monod, *Store Wars,* 158.

39. Advertisement for Butterick Company, *RD&C,* 3 November 1920, 3.

40. "Under 10,000," *Dry Goods Journal,* June 1936, 30.

41. Monod, *Store Wars,* 159

42. H. L. Post, "The Independent Does Not Need to Surrender," 3rd in a series, *DGMTJ,* March 1934, 27.

43. H. L. Post, "The Independent Does Not Need to Surrender," 2nd in a series, *DGMTJ,* February 1934, 21.

44. H. L. Post, "The Independent Does Not Need to Surrender," 3rd in a series, *DGMTJ,* March 1934, 28.

45. H. L. Post, "The Independent Does Not Need to Surrender," 4th in a series, *DGMTJ,* April 1934, 99, 106.

46. "Report on the Committee on Definitions," *NATMA Bulletin,* 1933 Series, no. 4 (November 1933): 2–3.

47. J. Frank Grimes and Godfrey M. Lebhar, "A Debate on the Chain Store System between J. Frank Grimes, President, Independent Grocers' Alliance and Godfrey M. Lebhar, Chain Store Age," Omaha, Nebraska, 16 September 1929, McGarry Papers, Carton 27/F455, Box 2, Folder "Chain Stores Literature," UBA, 5, 21.

48. National Wholesale Grocers' Association of the United States, "America Chained or Unchained" [pamphlet], New York, n.d., McGarry Papers, Carton

27/F455, Box 2, Folder "Chain Stores—Correspondence and Clippings, 1928–1929," UBA.

49. Advertisement for IGA, *BEN*, 31 October 1929, 36.

50. Perry O. Snider, "The Independent Grocers' Alliance of America," *NATMA Bulletin*, 1934 Series, no. 3 (November 1934): 4, 6, 14, 18.

51. Advertisement for McKesson Drugstores, *BEN*, 20 November 1929, 16.

52. Godfrey Lebhar, message from editor, *CSA* 3, no. 5 (May 1927): 72.

53. Advertisement for Wegmans, *RD&C*, 20 November 1936, 11.

54. "This Is the Real Chain Store Giant," *CSM* 1, no. 5 (March 1926): 28.

55. C. O. Sherrill, "Across the Chain Store Counter," *The Rotarian*, June 1931, BBR Archives, Case 19, Folder "Chain—General Publicity and Clippings 1929–1932 (Not Bureau Studies)," BLHU.

56. *CSA*, July 1927, 39.

57. Palmer, "Social and Economic Aspects of Chain Stores," 6.

58. Ibid., 7.

59. Advertisement for Walgreens, *RD&C*, 13 November 1936, 14.

60. *BCE*, 14 June 1938, *Industry in Buffalo and the Niagara Frontier* 4, 322, BECPL.

61. Advertisement for Loblaws Grocers, *BEN*, Inter-Urban Edition, 8 June 1931, 17.

62. "Grant's New Store Open to Public Today," *BCE*, 1 November 1939, *Industry in Buffalo and the Niagara Frontier* 4, 360, BECPL.

63. For a brief overview of the origins of the Hart chain, see Stuart E. Rosenberg, *The Jewish Community in Rochester, 1843–1925*, 161–62.

64. Advertisement for Hart Markets, *RD&C*, 21 November 1923, 19.

65. *CSA*, July 1927, 40.

66. Advertisement for Wegmans, *RD&C*, 20 November 1936, 11.

67. Advertisement for Wegmans, *RD&C*, 18 December 1936, 19.

68. Advertisement for Wegmans, *RD&C*, 20 November 1936, 11.

69. Advertisement for S. M. Flickinger, *BEN*, 11 November 1929, 13.

70. S. M. Flickinger, "Taking the Independent into the Fold," *CSA*, January 1926, 12.

71. R. W. Barker, "How the Red and White System is Operated," *CSA*, December 1928, 32.

72. Flickinger, "Taking the Independent," 12.

73. W. L. Pohn, "How We Run a Chain of Independent Stores," *CSA*, February 1928, 21.

74. Advertisement for Danahy-Faxon, *TT*, May 1931, 57.

75. Advertisement for Texaco, *BEN*, 3 September 1931, 63.

76. All figures are from the *J. Walter Thompson News Bulletin*, September 1927, 9, 11. J. Walter Thompson Company Collection, Duke University.

77. McGarry, "Structure and Stability," 2, table 1.

78. Ibid.

79. H. L. Post, "The Independent Need Not Surrender," *DGMTJ*, March 1934, 27.

80. *NATMA Bulletin*, 1931 Series, no. 4 (October 1931): 22, table 8.

81. See Jonathan Bean's brief account of antichain store activists such as W. K. Henderson of Louisiana, who used the radio and a fleet of "Minute Men" to bring the public's attention to the abuses of the chain store. Jonathan J. Bean, *Beyond the Broker State: Federal Policies toward Small Business, 1936–1961*, 27–31. See also David A. Horowitz, "The Crusade against Chain Stores."

82. "Fraudulent Anti-Chain Associations," *Better Business* 3, no. 8 (15 April 1930), issued semimonthly by the Bureau of Business and Government Research, University of Colorado, Boulder, Colorado, McGarry Papers, Box 2, Folder "Chain Stores—Correspondence and Clippings, 1928–1929," UBA.

83. "Anti-Chain Bolsheviks Active," *CSM* 3, no. 3 (March 1927): 5.

84. Bean, *Beyond the Broker State*, 28, 33–34; Horowitz, "The Crusade against Chain Stores," 359–63.

85. "The Publisher's Page," *Dry Goods Journal*, August 1936, 10.

86. Ibid.

87. Ellis W. Hawley, *The New Deal and the Problem of Monopoly: A Study in Economic Ambivalence*, 268.

88. Bean, *Beyond the Broker State*, 39–40, 62–65.

Chapter 5

1. Lewis Lansky, "Buffalo and the Great Depression, 1929–1933," 207; *BEN*, 26 August 1931, 23; "Buffalo Day Plans to Be Made Friday—Mayor Roesch Will Speak at Merchants' Session," *BEN*, 27 August 1931, 30; "Stores Get Stocks in Order as Buffalo Day Draws Near—Carnival Spirit Runs High on Eve of Great Community Selling Event," *BEN*, 3 September 1931, 1

2. Advertisement for Adam, Meldrum and Anderson, *BEN*, 5 September 1931, 14.

3. Advertisement for Bing and Nathan, *BEN*, 3 September 1931, 22.

4. *BEN*, 2 September 1931, 1.

5. Ibid., 5.

6. For example, see Bonnie Fox Schwartz, "Unemployment Relief in Philadelphia, 1930–1932: A Study of the Depression's Impact on Voluntarism," and David M. Katzman, "Ann Arbor: Depression City," in Bernard Sternsher, ed., *Hitting Home: The Great Depression in Town and Country*, 60–84, 47–59; Roman Heleniak, "Local Reaction to the Great Depression in New Orleans, 1929–1933."

7. Lansky, "Buffalo and the Great Depression," 205.

8. Goldman, *High Hopes*, 225.

9. "Mr. National Advertiser—If You Seek Optimism, Come to Rochester!" *RD&C*, 25 October 1931, 11C.

10. Ibid.

11. T. J. Jackson Lears, "From Salvation to Self-Realization: Advertising and the Therapeutic Roots of the Consumer Culture, 1880–1930," in Richard Wightman Fox and T. J. Jackson Lears, eds., *The Culture of Consumption: Critical Essays in American History, 1880–1980*, 3–38.

12. Daniel Horowitz, *Morality of Spending: Attitudes toward the Consumer Society in America, 1875–1940*, 135.

13. Richard Wightman Fox, "Epitaph for Middletown: Robert S. Lynd and the Analysis of Consumer Culture," in Fox and Lears, eds., *The Culture of Consumption*, 140.

14. Marchand, *Advertising the American Dream*, 238–47; Schneirov, *Dream of a New Social Order*, 200.

15. Lendol Calder, *Financing the American Dream: A Cultural History of Consumer Credit*, 30–31.

16. Michael E. Parrish, *Anxious Decades: America in Prosperity and Depression, 1920–1941*, 244.

17. Quoted in Jo Ann E. Argersinger, *Toward a New Deal in Baltimore: People and Government in the Great Depression*, xv.

18. *Kodak Magazine* 9, no. 6 (November 1928): 12.

19. *BCE*, 23 November 1930, 7.

20. William B. Waits, *The Modern Christmas in America: A Cultural History of Gift Giving*.

21. *BCE*, 2 December 1930, 1.

22. *BCE*, 6 December 1930, 1.

23. Goldman, *High Hopes*, 217.

24. *BCE*, 8 December 1931, 4.

25. Waits, *Modern Christmas*, 170–77. Even though personal, individualized Christmas charity was on the wane, Waits notes, the Depression years "once again encouraged Americans to perform small acts of kindness or to give small remembrances to the poor at Christmas," 175.

26. See T. H. Breen, "Narrative of Commercial Life: Consumption, Ideology and Community on the Eve of the American Revolution," in Glickman, ed., *Consumer Society in American History*, 100–29; Dana Frank, in *Buy American: The Untold Story of Economic Nationalism*, explores how consuming could be a powerful political act for organized labor and other groups.

27. "Buy Out Depression," *BEN*, 20 November 1930, 1.

28. *BEN*, 2 December 1930, 29.

29. *TT*, April 1932, reprinted in *TT*, June 1936, 34.

30. Ibid.

31. Advertisement for Mitchell Knitting Mills, *BEN*, Home Edition, 8 December 1930, 6.

32. *RD&C*, 3 October 1932, 19.

33. For a discussion of the perception of the consumer as female during the nineteenth century, see Kathleen G. Donohue, "What Gender Is the Consumer? The Role of Gender Connotations in Defining the Political," 21–23. See also Roland Marchand's chapter on how advertisers perceived their audience in his *Advertising the American Dream*, 52–87.

34. Advertisement for J. N. Adam, *BEN*, 26 June 1931, 6.

35. Advertisement for J. N. Adam, *BEN*, 23 June 1931, 7.

36. Advertisement for J. N. Adam, *BEN*, 25 June 1931, 7.

37. Advertisement for McCurdy and Company, *RD&C*, 8 December 1931, 5.

38. Abelson, *When Ladies Go A-Thieving*, 13–41, 120–72, quote on page 169.

39. Advertisement for J. N. Adam, *BEN*, 22 June 1931, 7.

40. Buffalo, in particular, had a tradition of merchants playing a large role in local politics. J. N. Adam, founder of the department store of the same name, even served as mayor of Buffalo. *BEN*, 11 April 1935, *Industry in Buffalo and the Niagara Frontier* 4, 297, BECPL.

41. Lynda McCurdy Hotra, "McCurdy & Company Timeline," 9.

42. Store workers were presumably not included in the "community" benefiting from these events, which would prevent them from earning a day's wages when volunteers took over their jobs. Some store clerks may have enjoyed a holiday, even if it was unpaid. "Today—Members of the Chatterbox Club, Junior Workers' Association, General Hospital Twigs Unite in Becoming 'Storekeepers for a Day!'" *RD&C*, 3 December 1931, 2.

43. *BEN*, 2 September 1931, 3.

44. *BEN*, 26 August 1931, 23.

45. Among those advertising with special reference to Buffalo Day in the Thursday, 3 September 1931 edition of the *Buffalo Evening News* were: J. N. Adam and Company (department store), Adam, Meldrum and Anderson Company (department store), Sears, Roebuck Company, Berger's Specialty Shop, Flickinger's Food Shops, Bing and Nathan (furniture store), Harvey Marshall (dress shop), Palmer's (specialty shops), Alexander Kornhauser (dress shop), A.M. Keating Millinery Importer, Peter Young (men's clothing), Hy-Pure Drug Stores, Scher Shop (women's dresses and coats), Jean Smart Dress Shop, Matrix Shoes, and Joan Baker (beauty salon).

46. Advertisement for Sears, Roebuck, *BEN*, 3 September 1931, 48–49.

47. *BEN*, 2 September 1931, 3.

48. "Buffalo Day Finds Store Aisles Filled," *BEN*, Stocks Edition, 4 September 1931, 1.

49. "Index of Sales of Department Stores," BBSR Records, Box 2, Folder

"Department Store Sales," UBA. With average monthly sales from January 1925 to December 1927 taken as 100 percent, monthly sales in September 1931 were 79.6 percent, while those of September 1930 were 100.2 percent. See Appendix.

50. Blake McKelvey, *Rochester, the Emerging Metropolis, 1925–1961*, 42.

51. Richard E. Holl, "Marion B. Folsom and the Rochester Plan of 1931," 5.

52. Ibid., 7.

53. Ibid., 10.

54. Ibid., 16. Folsom would eventually endorse the federal-state unemployment insurance system proposed by FDR in 1934 and 1935 as a way to expand unemployment insurance to a majority of American companies. He would be active as a member of the Advisory Council on Economic Security, working for the passage of the Social Security Act of 1935.

55. Federal Writers' Project, *Rochester and Monroe County*, 110.

56. Civic Committee on Unemployment, "Let This Be Your Christmas Gift" [full page ad], *RD&C*, 9 December 1931, 2.

57. "Have You Signed the Pledge?" *RD&C*, 14 December 1931, Section 2, 15.

58. "Sign the Pledge for Prosperity," *RD&C*, 3 December 1931, 8.

59. Ibid.

60. "Have You Signed the Pledge for Prosperity?" *RD&C*, 9 December 1931, 2.

61. Ibid.

62. Ibid.

63. "How You Can Help," *RD&C*, 3 December 1931, 8. Emphasis in original.

64. Calder, *Financing the American Dream*, 89.

65. Horowitz, *Morality of Spending*, xvii.

66. "Have You Signed the Pledge for Prosperity?" *RD&C*, 9 December 1931, 2.

67. "Continuous Thrift," *Rochester Gas and Electric News* 8 (February 1920): 146.

68. "Sign the Pledge for Prosperity," *RD&C*, 3 December 1931, 8.

69. Ibid.

70. McKelvey, *Rochester on the Genesee*, 164–65.

71. James R. Mock and Cedric Larson, *Words That Won the War: The Story of the Committee on Public Information*, 169.

72. "How You Can Help," *RD&C*, 3 December 1931, 8. Emphasis in original.

73. Marchand, *Advertising the American Dream*, 212–13.

74. "Take a 'Guest-Eye' Inventory Today—Be Ready," *RD&C*, 6 December 1931, 10C.

75. "Have You Signed the Pledge for Prosperity?" *RD&C*, 9 December 1931, 2.

76. "Have You Signed the Pledge?" *RD&C*, 14 December 1931, Section 2, 16.

77. Tom Pettey, "Real Boost to Business in City's 'Spending Drive,'" *RD&C*, 14 December 1931, section 2, 15.

78. "Canvass Goes Beyond Hopes of Sponsors," *RD&C*, 15 December 1931, 14.

79. Ibid.

80. *RD&C*, Financial Edition, 26 February 1932, Section 2, 17. The story featured a copy of Hoover's letter, including his signature.

81. "Canvass Goes Beyond Hopes of Sponsors," *RD&C*, 15 December 1931, 1, 14.

82. Ibid., 1.

83. Ibid., 14.

84. "Have You Signed the Pledge for Prosperity?" *RD&C*, 9 December 1931, 2. Emphasis added.

85. Marchand, *Advertising the American Dream*, 217–22.

86. "Let This Be Your Christmas Gift," *RD&C*, 9 December 1931, 2.

87. "Have You Signed the Pledge?" *RD&C*, 14 December 1931, Section 2I, 15.

88. Ibid.

89. "Twenty Million Citizens Back Hoover Anti-Hoarding Drive," *RD&C*, 7 February 1932, 1A, quote on page 7A.

90. Ibid., 1A. The relationship between black leaders and efforts to encourage consumer spending was ambivalent at best. During the mid-1930s, black consumers in Harlem would mobilize to boycott stores that refused to hire blacks in white-collar positions. Instead of participating in "Buy American" campaigns, black housewives were reminded not to buy where they could not work. See Cheryl Greenberg, "Don't Buy Where You Can't Work," in Glickman, ed., *Consumer Society*, 241–73.

91. Dana Frank devotes a chapter to Hearst's Buy American campaigns, in his *Buy American*, 56–78, quote on page 61.

92. Ibid., 64–65.

93. Merryle Stanley Ru Keyser, "The Buy American Movement," *MM*, February 1933.

94. "Around the Town," *TT*, February 1933, 7.

95. Niles Carpenter, "Trends in Relief Expenditures in Buffalo," *SS* 9 (February 1934): table 2.

96. "What We'll Use for Money!" *TT*, April 1934, 8.

97. McKelvey, *Rochester, the Emerging Metropolis*, 66.

98. Ibid., 67. McKelvey argues that Eastman's suicide had no connection with the Depression and instead resulted from "his desire to escape the debilitating pains of advancing age and threatened infirmities." The Kodak founder's final message stated, "My work is done. Why wait?" Despite Eastman's assertion that it was time for him to go, his death was still shocking to local residents and hardly helped the community to view conditions with optimism.

99. Goldman, *High Hopes*, 227.

100. "What We'll Use for Money!" *TT*, April 1934, 8.

101. Parrish, *Anxious Decades*, 328–29.

102. Alan Brinkley, *Voices of Protest: Huey Long, Father Coughlin, and the Great Depression*, 223; James R. McGovern, *And a Time for Hope: Americans in the Great Depression*, 51.

103. Brinkley, *Voices of Protest*, 223.

104. Ibid., 71–72.

105. *Buffalo Times*, 13 October 1935, n.p., BBSR Records, Scrapbook "Bureau of Business Research, 1932–1934," UBA.

Chapter 6

1. Robert H. Wiebe, *The Search for Order, 1877–1920*.

2. See Marchand, *Advertising the American Dream*, 77–87.

3. See Schneirov, *Dream of a New Social Order*, 3–6, 103–24; Scanlon, *Inarticulate Longings*, 232.

4. "Enormous Old Map Is Anniversary Feature," *DGMTJ*, August 1934, 24.

5. *RD&C*, 9 December 1936, 10.

6. Ibid.

7. For example, see the description of a "Buy-at-Home Drive" in The Dalles, Oregon, *Dry Goods Journal*, September 1938, 32. The ads featured in the articles had slogans such as "Why not spend your money in the city where you make it?"

8. Sibley's net sales were $12,606,898 in 1929, almost $900,000 lower than in the store's peak year of 1926. Still, the late 1920s would be recalled fondly after the Depression hit, when sales reached a low of $7,710,850 in 1933. The figure climbed slowly for the rest of the 1930s but did not reach $12,000,000 again until 1943. See table 4 in Appendix. All figures from table 18, "Net Sales, Gross Earnings and Net Earnings, 1915–1952," March 1953, Carton "Annual Reports, Homer Hoyt, Market Survey and Appraisal," Sibley Collection, Strong Museum.

9. "Index of Sales of Department Stores," BBSR, Box 2 "Sales," Folder "Department Stores, Data from *Statistical Survey*," UBA.

10. See Marchand, *Advertising the American Dream*, 288–92, 296–99.

11. The Main Street Association, Inc., Sidewalk Pedestrian Counts, issued June 1938.

12. "Interesting Items" [2 typed sheets, ca. 1940], Carton "Sibley's Misc. Store History," Sibley Collection, Strong Museum.

13. "3,000 Crowd into Sibley's to See New Escalators Start When Mayor Presses Button during Unveiling Ceremony," Scrapbook "Clippings, Local Press, 1936–1941" [no newspaper or page indicated], 1 October 1936, Sibley Collection, Strong Museum.

14. "Throng Sees Sibley Escalator Unveiled," Scrapbook "Clippings, Local Press, 1936–1941" [no newspaper or page indicated], 30 September 1936, Sibley Collection, Strong Museum.

15. *Buffalo Courier*, 22 September 1937, *Industry in Buffalo and the Niagara Frontier* 4, 292, BECPL.

16. "U.S. URGED TO GIVE BUSINESS CHANCE," *BEN*, 24 June 1935, *Industry in Buffalo and the Niagara Frontier* 4, 303, BECPL.

17. Ibid.

18. "J. N. Adam & Co. Plans $500,000 Store Building," *BCE*, 1 March 1936, *Industry in Buffalo and the Niagara Frontier* 4, 295, BECPL. Lord and Taylor was another Associated Dry Goods store, suggesting a long-term relationship between the parent company and the architects.

19. "Bright New Face in Store for Downtown Skyline" *BEN*, 11 April 1935, *Industry in Buffalo and the Niagara Frontier* 4, 296–97, BECPL.

20. "Merchants Who Bring Beauty to Main Street are Honored—New Store of J. N. Adam & Co. Takes Award," *Buffalo Courier*, 5 June 1936, *Industry in Buffalo and the Niagara Frontier* 4, 291, BECPL.

21. "Hengerer Store is Modernized," *BEN*, 30 March 1938, *Industry in Buffalo and the Niagara Frontier* 4, 314, BECPL.

22. Ibid.

23. "Edwards' New Store Viewed by Huge Crowd," *BCE*, 3 May 1938, *Industry in Buffalo and the Niagara Frontier* 4, 312, BECPL.

24. Ibid.

25. "Kleinhans Plans New Store Front," *Buffalo Times*, 17 January 1938, *Industry in Buffalo and the Niagara Frontier* 4, 319, BECPL.

26. "Please Patrons Neisner's Aim," *BEN*, 21 September 1938, *Industry in Buffalo and the Niagara Frontier* 4, 322, BECPL. On 19 September 1938, the *Buffalo Times* reported that Neisner was a chain of 115 stores.

27. *Buffalo Times*, 20 September 1938, *Industry in Buffalo and the Niagara Frontier* 4, 320, BECPL.

28. Ibid.

29. *Buffalo Times*, 19 September 1938, *Industry in Buffalo and the Niagara Frontier* 4, 319, BECPL.

30. *BEN*, 26 September 1939, *Industry in Buffalo and the Niagara Frontier* 4, 352, BECPL.

31. "Grant's New Store Open to Public Today," *BCE*, 1 November 1939, *Industry in Buffalo and the Niagara Frontier* 4, 360, BECPL.

32. Ibid.

33. "Sears, Roebuck Enlarging Store," *BEN*, 18 April 1939, *Industry in Buffalo and the Niagara Frontier* 4, 48, BECPL.

34. A study conducted by the University of Buffalo Bureau of Business and Social Research indicated a decline of thirty thousand in the population of the midtown section of Buffalo between 1920 and 1930; this was, however, more than offset by gains in the outer city, so during the decade, the city as a whole grew by 66,301. The metropolitan areas surrounding Buffalo outside the city limits (including Amherst, Lancaster, Aurora, Cheektowaga, West Seneca, Tonawanda, Lackawanna,

Grand Island, Hamburg, and East Hamburg) grew by 56,369 residents during the same period. Edmund D. McGarry, "Population Shifts in Buffalo, 1920–1930," *SS Supplement* 10, no. 10A (June 1935): 1, 4.

35. Associated Dry Goods Corporation, "Annual Report, Year Ended January 31, 1937," 5, Carton "Annual Reports R. E. Committee Minutes," Folder "Annual Reports, Associated Dry Goods Corporation, 1924–1971," Sibley Collection, Strong Museum.

36. *RD&C*, 24 April 1938, Scrapbook "Clippings, Local Press 1936–1941," Sibley Collection, Strong Museum.

37. "Walter Johnson in Hengerer's Toyland Today!" *BCE*, 4 December 1930, 12.

38. "Quins [sic] Cause Fun and Headaches, Admits Nurse of Famous Babies," *Rochester Times-Union* (hereafter *RTU*), 30 September 1937, Scrapbook "Local Clippings, 1936–1941," Sibley Collection, Strong Museum.

39. "Thousands Attend Sibley Style Show" [no newspaper name indicated], 30 September 1936, Scrapbook "Clippings, Local Press 1936–1941," Sibley Collection, Strong Museum.

40. See, for example, "McCurdy's Today at Four O'clock a PRE-HOLIDAY FASHION SHOW with 75 Rochester College and High School Girls," *RD&C*, 18 November 1936, 6.

41. The definitive work on American international expositions is Robert Rydell, *All the World's a Fair: Visions of Empire at American International Expositions, 1876–1916*. In particular, see the photos of the Igorot tribespeople from the Philippines at the Louisiana Exposition of 1916 on pages 174–76.

42. "SCHOOL CHILDREN Last chance to see the HOPI INDIANS This Morning—9 to 11," *RD&C*, 19 November 1932, 2.

43. "Many View Odditorium," *BCE*, 5 December 1933, 20. See also Andrea Stulman Dennett, *Weird and Wonderful: The Dime Museum in America*, 129–30.

44. Edward J. Fitzmorris, "Income of Motion Picture Theaters in Buffalo, 1932–1936," *SS Supplement* no. 9A (May 1937): 3, 6.

45. "'Snappy Steppin' Applauded at McCurdy Minstrel Show," *RD&C*, 25 October 1934, Section 2, 16. See Shawn Lay, *Hooded Knights on the Niagara: The Ku Klux Klan in Buffalo, New York*; Lewis A. Erenberg, *Steppin' Out: New York and the Transformation of American Culture, 1890–1930*, 68, 256–57.

46. "Light Advances over 50 Years Are on Display," *Buffalo Courier*, 1 March 1936, *Industry in Buffalo and the Niagara Frontier* 4, 294, BECPL.

47. Ibid.

48. "Store Plans Display of City Products" [n.d., pencil date 1938 on back], Scrapbook "Clippings, Local Press, 1936–1941," Sibley Collection, Strong Museum. Other articles indicate the exhibition was in May 1938.

49. "100,000 Inspect Home Products," *RTU*, 13 May 1938, Scrapbook "Clippings, Local Press, 1936–1941," Sibley Collection, Strong Museum.

50. "Exhibits Give New Facts on City Industry," *RD&C*, 18 May 1939; "Products of 106 Home Industries Shine at City's Own 'World's Fair,'" *RTU*, 18 May 1939; Scrapbook "Clippings, Local Press 1936–1941," Sibley Collection, Strong Museum.

51. Edmund W. Peters, "Rochester in 1839."

52. See Steven Conn, *Museums and American Intellectual Life, 1876–1926*, 13–15.

53. Leach, *Land of Desire*, 335.

54. "Balloon Zoo Led by Santa Attracts 80,000 Downtown," *RD&C*, 22 November 1936, 2, Scrapbook "Clippings, Local Press 1936–1941," Sibley Collection, Strong Museum.

55. "Circus Parade to Help Santa—Circus Day November 21," *RD&C*, 8 November 1936, Scrapbook "Clippings, Local Press 1936–1941," Sibley Collection, Strong Museum.

56. "Downtown Jammed for Sibley's Parade," *Journal*, 21 November 1936, Scrapbook "Clippings, Local Press 1936–1941," Sibley Collection, Strong Museum.

57. "Animal-shaped Balloons of Sizes Seldom Imagined," *RTU*, 11 November 1937, Scrapbook "Clippings, Local Press 1936–1941," Sibley Collection, Strong Museum.

58. See Appendix.

59. "Excerpts from a Statement by W.H. Bramley, Director, Sibley, Lindsay & Curr Company, Rochester, N.Y.," *Bulletin of the National Retail Dry Goods Association* (hereafter *NRDGA*), April 1933, 23.

60. Ibid., 22.

61. Ibid.

62. "Militant Action by New York Merchants and Civic Organizations against the Retail Sales Tax," *NRDGA*, February 1934, 113.

63. *NRDGA*, June 1934, 81.

64. Weldon D. Smith, "The Sales Tax Should Be Repealed Instead of Increased," *NRDGA*, January 1934, 70.

65. Gilbert J. C. McCurdy, "A Sales Tax a Stumbling Block to Recovery," *NRDGA*, January 1934, 71.

66. Advertisement for Arpeako Sausage, *BEN*, 13 November 1930, 19. This ad appeared in the "Western New York" edition of the paper, which may be why the ad refers to a "Rochester couple" rather than one from Buffalo.

67. Advertisers increasingly embraced this style of selling following the success of campaigns by Fleishmann's Yeast, Listerine, and Kotex. See Marchand, *Advertising the American Dream*, 14–22. Stephen Fox argues that during World War I, letters from soldiers praising razors and other personal items provided advertisers with highly effective testimonials. Stephen Fox, *The Mirror Makers: A History of American Advertising and Its Creators*, 88–89; see also Scanlon, *Inarticulate Longings*, 216.

68. Marchand, *Advertising the American Dream*, 112.

69. Advertising Federation of America, "Memo to the Board of Governors, the Advertising Commission, Presidents of Affiliated Clubs and Associations, Editors of Advertising Club and Association Publication" [mimeographed bulletin], 430 Lexington Avenue, 21 August 1929, McGarry Papers, F27/455, Box 2, Folder "Professional Organizations General, 1928–1947," UBA.

70. On the history of the Pond's campaign, see Fox, *Mirror Makers*, 88–90; Scanlon, *Inarticulate Longings*, 216–19.

71. Marchand, *Advertising the American Dream*, 14.

72. Advertisement for Rinso soap, *BEN*, Inter-Urban Edition, 4 June 1931, 30.

73. Advertisement for Lux soap, *BEN*, 1 December 1929, 12.

74. Advertisement for Rinso soap, *BEN*, Inter-Urban Edition, 4 June 1931, 30.

75. Advertisement for Chipso soap, *RD&C*, 23 November 1934, 24.

76. Advertisement for Chipso Soap, *RD&C*, 9 November 1934, 24.

77. "Be Rid of That Nagging Backache!" *RD&C*, 11 October 1920, 11.

78. Advertisement for Doan's Pills, *RD&C*, 23 November 1925, 13. The statement of the testimonial was dated 27 May 1922. This ad also used the "Ask Your Neighbor" tag line.

79. Advertisement for Konjola, *BEN*, Mail Edition, 9 November 1929, 18.

80. Advertisement for Konjola, *BEN*, 18 November 1929, 7.

81. Advertisement for Lifebuoy soap, *BEN*, 2 December 1929, 15.

82. Fox, *Mirror Makers*, 99.

83. *BEN*, Mail Edition, 6 November 1930, 36.

84. Advertisement for Lux soap, *BEN*, 1 December 1929, 12. The same ad featured a testimonial from a woman in Stamford, Connecticut.

85. Scripps-Howard Newspapers, *Market Records: From a Home-Inventory Study of Buying Habits and Brand Preferences of Consumers in Sixteen Cities: Buffalo, Washington, D.C., Pittsburgh, Akron, Cleveland, Columbus, Toledo, Cincinnati, Evansville, Indianapolis, Knoxville, Birmingham, Fort Worth, Houston, San Diego, San Francisco*, 5.

86. Ibid., 247.

87. Ibid., 19.

88. Ibid., 102.

89. Ibid., 257. The percentage of people selecting Campbell's tomato soup in the top income group was 80.1 percent, versus 82.9 percent in the middle group, and 82.3 percent in the lowest income group.

90. Ibid., 96.

91. Ibid., 76. The research indicated that 51.2 percent of Buffalo households chose Kraft's packaged cheese, compared with 76.1 percent in Cleveland, 68.2 percent in Columbus, and 74.3 percent in Washington.

92. Ibid., 50.

93. Ibid., 52–53.

94. Ibid., 248.

95. Ibid., 251.
96. Ibid., 247.
97. Ibid., 262.
98. Ibid., 262–63.

Epilogue

1. The paper reported that approximately 220,000 shares were held by descendants of the store's founders or of early investors, with only 33,000 shares held by the public. There were four hundred stockholders in the company. Associated Dry Goods Corporation's offer was $40 per share, totaling over $10 million. "Sibley's Offered 10 Million for Store by National Firm—Sale Negotiations Started," *RD&C*, 21 August 1957, Folder "1950s," Sibley Collection, RHS.

2. "Founder's Son Tells Reason for Sale," *RTU*, 21 August 1957, Folder "1950s," Sibley Collection, RHS.

3. Ibid.

4. Bruce Mann, "Business of Living—Not a Chain Store Operation, Writes Associated Chief—Now Head of Sibley's," *RTU*, 10 September 1957, Folder "1950s," Sibley Collection, RHS.

5. "Sibley's Offered 10 Million for Store by National Firm," *RD&C*, 21 August 1957, Folder "1950s," Sibley Collection, RHS.

6. Ernest Grogan Brown, "The Automobile and Leisure in Buffalo, New York during the 1920s: Local Institutions Shaping Mass Leisure," 295.

Bibliography

Primary Sources

NEWSPAPERS AND REGIONAL PUBLICATIONS

Buffalo Courier
Buffalo Courier-Express
Buffalo Evening News
Buffalo Live Wire (official publication of the Buffalo Chamber of Commerce)
Buffalo Morning Express
Buffalo Saturday Night
Buffalo Times
Niagara Area
Rochester Democrat and Chronicle
Rochester Times-Union
Town Tidings (Buffalo)

NATIONAL PERIODICALS

Bulletin of the National Retail Dry Goods Association
Chain Store Age
Chain Store Manager
Department Store Buyer
Dry Goods Merchants Trade Journal (later *Dry Goods Journal*)
Dry Goods Reporter
Merchandise Manager
Printer's Ink

ARCHIVAL MATERIALS

Buffalo and Erie County Historical Society

Adam, Meldrum and Anderson Company Papers
Flint and Kent Company Papers

Foster, Clarence P. "A Brief History of the Wm. Hengerer Co. Store." Buffalo, N.Y.: Wm. Hengerer Co., 1936. Vertical Files, Retailers.
Greater Buffalo Advertising Club Papers
Style Arch Boot Shop, *Sales Record Book*, 1929
Vertical Files: Celebrations, Retailers

Special Collections, Central Branch, Buffalo and Erie County Public Library, Buffalo, N.Y.

Business and Industry on the Niagara Frontier (Local history scrapbooks compiled by BECPL)
Holidays (Local history scrapbooks compiled by BECPL)

Rochester Gas and Electric Corporation Archives

Chamber of Commerce Ads, binder containing examples of company advertising
Kelly, Arthur P. *The R G and E Story: A Company Dedicated to the Public Service.* Rochester, N.Y.: Christopher Press, 1957.
Murphy, George. "History of the Home Service Department," photocopy, n.d. [1980].
R G & E Monthly Messenger
Service and Properties, Rochester Gas and Electric Corporation, binder containing essays prepared by the company and published 2 October 1922 to 2 December 1922
Speare, Jack W. *In Rochester One Hundred Years Ago and Now.* Rochester, N.Y.: Rochester Savings Bank, 1931.

Rochester Museum and Science Center Library, Rochester, N.Y.

Alice Colby Account Books, 1929–1942
Leah Covell Account Books, 1892–1920
Pfarrer Family Collection

Library and Research Collections, The Strong Museum, Rochester, N.Y.

Sibley, Lindsay and Curr Collection
Sibley, Lindsay and Curr. *Forty Years, 1868–1908.* Rochester: Sibley, Lindsay and Curr, 1908.
————. *Spreading beyond Old Walls.* Rochester: Sibley, Lindsay and Curr, 1926.
Wilson, Vera B. *One Hundred Years: A Century of Commerce in Rochester, N.Y.* Rochester, N.Y.: Rochester Chamber of Commerce, 1934.

Wolfe, Andrew D. *Bold Century, 1868–1968: 100 Adventurous and Happy Years of Merchandising—The Story of Sibley, Lindsay & Curr Company of Rochester, Monroe County, New York.* Rochester: n.p., 1968.

Special Collections, Rush Rhees Library, University of Rochester, Rochester, N.Y.

The Kodak Magazine, 1920–1932
Rochester Gas and Electric Company News
Sibley, Lindsay and Curr Company Financial Papers, 1868–1940

Rochester Historical Society, Rochester, N.Y.

Edwards Store Papers
"A Glorious Past." *News and Notes from the Rochester Historical Society,* Summer 1990.
Sibley, Lindsay and Curr Company. *Half a Century: 1868–1918.* Rochester: Sibley, Lindsay and Curr, 1918.
Sibley, Lindsay and Curr Company Papers

University Archives, University at Buffalo, SUNY

Bureau of Business and Social Research Papers and Research Files
Dr. Edmund D. McGarry Papers
Statistical Survey. Publication of the University of Buffalo Bureau of Business and Social Research.

Special Collections, Baker Library, Harvard Business School, Cambridge, Mass.

American Association of Advertising Agencies. *Chart Presentation of Income Data from Newspaper Reader Surveys in Boston, Buffalo, Detroit, Philadelphia, St. Louis, Washington.* New York: American Association of Advertising Agencies, 1932.
The American Consumer Market: A Study by The Business Week. Reprinted from *Business Week* issues of 27 April to 7 September 1932.
Buckley, Homer J. *The Science of Marketing by Mail.* New York: B. C. Forbes, 1924.
Bureau of Business Research Correspondence Files
Bureau of Business Research Notebooks on Retail Trade
Bureau of Business Research Office Files
House of Kuppenheimer. *Successful Selling in the Retail Clothing Store, A Series of Lectures.* New York: House of Kuppenheimer, 1921.
J. Walter Thompson Company. *Retail Shopping Areas: A Suggested Grouping of Counties*

about 683 Principal Shopping Centers, with 642 Sub-centers Indicated. Supplement to Part 4 of *Population and Its Distribution,* 4th ed., 1927, published by J. Walter Thompson Company.

The Manual of Variety Storekeeping. New York: Butler Brothers, 1925.

Scripps-Howard Newspapers. *Market Records: From a Home-Inventory Study of Buying Habits and Brand Preferences of Consumers in Sixteen Cities: Buffalo, Washington, D.C., Pittsburgh, Akron, Cleveland, Columbus, Toledo, Cincinnati, Evansville, Indianapolis, Knoxville, Birmingham, Fort Worth, Houston, San Diego, San Francisco.* Vol. 1. Scripps-Howard Newspapers, 1938, no place of publication listed, company's National Advertising Department is in New York.

U.S. Department of Commerce. *An Aid for Analyzing Markets in New York: Concentration of Markets for General Consumer Commodities.* Washington, D.C.: Government Printing Office, 1933.

Private Collection of Lynda McCurdy Hotra, Rochester, N.Y.

Colean, Miles L. "The Public Moves Away." Address presented at a forum sponsored by the American Retail Federation, Chicago, 16 May 1940.

Hotra, Lynda McCurdy. "McCurdy & Company Timeline," 1997.

Life at McCurdys. Golden Jubilee ed. Rochester, N.Y.: McCurdy and Company, 1951.

"Something about This New Store Here in Rochester." Rochester, N.Y.: n.p., Winter 1901–1902.

Science, Industry and Business Library, New York Public Library

Barton, Fred B. *How to Sell in Chain Stores: For the Man Anxious to Make Good with the Public, His Company, and Himself.* New York and London: Harper and Brothers, 1937.

Buehler, E. C. *Chain Store Debate Manual: A Digest of Material for Debate on the Chain Store Question.* New York: National Chain Store Association, 1931.

Flowers, Montaville. *America Chained: A Discussion of "What's Wrong with the Chain Store."* Transcript of radio addresses. Pasadena, Calif.: Montaville Flowers Publicists, Economic, Educational and Political Topics of the Times, 1931.

Haywood, Walter S., and Percy White. *Chain Stores, Their Management and Operation.* 3rd ed. New York: McGraw-Hill, 1928.

Lebhar, Godfrey M. *The Chain Store—Boon or Bane?* New York: Harper and Brothers, 1932.

OTHER PRINTED PRIMARY SOURCES

Barry, John F., and Robert W. Elmes. *Buffalo's Text Book.* Buffalo, N.Y.: Robert W. Elmes, 1924, 1929.

Boyd, John Taylor, Jr. "The Art of Commercial Display." *Architectural Record* 63, no. 1 (January 1928): 59–67.

Federal Writers' Project, Works Progress Administration, State of New York. *Rochester and Monroe County: A History and Guide.* Rochester, N.Y.: Scrantom's, 1937.

Foreman, Edward R., ed. *Centennial History of Rochester, New York.* Vol. 4. Rochester, N.Y.: Board of Trustees of the Rochester Public Library, 1934.

Gard, Anson A. "'A Tale of Two Cities' or a Race for a Million: Toronto and Buffalo." A reproduction taken from *The Busy Man's Canada,* June 1914, compliments of Buffalo Suburban Securities Corporation.

The Industries of Buffalo: A Resume of the Mercantile and Manufacturing Progress of the Queen City of the Lakes, Together with a Condensed Summary of Her Material Development and History and a Series of Comprehensive Sketches of Her Representative Business Houses. Buffalo, N.Y.: Elstner Publishing, 1887. Available online at the Cornell Library New York State Historical Literature Collection, http://encompass.library.cornell.edu/nys/.

Lewis, Sinclair. *Babbitt.* New York: Signet Classics, 1961.

———. *Main Street.* New York: Signet Classics, 1980.

National Retail Merchants Association. *25 Years of Retailing, 1911–1936.* New York: National Retail Dry Goods Association, 1936.

Nimmons, George C. "The Eastern Store of Sears, Roebuck & Company at Philadelphia, Geo. C. Nimmons & Co., Architects." *Architectural Record* 50, no. 2 (August 1921): 119–32.

The Pan-American Exposition, May 1 to November 1, 1901: Its Purpose and Plan. Buffalo, N.Y.: Pan-American Exposition, 1901. Available online at "Illuminations: Revisiting the Buffalo Pan-American Exposition of 1901," University at Buffalo Libraries, http://libris.lib.buffalo.edu/cgi-test/ublproj/panam/pancode.cgi?dir=purposeplan&gotopage=1.

U.S. Department of Commerce, Bureau of the Census. *Abstract of the Fourteenth Census of the United States: 1920.* Washington, D.C.: Government Printing Office, 1923.

Secondary Sources

Abelson, Elaine. *When Ladies Go A-Thieving: Middle-Class Shoplifters in the Victorian Department Store.* New York: Oxford University Press, 1989.

Adler, Selig, and Thomas E. Connolly. *From Ararat to Suburbia: The History of the Jewish Community of Buffalo.* Philadelphia: Jewish Publication Society of America, 1966.

Argersinger, Jo Ann E. *Toward a New Deal in Baltimore: People and Government in the Great Depression.* Chapel Hill: University of North Carolina Press, 1988.

Atherton, Lewis. *Main Street on the Middle Border.* Bloomington: Indiana University Press, 1954.

Badger, Anthony. *The New Deal: The Depression Years, 1933–1940.* New York: Basingstoke Macmillan Education, 1989.

Barber, William J. *From New Era to New Deal: Herbert Hoover, the Economists, and American Economic Policy, 1921–1933.* New York: Cambridge University Press, 1985.

Barnes, Joseph W. "The City's Golden Age." *Rochester History* 35, no. 2 (April 1973): 1–24.

Bean, Jonathan J. *Beyond the Broker State: Federal Policies toward Small Business, 1936–1961.* Chapel Hill: University of North Carolina Press, 1996.

Beckman, Theodore N., and Herman C. Nolen. *The Chain Store Problem: A Critical Analysis.* New York: McGraw-Hill, 1938.

Belk, Russell W. "A Child's Christmas in America: Santa Claus as Deity, Consumption as Religion." *Journal of American Culture* 10, no. 1 (1987): 87–100.

Benson, Susan Porter. *Counter Cultures: Saleswomen, Managers, and Customers in American Department Stores, 1890–1940.* Urbana: University of Illinois Press, 1986.

Bernstein, Michael A. *The Great Depression: Delayed Recovery and Economic Change in America, 1929–1939.* New York: Cambridge University Press, 1983.

Biles, Roger. *A New Deal for the American People.* Dekalb: Northern Illinois University Press, 1991.

Blackford, Mansel. *A History of Small Business in America.* New York: Twayne Publishers, 1991.

Blanke, David. *Sowing the American Dream: How Consumer Culture Took Root in the Rural Midwest.* Athens: Ohio University Press, 2000.

Blumin, Stuart M. *The Emergence of the Middle Class: Social Experience in the American City, 1760–1900.* Cambridge: Cambridge University Press, 1989.

Bogart, Michele. *Artists, Advertising, and the Borders of Art, 1890–1960.* Chicago: University of Chicago Press, 1995.

Boorstin, Daniel. *The Americans: The Democratic Experience.* New York: Random House, 1973.

Bourdieu, Pierre. *Distinction: A Social Critique of the Judgement of Taste.* London: Routledge, 1984.

Boyer, Paul. *Urban Masses and Moral Order in America, 1820–1920.* Cambridge, Mass.: Harvard University Press, 1978.

Briggs, John W. *An Italian Passage: Immigrants to Three American Cities, 1890–1930.* New Haven, Conn.: Yale University Press, 1970.

Brinkley, Alan. *Voices of Protest: Huey Long, Father Coughlin, and the Great Depression.* New York: Knopf, 1982.

Bronner, Simon J., ed. *Grasping Things: Folk Material Culture and Mass Society in America.* Lexington: University of Kentucky Press, 1986.

———. *Consuming Visions: Accumulation and Display of Goods in America, 1880–1920.* New York: W. W. Norton, 1989.

Brown, Ernest Grogan. "The Automobile and Leisure in Buffalo, N.Y., during the

1920s: Local Institutions Shaping Mass Leisure." Ph.D. diss., State University of New York at Buffalo, 1995.

Calder, Lendol. *Financing the American Dream: A Cultural History of Consumer Credit.* Princeton, N.J.: Princeton University Press, 1999.

Carpenter, Niles. *Nationality, Color, and Economic Opportunity in the City of Buffalo.* New York and Buffalo: University of Buffalo, 1927.

Chandler, Alfred D. *The Visible Hand: The Managerial Revolution in American Business.* Cambridge, Mass.: Harvard University Press, 1977.

Cohen, Lizabeth. "Encountering Mass Culture at the Grassroots: The Experience of Chicago Workers in the 1920s." *American Quarterly* 41 (Spring 1989): 6–33.

———. *Making a New Deal: Industrial Workers in Chicago, 1919–1939.* Cambridge: Cambridge University Press, 1990.

———. "From Town Center to Shopping Center: The Reconfiguration of Community Marketplaces in Postwar America." *American Historical Review* 101 (October 1996): 1050–81.

———. "Is There an Urban History of Consumption?" *Journal of Urban History* 29, no. 2 (January 2003): 87–106.

Conn, Steven. *Museums and American Intellectual Life, 1876–1926.* Chicago: University of Chicago Press, 1998.

Cotkin, George. *Reluctant Modernism: American Thought and Culture, 1880–1900.* New York: Twayne Publishers, 1992.

Couvares, Francis G. *The Remaking of Pittsburgh: Class and Culture in an Industrializing City, 1877–1919.* Pittsburgh, Pa.: University of Pittsburgh Press, 1984.

Cronon, William. *Nature's Metropolis: Chicago and the Great West.* New York: W. W. Norton, 1991.

Cross, Gary. *An All-Consuming Century: Why Commercialism Won in Modern America.* New York: Columbia University Press, 2000.

Curtis, Susan. *A Consuming Faith: The Social Gospel and Modern American Culture.* Baltimore: Johns Hopkins University Press, 1991.

Damon-Moore, Helen. *Magazines for the Millions: Gender and Commerce in the* Ladies' Home Journal *and the* Saturday Evening Post, *1880–1910.* Albany: State University of New York Press, 1994.

de Grazia, Victoria, and Ellen Furlough, eds. *The Sex of Things: Gender and Consumption in Historical Perspective.* Berkeley: University of California Press, 1996.

Dennett, Andrea Stulman. *Weird and Wonderful: The Dime Museum in America.* New York: New York University Press, 1997.

Denning, Michael. *Mechanic Accents: Dime Novels and Working-Class Culture in America.* London: Verso Press, 1987.

Dicke, Thomas S. *Franchising in America: The Development of a Business Method, 1840–1980.* Chapel Hill: University of North Carolina Press, 1992.

Donohue, Kathleen G. "What Gender Is the Consumer?: The Role of Gender

Connotations in Defining the Political." *Journal of American Studies* 33, no. 1 (1999): 19–44.

Douglas, Ann. *The Feminization of American Culture.* New York: Avon, 1977.

———. *Terrible Honesty: Mongrel Manhattan in the 1920s.* New York: Farrar, Straus and Giroux, 1995.

Edsforth, Ronald. *Class Conflict and Cultural Consensus in Flint, Michigan.* New Brunswick, N.J.: Rutgers University Press, 1987.

Emmet, Boris, and John E. Jeuk. *Catalogues and Counters: A History of Sears, Roebuck and Co.* Chicago: University of Chicago Press, 1950.

Erenberg, Lewis A. *Steppin' Out: New York and the Transformation of American Culture, 1890–1930.* Chicago: University of Chicago Press, 1981.

Ewen, Elizabeth. *Immigrant Women in the Land of Dollars: Life and Culture on the Lower East Side, 1890–1925.* New York: Monthly Review Press, 1985.

Ewen, Stuart. *Captains of Consciousness: Advertising and the Social Roots of the Consumer Culture.* New York: McGraw-Hill, 1976.

Fass, Paula S. *The Damned and the Beautiful: American Youth in the 1920s.* New York: Oxford University Press, 1977.

Fisher, Jack C. *Stolen Glory: The McKinley Assassination.* La Jolla, Calif.: Alamar Books, 2001.

Fishman, Robert. *Bourgeois Utopias: The Rise and Fall of Suburbia.* New York: Basic Books, 1987.

Fox, Richard Wightman, and T. J. Jackson Lears, eds. *The Culture of Consumption: Critical Essays in American History, 1880–1980.* New York: Pantheon Books, 1983.

Fox, Stephen. *The Mirror Makers: A History of American Advertising and Its Creators.* New York: William Morrow, 1984.

Frank, Dana. *Purchasing Power: Consumer Organizing, Gender, and the Seattle Labor Movement, 1919–1929.* New York: Cambridge University Press, 1993.

———. *Buy American: The Untold Story of Economic Nationalism.* Boston: Beacon Press, 1999.

Frish, Michael, and Daniel J. Walkowitz, eds. *Working-Class America: Essays on Labor, Community, and American Society.* Urbana: University of Illinois Press, 1983.

Galbraith, John Kenneth, *The Affluent Society.* 3rd ed. Boston: Hougton Mifflin, 1976.

Garvey, Ellen Gruber. *The Adman in the Parlor: Magazines and the Gendering of Consumer Culture, 1880s to 1910s.* New York: Oxford University Press, 1993.

Gerber, David A. *The Making of an American Pluralism: Buffalo, New York, 1825–1860.* Urbana: University of Illinois Press, 1989.

Gerling, Curt. *Smugtown, USA.* Webster, N.Y.: Plaza Publishers, 1957.

Glickman, Lawrence B. *A Living Wage: American Workers and the Making of Consumer Society.* Ithaca, N.Y.: Cornell University Press, 1997.

Glickman, Lawrence B., ed. *Consumer Society in American History: A Reader.* Ithaca, N.Y.: Cornell University Press, 1999.

Goldberg, David J. *Discontented America: The United States in the 1920s*. Baltimore: Johns Hopkins University Press, 1999.

Goldman, Mark. *High Hopes: The Rise and Decline of Buffalo, New York*. Albany: State University of New York Press, 1983.

Hammett, Ralph W. *Architecture in the United States: A Survey of Architectural Styles since 1776*. New York: John Wiley and Sons, 1976.

Harris, Leon A. *Merchant Princes: An Intimate History of Jewish Families Who Built Great Department Stores*. New York: Harper and Row, 1979.

Hawley, Ellis W. *The New Deal and the Problem of Monopoly: A Study in Economic Ambivalence*. Princeton, N.J.: Princeton University Press, 1966.

Heinze, Andrew. *Adapting to Abundance: Jewish Immigrants, Mass Consumption, and the Search for American Identity*. New York: Columbia University Press, 1990.

Heleniak, Roman. "Local Reaction to the Great Depression in New Orleans, 1929–1933," *Louisiana History* 10 (Fall 1969): 283–306.

Hendrickson, Robert. *The Grand Emporiums: The Illustrated History of America's Great Department Stores*. New York: Stein and Day, 1980.

Holl, Richard E. "Marion B. Folsom and the Rochester Plan of 1931." *Rochester History* 61, no. 1 (Winter 1999): 1–22.

Horowitz, Daniel. *The Morality of Spending: Attitudes toward the Consumer Society in America, 1875–1940*. Baltimore: Johns Hopkins University Press, 1985.

Horowitz, David A. "The Crusade against Chain Stores: Portland's Independent Merchants, 1928–1935." *Oregon Historical Quarterly* 89, no.4 (Winter 1988): 340–68.

Hounshell, David A. *From the American System to Mass Production, 1800–1932: The Development of Manufacturing Technology in the United States*. Baltimore: Johns Hopkins University Press, 1984.

Hower, Ralph M. *History of Macy's of New York, 1858–1919: Chapters in the Evolution of the Department Store*. Cambridge, Mass.: Harvard University Press, 1967.

Illingworth, Charles S. "This I Remember—VIII: Down Town." *Niagara Frontier* 2 (Spring 1955–Winter 1956): 89–90.

———. "Buffalo Theatres—1898–1908." *Niagara Frontier* 6 (Spring 1959–Winter 1960): 42–43.

Isenberg, Alison Ellen. "Downtown Democracy: Rebuilding Main Street Ideals in the Twentieth-Century American City." Ph.D. diss., University of Pennsylvania, 1995.

Jackson, Kenneth T. *The Crabgrass Frontier: The Suburbanization of the United States*. New York: Oxford University Press, 1985.

Johnson, Paul E. *A Shopkeeper's Millennium: Society and Revivals in Rochester, New York, 1815–1837*. New York: Hill and Wang, 1978.

Karl, Barry. *The Uneasy State: The United States from 1915 to 1945*. Chicago: University of Chicago Press, 1983.

Kline, Ronald R. *Consumers in the Country: Technology and Social Change in Rural America.* Baltimore: Johns Hopkins University Press, 2000.

Klinkenborg, Verlyn. *The Last Fine Time.* New York: Knopf, 1991.

Kowsky, Francis R. "Municipal Parks and City Planning; Frederick Law Olmsted's Buffalo Park and Parkway System." *Journal of the Society of Architectural Historians* 44 (March 1987): 49–64.

Kraus, Neil. *Race, Neighborhoods, and Community Power: Buffalo Politics, 1934–1997.* Albany: State University of New York Press, 2000.

Laird, Pamela Walker. *Advertising Progress: American Business and the Rise of Consumer Marketing.* Baltimore: Johns Hopkins University Press, 1998.

Lansky, Lewis. "Buffalo and the Great Depression, 1929–1933." In Milton Plesur, ed., *An American Historian: Essays to Honor Selig Adler.* Buffalo: State University of New York at Buffalo, 1980, 204–13.

Lay, Shawn. *Hooded Knights on the Niagara: The Ku Klux Klan in Buffalo, New York.* New York: New York University Press, 1995.

Leach, William. "Transformations in a Culture of Consumption: Women and Department Stores, 1890–1925." *Journal of American History* 71 (September 1984): 319–42.

———. *Land of Desire: Merchants, Power, and the Rise of a New American Culture.* New York: Pantheon Books, 1993.

———. *Country of Exiles: The Destruction of Place in American Life.* New York: Pantheon Books, 1999.

Lears, T. J. Jackson. *No Place of Grace: Antimodernism and the Transformation of American Culture, 1880–1920.* New York: Pantheon Books, 1981.

———. "Packaging the Folk: Tradition and Amnesia and American Advertising, 1880–1940." In Jane Becker and Barbara Franco, eds., *Folk Roots, New Roots: Folklore in American Life.* Lexington, Mass.: Museum of Our National Heritage, 1988.

———. *Fables of Abundance: A Cultural History of Advertising in America.* New York: Basic Books, 1994.

Lebhar, Godfrey M. *Chain Stores in America, 1859–1962.* New York: Chain Store Publishing, 1963.

Levine, Lawrence. *Highbrow/Lowbrow: The Emergence of Cultural Hierarchy in America.* Cambridge, Mass.: Harvard University Press, 1988.

———. *The Unpredictable Past: Explorations in American Cultural History.* New York: Oxford University Press, 1993.

Lipman, Andrew David. "The Rochester Subway: Experiment in Municipal Rapid Transit." *Rochester History* 36, no. 2 (April 1974): 1–24.

Loeb, Lori Anne. *Consuming Angels: Advertising and Victorian Women.* New York: Oxford University Press, 1994.

Marchand, Roland. *Advertising the American Dream: Making Way for Modernity, 1920–1940.* Berkeley: University of California Press, 1985.

———. *Creating the Corporate Soul: The Rise of Public Relations and Corporate Imagery in American Big Business.* Berkeley: University of California Press, 1998.

Marcus, Leonard S. *The American Store Window.* New York: Whitney Library of Design, an imprint of Watson-Guptill Publications, 1978.

Marquis, Alice G. *Hopes and Ashes: The Birth of Modern Times, 1929–1939.* New York: Free Press, 1986.

Matt, Susan J. *Keeping Up with the Joneses: Envy in American Consumer Society, 1890–1930.* Philadelphia: University of Pennsylvania Press, 2003.

May, Larry. *Recasting America: Culture and Politics in the Age of the Cold War.* Chicago: University of Chicago Press, 1989.

McAllister, Matthew P. *The Commercialization of American Culture: New Advertising, Control, and Democracy.* Thousand Oaks, Calif.: Sage Publications, 1996.

McGarry, Edmund D. *Retail Trade Mortality in Buffalo, 1918–1928: Groceries, Drugs, Hardware, Shoes.* Buffalo, N.Y.: University of Buffalo Bureau of Business and Social Research, 1929.

McGovern, James R. *And a Time for Hope: Americans in the Great Depression.* Westport, Conn.: Praeger, 2000.

McKelvey, Blake. *Rochester, the Flower City—1855–1890.* Cambridge, Mass.: Harvard University Press, 1949.

———. "The Physical Growth of Rochester." *Rochester History* 13, no. 4 (October 1951): 1–24.

———. *Rochester, the Quest for Quality, 1890–1925.* Cambridge, Mass.: Harvard University Press, 1956.

———. "The Men's Clothing Industry in Rochester's History." *Rochester History* 22, no. 3 (July 1960): 1–32.

———. *Rochester, the Emerging Metropolis, 1925–1961.* Rochester, N.Y.: Christopher Press, 1961.

———. "The Changing Face of Rochester." *Rochester History* 26, no. 2 (April 1964): 1–24.

———. "Historic Predecessors of the Central Business District." *Rochester History* 34, no. 2 (April 1972): 1–24.

———. *Rochester on the Genesee: The Growth of a City.* Syracuse, N.Y.: Syracuse University Press, 1973.

McKendrick, Neil, Colin Brewer, and J. H. Plumb, eds. *The Birth of a Consumer Society: The Commercialization of Eighteenth-Century England.* London: Europa, 1982.

Miller, Perry. *The Bon Marche: Bourgeois Culture and the Department Store, 1869–1920.* Princeton, N.J.: Princeton University Press, 1981.

Mock, James R., and Cedric Larson. *Words That Won the War: The Story of the Committee on Public Information.* Princeton, N.J.: Princeton University Press, 1939.

Monod, David. *Store Wars: Shopkeepers and the Culture of Mass Marketing, 1890–1939.* Toronto, Canada: University of Toronto Press, 1996.

Monti, Daniel J. *The American City: A Social and Cultural History.* Malden, Mass.: Blackwell Publishers, 1999.

Nasaw, David. *Going Out: The Rise and Fall of Public Amusements.* New York: Basic Books, 1993.

Nienburg, Bertha M. *The Woman Home-Maker in the City: A Study of Statistics Relating to Married Women in the City of Rochester, N.Y., at the Census of 1920.* Washington, D.C.: Government Printing Office, 1923.

Nissenbaum, Stephen. "Revisiting 'A Visit from St. Nicholas': The Battle for Christmas in Early Nineteenth-Century America." In James Gilbert, Amy Gilman, Donald Scott, and Joan W. Scott, eds., *The Mythmaking Frame of Mind: Social Imagination and American Culture.* Belmont, Calif.: Wadsworth, 1992, 25–70.

Norris, James D. *Advertising and the Transformation of American Society, 1865–1920.* Westport, Conn.: Greenwood Press, 1990.

Nye, David. *Electrifying America: Social Meanings of a New Technology.* Cambridge, Mass.: MIT Press, 1990.

Ohmann, Richard. *Selling Culture: Magazines, Markets, and Class at the Turn of the Century.* New York: Verso, 1996.

Olney, Martha L. *Buy Now, Pay Later: Advertising, Credit, and Consumer Durables in the 1920s.* Chapel Hill: University of North Carolina Press, 1991.

Orvell, Miles. *The Real Thing: Imitation and Authenticity in American Culture, 1865–1920.* Chapel Hill: University of North Carolina Press, 1989.

Ownby, Ted. *American Dreams in Mississippi: Consumers, Poverty, and Culture, 1830–1998.* Chapel Hill: University of North Carolina Press, 1999.

Painter, Nell Irvin. *Standing at Armageddon: The United States, 1877–1919.* New York: W. W. Norton, 1987.

Parrish, Michael E. *Anxious Decades: America in Prosperity and Depression, 1920–1941.* New York: W. W. Norton, 1992.

Peiss, Kathy. *Cheap Amusements: Working Women and Leisure in Turn-of-the-Century New York.* Philadelphia: Temple University Press, 1986.

———. *Hope in a Jar: The Making of America's Beauty Culture.* New York: Metropolitan Books, 1998.

Pendergast, Tom. "Consuming Questions: Scholarship on Consumerism in America to 1940." *American Studies International* 36, no. 2 (1998): 23–42.

Peters, Edmund W. "Rochester in 1839." *Museum Service: The Bulletin of the Rochester Museum of Arts and Sciences* 13 (January–February 1940): 8.

Pope, Daniel. *The Making of Modern Advertising.* New York: Basic Books, 1982.

Porter, Glenn, and Harold C. Livesay. *Merchants and Manufacturers: Studies in the Changing Structure of Nineteenth-Century Marketing.* Baltimore: Johns Hopkins University Press, 1971; Chicago: Elephant Paperbacks, 1989.

Potter, David. *People of Plenty: Economic Abundance and American Character.* Chicago: University of Chicago Press, 1954.

Ralph, Henry Gabriel, ed. *The Pageant of America: A Pictorial History of the United States.* Vol. 13. New Haven, Conn.: Yale University Press, 1926.

Rappaport, Erika. *Shopping for Pleasure: Women in the Making of London's West End.* Princeton, N.J.: Princeton University Press, 2000.

Restad, Penne. *Christmas in America: A History.* New York: Oxford University Press, 1995.

Rosenberg, Stuart E. *The Jewish Community in Rochester, 1843–1925.* New York: Columbia University Press, 1954.

Rosenof, Theodore. *Economics in the Long Run: New Deal Theorists and Their Legacies, 1933–1993.* Chapel Hill: University of North Carolina Press, 1997.

Rosenzweig, Roy. *Eight Hours for What We Will: Workers and Leisure in an Industrial City, 1870–1920.* Cambridge: Cambridge University Press, 1983.

Rydell, Robert. *All the World's a Fair: Visions of Empire at American International Expositions, 1876–1916.* Chicago: University of Chicago Press, 1984.

Sanchez, George. *Becoming Mexican American: Ethnicity, Culture, and Identity in Chicano Los Angeles, 1900–1945.* New York: Oxford University Press, 1993.

Scanlon, Jennifer. *Inarticulate Longings: The* Ladies' Home Journal, *Gender, and the Promises of Consumer Culture.* New York: Routledge, 1995.

Schmidt, Leigh Eric. "The Commercialization of the Calendar: American Holidays and the Culture of Consumption, 1870–1930." *Journal of American History* 78 (December 1991): 894.

———. "Joy to (Some of) the World: Christianity in the Marketplace—Christmas and the Consumer Culture." *Cross Currents* 42 (1992): 350–51.

———. *Consumer Rites: The Buying and Selling of American Holidays.* Princeton, N.J.: Princeton University Press, 1995.

Schneirov, Matthew. *The Dream of a New Social Order: Popular Magazines in America, 1893–1914.* New York: Columbia University Press, 1995.

Schudson, Michael. *Advertising, the Uneasy Persuasion: Its Dubious Impact on American Society.* New York: Basic Books, 1984.

Schwartz, Jordan A. *The New Dealers: Power Politics in the Age of Roosevelt.* New York: Knopf, 1993.

Scranton, Phil. *Endless Novelty: Specialty Production and American Industrialization, 1865–1925.* Princeton, N.J.: Princeton University Press, 1997.

Scully, Vincent. *American Architecture and Urbanism.* New rev. ed. New York: Henry Holt, 1969.

Sheriff, Carol. *The Artificial River: The Erie Canal and the Paradox of Progress, 1817–1862.* New York: Hill and Wang, 1996.

Shi, David. "Advertising and the American Literary Imagination in the Jazz Age." *Journal of American Culture* 2 (Summer 1979): 167–75.

———. *The Simple Life: Plain Living and High Thinking in American Culture.* New York: Oxford University Press, 1985.

Stearns, Peter N. "Stages of Consumerism: Recent Work on the Issue of Periodization." *Journal of Modern History* 69 (March 1997): 102–17.

Sternsher, Bernard, ed. *Hitting Home: The Great Depression in Town and Country.* Chicago: Quadrangle Books, 1970.

Strasser, Susan. *Satisfaction Guaranteed: The Making of the American Mass Market.* New York: Pantheon, 1989.

Suozzi, Paul. *Three Walking Tours of Buffalo, New York* [booklet]. Buffalo, N.Y.: Landmark Society of the Niagara Frontier, [198?].

Susman, Warren I. *Culture as History: The Transformation of American Society in the Twentieth Century.* New York: Pantheon Books, 1984.

Tedlow, Richard S. *New and Improved: The Story of Mass Marketing in America.* New York: Basic Books, 1990.

Tomlinson, Alan, ed. *Consumption, Identity, & Style: Marketing, Meanings, and the Packaging of Pleasure.* London: Routledge, 1990.

Trachtenberg, Alan. *The Incorporation of America: Culture and Society in the Gilded Age.* New York: Hill and Wang, 1982.

Trout, Charles H. *Boston, the Great Depression, and the New Deal.* New York: Oxford University Press, 1977.

Tyler, Linda L. "'Commerce and Poetry Hand in Hand': Music in American Department Stores, 1880–1930." *Journal of the American Musicological Society* 45 (1992): 75–120.

Waits, William B. *The Modern Christmas in America: A Cultural History of Gift Giving.* New York: New York University Press, 1993.

Walden, Keith. "Speaking Modern: Language, Culture and Hegemony in Grocery Window Displays, 1887–1920." *Canadian Historical Review* 80, no. 3 (1989): 285–310.

Weil, Gordon L. *Sears, Roebuck, USA: The Great American Catalogue Store and How It Grew.* New York: Stein and Day, 1977.

Wendt, Lloyd, and Herman Kogan. *Give the Lady What She Wants: The Story of Marshall Field & Co.* Chicago: Rand McNally, 1952.

Wiebe, Robert H. *The Search for Order, 1877–1920.* New York: Hill and Wang, 1967.

Williams, Rosalind H. *Dream Worlds: Mass Consumption in Late Nineteenth-Century France.* Berkeley: University of California Press, 1982.

Wilson, Joan Hoff. *Herbert Hoover, Forgotten Progressive.* Boston: Little, Brown, 1975.

Yans-McLaughlin, Virginia. *Family and Community: Italian Immigrants in Buffalo, 1880–1930.* Ithaca, N.Y.: Cornell University Press, 1977.

Index